T0344377

Logic Programming
New Frontiers

Edited by
D R Brough
Imperial College
University of London

intellect
Oxford, England

SPRINGER-SCIENCE+BUSINESS MEDIA, B.V.

Consulting editor: Masoud Yazdani
Copy editor: Pamela Clements
Cover Design: Mark Lewis

British Library Cataloguing in Publication Data

Brough, D. R.
    Logic Programming.
    I. Title
    005.131

        ISBN 978-0-7923-1546-9   ISBN 978-94-011-2562-8 (eBook)
        DOI 10.1007/978-94-011-2562-8

Library of Congress Cataloging-in-Publication Data

Logic programming : new frontiers / edited by D.R. Brough
        p.   cm.
    ISBN 978-94-010-5131-6
    1. Logic programming.   I. Brough, D. R.
QA76.63.L633   1992
005. 1--dc20   91-405443

ISBN 978-0-7923-1546-9

Contents

Authors

Edward Babb
    Strategic Systems Technology, ICL, Lovelace Road, Bracknell, Berks
    babb@sst.icl.co.uk

Paul Brna
    DAI, Edinburgh University, 80 South Bridge, Edinburgh EH1 1HN
    paul@aisb.ed.ac.uk

Derek Brough
    Dept. of Computing, Imperial College, London

Alan Bundy
    DAI, Edinburgh University, 80 South Bridge, Edinburgh EH1 1HN
    bundy@ed.ac.uk

Andrew Casson
    DAI, Edinburgh University, 80 South Bridge, Edinburgh EH1 1HN
    andrewc@uk.ac.ed.aiai

Subratra Kumar Das
    Dept. of Computer Science, Heriot-Watt University,
    79, Grassmarket, Edinburgh EH1 2HJ
    das@uk.ac.hw.cs

Yves Deville
    Unité d'Informatique, Université Catholique de Leuven
    Place Ste Barbe 2, B-1348 Louvain-la-Neuve, Belgium
    yde@info.ucl.ac.be

P. W. Grant
    Department of Computer Science, University College of Swansea,
    Singleton Park, Swansea SA2 8PP
    csphil@uk.ac.swan.pyr

Keith Harrison
    Information Systems Centre, Hewlett-Packard Laboratories,
    Filton Road, Stoke Gifford, Bristol BS12 6QZ

C. P. Jobling
    Department of Electronic and Electrical Engineering,

University College of Swansea, Singleton Park, Swansea SA2 8PP
eechris@uk.ac.swan.pyr

Ron Knott
Maths Dept, Surrey University, Guildford, Surrey GU2 5XH

Professor Simon Lavington
Dept. of Computer Science, University of Essex, Colchester CO4 3SQ
lavington@uk.ac.sx

Chris Mellish
DAI, Edinburgh University, 80 South Bridge, Edinburgh EH1 1HN
c.mellish@uk.ac.edinburgh

Chris Moss
Dept. of Computing, Imperial College, London
cdsm@doc.ic.ac.uk

Helen Pain
DAI, Edinburgh University, 80 South Bridge, Edinburgh EH1 1HN
helen@aisb.ed.ac.uk

C. Rezvani
Department of Computer Science, University College of Swansea,
Singleton Park, Swansea SA2 8PP

S. M. S. Syed-Mustaffa
Dept. of Computer Science, University of Manchester, Oxford Road,
Manchester M13 9PL
salleh@uk.ac.man.cs.r4

Hamish Taylor
Dept. of Computer Science, Heriot-Watt University,
79, Grassmarket, Edinburgh EH1 2HJ
hamish@uk.ac.hw.cs

Pascal van Hentenryck
Department of Computer Science, Brown University,
Box 1919, Providence, RI 02912, USA
pvh@cs.brown.edu

Jiwei Wang

Dept. of Computer Science, University of Essex, Colchester CO4 3SQ
jiwei@uk.ac.sx

M. H. Williams
Dept. of Computer Science, Heriot-Watt University,
79, Grassmarket, Edinburgh EH1 2HJ
howard@uk.ac.hw.cs

Preface

In Logic Programming, as in many other areas, Theory is often best tested by Application and attempted Application frequently necessitates advances in Theory, so both theoretical and practical work is essential for effective progress. This is clearly evident in the following papers presented to the second UK Logic Programming Conference which was sponsored by the United Kingdom branch of the Association of Logic Programming and convened at Bristol University in March 1990.

This book contains 13 papers from that conference grouped under four headings:

Theory supporting practice motivating theory

In this first group of papers, difficulties experienced in practical application of Prolog and in debugging Prolog programs have motivated work on extensions to the language and its development environment.

Program development advances are represented by two papers on debugging and one on a development methodology for CLP programs. On the theoretical side a Pure(r) logic language is proposed as well as extensions to make logic more effective for integrity checking in deductive databases.

Applications

The next group contains three papers. The first describers the use of Prolog to develop a Control Engineering workStation (CES). The second investigates the use of a logic programming based KBMS for developing a prototype Financial Management Information System. In the last it is shown how a subset of prolog can provide a vehicle for the animation of Discrete Mathematics.

Theoretical Possibilities

Next follow two papers which respectively develop theoretical aspects of and constraints on the types of problem which can be tackled by Logic in particular and computing machines in general. One paper investigates requirements for the encoding of Description spaces and the other discusses the limitations of symbolic systems and their relation to "Intelligence".

Implementation Techniques

The final group of papers investigates various implementation techniques for Prolog. Two in particular look at parallelism, one considering a graph reduction implementation model for OR-Paralleelism while the other investigates the wider scope for parallelisms. The final paper looks at thge implementation problems of combining both knowledge processing and systems handling capabilities.

Acknowledgements

We would also like to thank Professor Mike Rogers and his colleagues at Bristol, without whom there would have been no conference. Also thanks are due to all those involved in the production process, particularly the authors who went to considerable trouble to send in machine readable copy for their papers and so carefully checked their proofs.

Metalevel and Constraint Technology in a Pure Logic Language

Edward Babb*

Abstract

The Pure Logic Language — PLL — is designed primarily to improve the match between the application builder and his problem. To facilitate this match the language includes a number of features: *Classical conjunction* so that terms can be written in any order — important in logic spreadsheets, one of the main current uses of PLL. *Classical negation* to match the end user's requirement and to give guaranteed order independence. *Rewrite definitions* so that commonly used expressions can be defined as predicates. The crucial feature of the language is that any query Q and its answer Q' are logically equivalent under this set of definitions Π.[1] The ability of the language to return formulas as well as definite answers means that the answer to one query can be used instead of the original query thus saving unnecessary recomputation.

Emphasis is placed on the use of the metalevel capability of the language where a clean separation is made between the variables in the meta and object level. At the metalevel all expressions are held as strings. When these strings are passed to the object level the symbols in the string take on their normal logical meaning — so that a string "x" becomes a variable x . All these ideas are illustrated by reference to a railway timetable example.

1   Introduction

This paper in contrast to an earlier paper [6] concentrates on the use of the metalevel and constraint capabilities of PLL. However, because this earlier paper may not be available, PLL is summarised in the *appendix*.

---

*Research carried out at Strategic Systems Technology, ICL, Lovelace Road, Bracknell, Berks with the support of ICL and ALVEY under grants IKBS 084 & 092
    [1]formally ($\Pi \vdash Q \Leftrightarrow Q'$).

1

The philosophy behind PLL is to make logic more accessible to end users by:

- Rewriting to more solvable logic in such a way that the query and the answer are logically equivalent under the set of rewrites available in the language:

  – ie: $(\Pi \vdash Q \Leftrightarrow Q')$

  – for example, a query $not\ 2 * x = 1 + 15$ rewrites to $not\ x = 8$

- Using a familiar and easily transformable mathematical or logic notation:

  – for example, $not\ some(x)(2 * x = 1 + 15\ \&\ weight(x, y))$ simplifies to $not\ weight(8, y)$

2 Railway timetable problem

2.1 Introduction

In the railway timetable problem we investigate the construction of a timetable and use it to illustrate how useful the flexible execution order in PLL can be in answering queries about the time table. The ability to return generalised answers as formulas is used to improve the answer given back by queries about trains. Finally the operation of the timetable model is checked with some real observations and in the case of a contradiction, the ability of PLL to return expressions, at the metalevel, is used to help identify the causes of the contradiction.

2.2 Generating a timetable

In Figure 1, there are two routes between station 1 and station 4, based on a small fragment of the London underground. One route goes to station 4 via stations 2 and 3 and takes 9 minutes in total. The second route goes direct and takes only 5 minutes. Each train must be more than 1 minute apart from the others at stations 1 and 4.

The timetable Logic Spreadsheet[7] representing how the PLL user might see this network is shown in Table 1. Train "A" is represented by the A column with a succession of additions representing the time delay between stations. Trains "B" and "C" are on the fast route and include a constraint which says

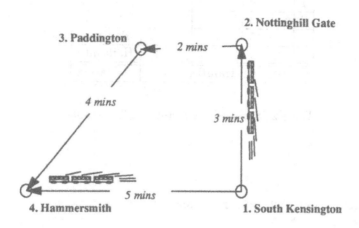

Figure 1: Simple Railway Network

	A	B	C	D
1	0	2 & $\neg near(A1)$	6 & $\neg near(A1, B1)$	Sth Ken
2	$A1 + 3$			Not Hill
3	$A2 + 2$			Padingtn
4	$A3 + 4$	$B1 + 5$ & $\neg near(A4)$	$C1 + 5$ & $\neg near(A4, B4)$	Hamsmth
	trainA	trainB	trainC	Station

Table 1: Spreadsheet formulas for Timetable

	A	B	C	D
1	0	2	6	Sth Ken
2	3			Not Hill
3	5			Padingtn
4	9	7	11	Hamsmth
	trainA	trainB	trainC	Station

Table 2: Spreadsheet results for Timetable

```
define route1(x1, x2, x3, x4) tobe
    x2 = x1 + 3 &
    x3 = x2 + 2 &
    x4 = x3 + 4?

define route2(x1, x4) tobe
    x4 = x1 + 5?

define near(x, y) tobe
    x <= y + 1
    &   x + 1 >= y?
```

Figure 2: PLL definition of railway network

```
define timetable(A1,A2,A3,A4,B1,B4) tobe
    route1(A1, A2, A3, A4) &
    route2(B1, B4) &
    not near(A1, B1) &
    not near(A4, B4) ?
```

Figure 3: PLL definition of train timetable

they must not be near in time to the other two trains. One solution obeying these constraints is shown in Table 2.

The predicates describing the routes in this diagram are shown in Figure 2. The predicates *route1* and *route2* represent the fast and slow routes from station 1 to station 4. The PLL predicate *timetable* for two trains "A" and "B" using this network is then shown in Figure 3.

Using this definition we set the first train off at time zero and ask what times the second train "B" could leave by listing a number of alternative values for B1:

```
QUERY:
(B1=0 or ... B1=6)&
timetable(0,A2,A3,A4,B1,B4)?
ANSWER:
   B1 = 2 &  B4 = 7  &
   A2 = 3 &  A3 = 5  & A4 = 9 &
   or
   B1 = 6     B4 = 11 &
   A2 = 3 &  A3 = 5  & A4 = 9
```

Notice that the same answer is obtained even if we specify the arrival time B4 of the second train:

```
(B4=7 or ... B4=11)&
timetable(0,A2,A3,A4,B1,B4)?
ANSWER:
   B1 = 2 &  B4 = 7  &
   A2 = 3 &  A3 = 5  & A4 = 9 &
   or
   B1 = 6     B4 = 11 &
   A2 = 3 &  A3
```

The answer is either B1 = 2 minutes (arriving before the first train) or B1 = 6 minutes (arriving after the first train).

In Figure 4 is a timetable for three trains. Using this timetable we can obtain the time of the third train "C" assuming the first and second train leave at times 0 and 2 respectively and train "C" leaves at possible times 5 or 6:

```
QUERY:
```

```
define timetable3(A1,A2,A3,A4,B1,B4,C1,C4)
  tobe
    timetable(A1, A2, A3, A4, B1, B4) &
    route2(C1, C4) &
    not near(A1, C1) &
    not near(A4, C4) &
    not near(B1, C1) &
    not near(B4, C4) ?
```

Figure 4: Three train timetable

```
(C1=5 or C1=6)
 & timetable3(0,A2,A3,A4,2,B4,C1,C4)?
ANSWER:
    C1 = 6 &
    C4 = 11 &
    B4 = 7 &
    A2 = 3 &
    A3 = 5 &
    A4 = 9 &
```

The answer is train "C" must leave at time 6.

Observe that we could have avoided unnecessary recomputation by replacing the `timetable(...)` term in the definition of `timetable3(...)` in Figure 4 by the solution we are assuming for the first two trains.

2.3   Using interval constraints

In the earlier examples, we needed to drive the timetable predicate with a range of values. It was really *just luck* that the right values were chosen. The problem would have been even worse if we had chosen seconds rather that minutes for our time units or if the search space had been real numbers. The alternative is to use constraint technology and just reason about intervals and return a generalised answer. In order to explain the operation of the constraint technology the predicates used in the definition of timetable have been left undefined except *route 1*:

```
QUERY: some(A2,A3,A4) (B1 >=0 &
    timetable(0,A2,A3,A4, B1,B4))?
```

```
ANSWER: ... with only "route1" defined
   0<=B1
   & route2(B1, B4)
   & notnear(9, B4)
   & notnear(0, B1)
```

This generalised answer says the departure time of the second train must not be near time 0 and its arrival time must not be near time 9. This answer is then reentered as a query with the predicate *route 2* defined:

```
ANSWER: ... with "route2" defined
   0<=B1 & 5<=B4
   & B4 - B1 = 5
   & notnear(9, B4)
   & notnear(0, B1)
```

Because B4 is B1 + 5 and B1 greater than or equal to zero then the system has deduced that B4 must be greater than or equal to 5. This answer is then reentered as a query with *near* defined:

```
ANSWER: ... with "near" defined
   B1=2 &   B4=7

or 6 <=B1 & 11<=B4 &
   B4 - B1 = 5
```

The result is a definite solution at B1=2 and B4=7. However, the interesting solution is the indefinite second solution, that shows train B must start at or after 6 minutes and arrive at or after time 11 minutes. The apparently spurious formulas are there to allow this answer to be incrementally re-entered as a further query. On the Logic Spreadsheet these results are displayed as in Table 3.

2.4   Checking the timetable against observations

2.4.1   Object level

Once a timetable has been constructed it is essential to check this timetable against actual data. For example, suppose we observe that train "A" leaves

	A	B	C	D
1	0	≥ 6		Sth Ken
2	3			Not Hill
3	5			Padingtn
4	(	$\geq$		Hamsmth
	trainA	trainB	trainC	Station

Table 3: Spreadsheet results for Timetable

```
define timetablex(A1,A2,A3,A4, B1,B4)
tobe
    route1(A1, A2, A3, A4) &
    undefroute2(B1, B4)    &
    not undefnear(A1, B1) &
    not near(A4, B4) ?
```

Figure 5: Making *route2* and *near* undefined

at time 0 and arrives at station 4 at time 9. We also observe that train "B" leaves station 1 at time 1 and arrives at station 4 at time 3. Is this consistent with our timetable? Can we abduce the changes to restore consistency?

The answer to the query *timetable*(0, 3, 5, 9, 1, 3)? is false and so there is clearly either a fault in our observation or a fault in the timetable. To find the source of the contradiction in our timetable, we progressively undefine predicates in the body of the timetable until it ceases to be false. It turns out that at least the route2 predicate and one of the near predicates must be undefined for a non false answer to be obtained. In Figure 5 the new *timetable* predicate is called *timetablex*. Using this definition gives an answer that is a formula that the user must make true to restore consistency:

```
QUERY:
    timetablex(0,3,5,9, 1,3)?
ANSWER:
    undefroute2(1, 3)      &
    not (undefnear(0, 1))
```

```
define checktimetable(A1,A2,A3,A4,B1,B4)
  tobe  (route1(A1,A2,A3,A4)
          or not route1(A1,A2,A3,A4) &
          undefroute1(A1,A2,A3,A4) )&
        (route2(B1,B4)
          or not route2(B1,B4) &
          undefroute2(B1,B4) )&
        (not near(A1,B1)
          or not not near(A1,B1) &
          not undefnear(A1,B1) )&
        (not near(A4,B4)
          or not not near(A4,B4) &
          not undefnear(A4,B4) ) ?
```

Figure 6: Timetable with contradiction check

2.4.2 Meta level

Undefining each predicate by hand can be rather slow. However, we can use
the metalevel of PLL to partially automate this process. First we define, in
Figure 6, a new version of the timetable predicate that automatically checks
if each predicate is contradictory and calls an undefined predicate with the
same name but with "undef" in front. If we use this instead of the previous
timetable it will immediately give the predicates in the definition of timetable
that are false:

```
QUERY:
checktimetable(0,3,5,9, 1,3)?
ANSWER:
undefroute2(1, 3) & not(undefnear(0, 1))
```

However, we can define a meta predicate called *diag* in Figure 7. A predicate
reduce rewrites a query "q" using the PLL interpreter to an answer expression
"ans". If "q" rewrites to "false" then the above *checktimetable* predicate is
automatically used by including the string "check" on the front of query "q".

```
QUERY:
diagnostic("timetable(0,3,5,9, 1,3)",
             ans)?
ANSWER:
```

```
define diagnostic(q, ans) tobe
   reduce(q, ans2) &
   ( ans2 = "FALSE" &
       qq = "check" + q &
       reduce(qq, ans)
     or not(ans2 = "FALSE") &
         ans = ans2
   ) ?
```

Figure 7: Meta predicate to explain contradictions

```
define route2(x1,x4) tobe x4=x1+2 ?
```

Figure 8: Revised definition of *route2*

```
ans = "undefroute2(1, 3) &
       not(undefnear(0, 1))"
```

This shows that route2(1,3) is FALSE and route2 has to be modified to the new definition in Figure 8 and the query reissued:

```
QUERY: diagnostic("timetable(0,3,5,9, 1,3)",
                   ans )?
ANSWER:  ans = "not(undefnear(0, 1))"
```

It is now the turn of the predicate *near* to be modified as in Figure 9 and the query again reissued:

```
QUERY:
     diagnostic("timetable(0,3,5,9, 1,3)", ans )?
ANSWER:
     ans = "TRUE"
```

```
define near(x,y) tobe
   x <= y + 1 &
   x >= y?
```

Figure 9: Revised definition of *near*

```
define provable(query) tobe
   ["TRUE"] = rewrite(query) ?

define naf(query) tobe
   query1 = " """ + query + " ""
   & metaquery = "~ provable(" + query1 + ")"
   & provable(metaquery) ?
```

Figure 10: Definition of provable and negation as failure

We now finally have a timetable consistent with the observed data.

2.5   Negation as Failure

Negation as Failure [9], [19] in mathematical logic can be formalised as: ($\vdash$ $\neg(\vdash \phi)$) meaning that it is provable that ϕ *is not provable*, where ϕ has no free variables. Informally, it means *Do we have a contradiction?*

In PLL this can be defined using the metalevel predicate *rewrite*. We first define provable in PLL as a rewrite that rewrites an expression *query* to TRUE assuming that *query* contains no free variables. *Negation as failure* in PLL is then the same as the mathematical logic definition and is defined in Figure 10.

For this expression to be TRUE, *query* must rewrite to anything but TRUE. Furthermore, for this expression to be computable, all the free variables in *query* must be bound or quantified. For example, naf applied to some of the queries given earlier, to find if they are contradictory, gives the following results:

```
QUERY:
naf("timetable(0,3,5,9, 1,3)")?
ANSWER:    ... with only naf defined
   provable("not provable( "timetable(0,3,5,9, 1,3) ")")
ANSWER:    ... also with inner provable and timetable defined
   provable("not FALSE")
ANSWER:    ... also with outer provable defined
   TRUE

QUERY:
naf("timetable(0,3,5,9, 2,7)")?
```

```
define disj(exp, ans) tobe
    not some(a,b) exp = [a, "|", b]
    & somegt(exp, ans)
    or exp = [a, "|", b]
    & disj(a,aa)
    & disj(b,bb)
    & absorb(aa, bb, ans) ?
```

Figure 11: Definition of disj

```
ANSWER:   ... with only naf defined
    provable("not provable( "
        timetable(0,3,5,9, 2,7) ")") ?
ANSWER:   ... also with inner provable and timetable defined
    provable("not TRUE") ?
ANSWER:   ... also with outer provable defined
    FALSE

QUERY:
naf("some(B1,B4)timetable(0,3,5,9,
                    B1,B4)")?
ANSWER:   ... with only naf defined
    provable("not provable( "some(B1,B4)
        timetable(0,3,5,9, B1,B4) ")")?
ANSWER:   ... with timetable also defined
ANSWER:   ... also with inner provable and timetable defined
    provable("not FALSE")
ANSWER:   ... also with outer provable defined
    TRUE
```

Notice how the ability to return expressions allows some explanation of what would otherwise be very difficult to understand.

These examples illustrate how this kind of negation doesn't distinguish between something that is never true like $2 = 3$ and something which is simply undefined like $some(B1, B4)\ timetable(0, 3, 5, 9, B1, B4))$. The classical negation in PLL allows this distinction.

The classical negation in PLL allows a better modelling of reality by avoiding the need to assume undefined predicates are false and then subsequently to define them as true.

$$\phi \lor TRUE - R- > TRUE$$

```
define absorb(a,b,ans) tobe
  (a=["TRUE"] or b=["TRUE"]) & ans=["TRUE"]
  | not(a=["TRUE"] or b=["TRUE"]) &
    ans=[a,"|",b]?
```

Figure 12: Definition of *absorb*

```
define somegt(exp, ans) tobe
  exp = ["some",[t],[t,">",n]] &
  number(n)&
  ans = ["TRUE"]
  or not some(t,n)
        exp=["some",[t],[t,">",n]]
  & ans = exp ?
```

Figure 13: Definition of *somegt*

2.6   Meta level Reasoning

The example in this section shows how features that may be missing in PLL can be easily added at the metalevel. The feature missing is the ability to realise that $\exists x(x > c)$ can be rewritten to $TRUE$.

The first step is to attempt to rewrite our query to an answer just using conventional PLL:

```
QUERY:
      ans = rewrite("f(w) or some(t,now)
            (t>now & now=3+6)")?
ANSWER:
ans =
[["f",["w"]],"|",["some",
        ["q1"],["q1",">",9]]]
```

The particular metalevel predicate used here, unlike earlier, returns a tree structured list of quoted constants. This is much easier to manipulate than just a conventional string. The predicate *disj*, defined in Figures 11 to 13, is then used to break this answer down into elementary terms:

QUERY:
```
disj([["f",["w"]],"|", ["some",["q1"],["q1",">",9]]], ans)?
```

ANSWER: ... with disj defined
```
    some(q1, q2)
    (absorb(q2, q1, ans) &
    somegt(["f", ["w"]], q2) &
    somegt(["some", ["q1"], ["q1", ">", 9]], q1))
```

ANSWER: ... with somegt defined
```
    absorb(["f", ["w"]], ["TRUE"], ans)
```

ANSWER: ... with absorb defined
```
    ans = ["TRUE"]
```

As this trace shows the disj predicate breaks the expression down into *somegt* which looks for a term of the form *some ...* >. If it finds such a term it binds the variables q1 or q2 to TRUE, otherwise it returns the original expression. Finally, the absorb predicate returns TRUE if any arm of an *or* is true.

Of course this is only a tiny portion of a metalevel program. Its practical application to the timetable problem would be to answer temporal logic queries about whether a train was running some time in the future.

3 Conclusion

The major concern of PLL was to improve the match between an application builder's problem and the language used to describe his problem. Thus in the railway problem we only need specify the relationships between the times at the stations. The direction of the computation backwards or forwards is then automatic. To analyse the internal structure of a computation for explaining a contradiction, we simply leave some of our predicates undefined. Perhaps most importantly, it is easy to ask PLL to explain its mode of operation by temporarily undefining predicates. Furthermore, it is a simple matter at the metalevel to augment the reasoning power of PLL so that automatic problem solving capabilities not present can be added, but the speed of compiled PLL is retained. This can either be done as illustrated by predicates defined in PLL or by predicates defined in a conventional language such as C or *PROLOG*.

4 Acknowledgement

PLL is based on work performed mainly under ALVEY contracts *IKBS 084 Pure Logic Language* and *IKBS 092 Logic Database Demonstrator*. These contracts involved Imperial College, Edinburgh University, Bradford University and the Turing Institute. The funding by Alvey and ICL and the important contributions of Koos Rommelse, Ian Nairn, Peter McBrien[2], Joachim Achtzehnter [1][3] is gratefully acknowledged. In addition, we received background help from Bill O'Riordan Manager Future Systems Technology ICL, and from groups led by Professor Barry Richards at Edinburgh University, Professor Dov Gabbay at Imperial College and Professor Imad Torsun at Bradford University.

References

[1] J. Achtzehnter. Interval reduction in the pure logic language. ICL Internal Report, May 1989.

[2] K. R. Apt and M. H. van Emden. Contributions to the theory of logic programming. *JACM*, 29:841–863, 1982.

[3] E. Babb. Performing relational operations by means of specialised hardware. *ACM TODS*, March 1979.

[4] E. Babb. Finite computation principle: An alternative method of adapting resolution for logic programming. In *Proceedings of LP83*, Portugal, 1983.

[5] E. Babb. Pure logic language. *ICL Technical Journal*, May 1989.

[6] E. Babb. An incremental pure logic language with constraints and classical negation. In Dodd et al. [10].

[7] E. Babb and V. West. A spreadsheet with visible logic. *ICL Technical Journal*, 7(2), November 1990.

[8] *CHIP/SEPIA reference manuals*.

[9] K. L. Clark. Negation as failure. In H.Gallaire and J.Minker, editors, *Logic and Databases*, pages 293–322. Plenum Press, New York, 1978.

---

[2]Prototype implementation in C [14]
[3]Prototype constraint technology

[10] A. Dodd, R. Owens, and S. Torrance, editors. *Logic Programming: Expanding the Horizons*. Intellect, 1991.

[11] M. H. Van Emden and J. W. Lloyd. The logical reconstruction of prolog ii. *Journal of Logic Programming*, 1(2), August 1984.

[12] J. Jaffar, Michaylov, P. J. Stuckey, and R. H. C. Yap. The clp($\mathcal{R}$) language and system.

[13] J. W. Lloyd. Directions for metaprogramming. Technical report, Bristol University.

[14] P. J. McBrien. *PLL User Guide Version 0.32 Issue A*. ICL.

[15] P. J. McBrien. Implementing logic languages by graph rewriting. In Dodd et al. [10].

[16] Lee Naish. *MuPROLOG Reference manual*. Department of Computer Science, Melbourne.

[17] Lee Naish. Automating control for logic programs. *Journal of Logic Programming*, 2(3), October 1985.

[18] M. J. O'Donnell. *Equational Logic as a programming language*. MIT press, 1985.

[19] J. C. Shepherdson. Negation as failure. II. *Journal of Logic Programming*, 2(3), October 1985.

[20] Leon Sterling and Ehud Shapiro. *The Art of Prolog*. MIT Press, 1986.

[21] Pascal van Hentenryck. *Constraint Satisfaction in Logic Programming*. MIT Press, 1989.

A Summary of PLL

PLL is described in more detail in reference [6]. PLL has two broad classes of rewrites:

- Atomic formula rewrites which apply to *atomic formulas* involving data structures such as numbers, strings and lists.

- Compound formula rewrites which apply to a *set of formulas*.

A.1   Notation

Before continuing, it is worth noting some of the notations used in PLL. A query or definition [15] is written after the prompt *Query:* and is terminated by a question mark. The question mark "?" also closes off all unmatched brackets. The answer is written after the word *Answer:* In addition the *rewrite* symbol –R–> is used to show that something is rewritten using a rewrite definition. The Greek letter ϕ is used to denote a PLL expression such as $(x = 2 * 3)$. The letter c is used to represent bound variables or constants such as the number 12 or the list $[1, 2]$. Comments in PLL programs follow a % sign. The function $rewrite_{PLL}(\phi)$ rewrites the expression ϕ using the PLL interpreter.

A.2   Atomic Formula Rewrites

These rewrites apply to *atomic formulas* and try to reduce them to the solution *atomic formula* of the form $x_1 = c_1 \land \ldots \land x_m = c_m$.

Arithmetic

The arithmetic rewrites only occur on pairs of constants held in a tree to give a new state of the tree:

c1 + c2	$-R->$	the sum of c1 and c2
c1 - c2	$-R->$	the difference of c1 and c2
c1 * c2	$-R->$	the product of c1 and c2
c1 / c2	$-R->$	the division of c1 and c2
c1 = c2	$-R->$	TRUE if c1 equal to c2
	$-R->$	FALSE if c1 not equal to c2

List Structures

The list rewrites only occur on pairs of constants held in a tree to give a new state of the tree::

[x1, x2,...]=head::tail	$-R->$	x1 = head & [x2, ...] = tail
[x1, x2,...]=[y1, y2,...]	$-R->$	x1 = y1 & ...

A.3   Compound Formula Rewrites

Compound formula rewrites operate on sets of atomic formulas.

Conjunction

The atomic terms in a conjunction are reduced to bindings for variables, which are then available to any other atomic term involving that variable.

The primary rewrites cause expressions involving TRUE or FALSE to simplify as follows:

$$\phi \wedge TRUE \qquad -R-> \quad \phi$$
$$\phi \wedge FALSE \qquad -R-> \quad FALSE$$

Disjunction

The primary rewrites cause expressions involving TRUE or FALSE to simplify as follows:

$$\phi \vee TRUE \qquad -R-> \qquad TRUE$$
$$\phi \vee FALSE \qquad -R-> \qquad \phi$$

Existential Quantification

Existential quantification is a way of introducing local variables into an expression ϕ. In logic we write $(\exists x_1, x_2 \ldots)\phi$ and it means do there exist any bindings for the variables $x_1, x_2 \ldots$ that make the formula true.

To the user, the expression ϕ is locally reduced with the prevailing bindings. The complication is that we must restore the quantifier if we haven't bound all the variables mentioned in the list. Thus we have the rewrites:

$$\exists X \phi(Y) \qquad -R-> \quad \exists (X \cap Y')\phi'(Y'))$$
where $\phi'(Y') = rewrite_{PLL}(\phi(Y))$
and X , Y and Y' are sets of variables

$$\exists x(x = c \vee f(x,y)) \qquad -R-> \quad TRUE$$

$$\exists x(x = c \wedge f(x,y)) \qquad -R-> \quad f(c,y)$$

Universal Quantification and Implies

In PLL, *universal quantifiers* and *implies* are immediately written to a negative existential quantifier and a disjunction:

$$\forall x \phi \qquad\qquad -R-> \quad \neg \exists x \neg \phi$$
$$\phi_1 \Rightarrow phi_2 \qquad -R-> \quad \neg \phi_1 \vee \phi_2$$

Execution then proceeds as usual for existential quantifiers, negation and disjunctions.

Classical Negation

In the case of negation, the approach is more subtle than PROLOG *Negation As Failure*. In PLL we use standard tautologies of logic as rewrites:

$$\neg\neg\phi \qquad\qquad -R-> \quad \phi$$
$$\neg(\phi_1 \vee \phi_2) \qquad -R-> \quad (\neg\phi_1 \wedge \neg\phi_2)$$
$$\neg\phi \qquad\qquad -R-> \quad \neg rewrite_{PLL}(\phi)$$
$$\neg(\phi_1 \wedge \phi_2) \qquad -R-> \quad (\neg\phi_1 \vee \neg\phi_2)$$
$$\phi \qquad\qquad -R-> \quad \neg rewrite_{PLL}(\neg\phi_1)$$

Definitions

Instead of writing a formula directly, PLL allows user defined rewrites that rewrite to this formula with parameter substitution occurring:

define $<$ atomic head formula $>$ $<$ guard expression $>$ tobe ϕ ?

A.4   Constraint Technology

The constraint technology in PLL is based on the ECRC [8] work on Finite Domains and Intervals. Because PLL is a rewrite language the implementation [1] is different but the resulting prototype performance is very similar. However, because PLL can return general expressions, it can reason and give answers even about infinite domains.

The following are some of the rewrites that are implemented as an integral part of the interpreter.

Simplifying Interval Domains

$$x \geq c_1 \wedge x \geq c_2 - R- > x \geq c_1 \qquad \text{if } c_1 \geq c_2$$

$$x \geq c_1 \wedge x \geq c_2 - R- > x \geq c_2 \qquad \text{if } c_1 < c_2$$

Propagating Interval Domains through Linear Equations

$$x \geq c_1 \wedge x \leq c_2 \wedge y = ax + b$$
$$-R- >$$
$$x \geq c_1 \wedge x \leq c_2 \wedge$$
$$y \geq (ac_1 + b) \wedge y \leq (ac_2 + b) \wedge$$
$$y = ax + b$$

Restricting Real to Integer Domains

$$\text{if } integer(x) \wedge x \geq c_1 \wedge x \leq c_2$$
$$-R- >$$
$$x \in \{\text{set of integers encoded as bitmap from } c_1 \text{ to } c_2\}$$

Propagating Finite Domains through Linear Equations

$$x \in \{c_1, c_2, \ldots c_n\} \wedge y = x + b$$
$$-R- >$$
$$x \in \{c_1, c_2, \ldots c_n\} \wedge y \in \{c_1 + b, c_2 + b, \ldots c_n + b\} \wedge y = x + b$$

Restricting Finite Domains with $\neq$

The sets of constants are encoded by their upper and lower limit and by a bitmap:

$$x \in \{c_1, c_2, \ldots, c_i, \ldots, c_n\} \wedge x \neq c_i$$
$$-R- >$$
$$x \in \{c_1, c_2, (\text{without } c_i) \ldots c_n\}$$

The actual method of coding is very similar to the methods used in database query optimisation [3].

Metalevel

PLL expressions t held as strings can be rewritten by re-entering the PLL interpreter with a predicate called *rewrite* to give a list of strings t':

$$t' = rewrite(t)$$

```
Query:   ans = rewrite("x = 2 + 6")) ?
Answer:  ans = ["x" ,"=",8]
```

However, a PLL defined rewrite is also available called *reduce* that rewrites a string to a string:

$$reduce(t, t')$$

```
Query:   reduce("x = 2 + 6", ans)) ?
Answer:  ans = "x = 8"
```

A Framework for the Principled Debugging of Prolog Programs: How to Debug Non-Terminating Programs*

Paul Brna   Alan Bundy   Helen Pain

Abstract

The search for better Prolog debugging environments has taken a number of different paths of which three are particularly important: improvements to monitoring tools (notably the Transparent Prolog Machine [12]), providing for greater user control over the debugging process (notably as in Opium⁺ [11]), and partially automating the debugging process (notably in [17],[14],[18] and [15]).

A serious problem associated with this activity lies in providing a principled conceptual framework within which the programmer can work with a number of different debugging tools. Here, we outline a framework that we have developed for the debugging of Prolog programs. We point out the relationship that holds between this framework and each of these three advances in debugging.

In order to demonstrate how the framework can be used, we explore an issue that has received relatively little attention recently: the runtime detection of programs that do not appear to terminate.

Our analysis of (apparent) non-termination is based on a four level Bug Description Framework that we have developed. This analysis goes further than the consideration of programs that would normally be regarded as 'looping'. We describe a debugging strategy in conjunction with a range of monitoring tools that provide greater assistance than currently found. We indicate the increased efficiency that would be gained through a close-coupling of the program construction and execution phases.

From this analysis, we see that current (non-graphical) debugging tools do not provide the necessary help to deal with the case of (apparent) non-termination. We also note that even a graphical debugger

*This research was supported by SERC/Alvey Grant number GR/D/44287. Thanks to Alan Smaill for various discussions and helpful comments.

such as TPM [12] does not provide all the desired assistance that we would like.

1   Introduction

Recent developments in the provision of tools to aid in debugging Prolog programs have been impressive. We briefly summarise the current situation:

Monitoring: The Transparent Prolog Machine (TPM) is intended to provide a faithful representation of the execution of Prolog programs in terms of an extended AND/OR tree. We will not detail all the different ways in which this system is of use — the interested reader should refer to [1] for further information. It does, however, include a number of aids to navigation through the execution space of a Prolog program — e.g. it allows the user to choose between a 'course grained' view and a 'fine grained' one. There is a 'data-flow' representation of the results of unification. The programmer can hide subtrees and has some further control on the amount of detail. A Byrd box debugger is included within the system.

This kind of system has its associated difficulties. The programmer is offered a great deal of choice as to which way he/she should examine program execution. If, however, the programmer is to make full use of such facilities then an overarching debugging framework has the potential to be of great assistance.

Flexibility: The Opium+ debugger provides the user with the greatest degree of control. It allows the programmer to write his/her own debugging aids (in Prolog) — see [11] for details. In this way it avoids the problem of prescribing the precise way in which debugging should take place and hands over the decision to the programmer who then has the task of writing the necessary debugging tools in Prolog. This provides for flexibility but evades the issue of the conceptual framework in which debugging takes place. We hope that the designers of Opium+ will continue its development with a view to providing the necessary debugging framework.

Automation: The work on algorithmic debugging, inspired by Shapiro, is valuable because it provided a theoretical basis for the debugging of pure Prolog programs (ones not featuring the use of the cut, assert etc.). Other workers have tried to extend the theory to make it more useful for 'real' Prolog programming — e.g. [10]. Apart from various improvements in the efficiency of the diagnosis, we are particularly interested in an approach which respects the cognitive requirements of Prolog programmers. Thus we are interested in Lloyd's top-down diagnosis of wrong answers not because it can be shown to be more efficient that Shapiro's divide and query approach in some circumstances (in terms of queries answered by the programmer/oracle) but because the top-down approach (especially if this preserves the left-to-right order of subgoals) can be argued as providing a better mapping between the programmer's procedural expectations and the queries that the programmer/oracle has to answer [14].

Despite these various advances, many researchers have commented upon the difficulties facing the programmer in connection with non-terminating programs ([5],[8] and [22])

In this paper we explore the problem of debugging programs that do not appear to terminate. That is, the programmer expects that the program should terminate but it seems to be taking far too long. The purposes of this exploration are: to outline an approach to the top-down debugging of such programs; to expose problems with current environments; to show how the situation could be improved; and to show how the conceptual framework that we have developed can be used.

Basically, we have the same agenda as Hogger and Brough: how can we avoid creating programs that do not appear to terminate; how can we spot that a program is going to cause us problems before running it; and how can we pinpoint the reason for the surface manifestation of apparent non-termination.

In line with this, we presume that, ideally, Prolog environments should be augmented with tools for creating programs that can be guaranteed to terminate (as suggested, for example in [6]) and with tools for detecting non-terminating programs through some form of analysis of the whole program prior to execution. We also know that we will create programs (by accident or by design) that cannot be provided with a guarantee that they will terminate.

For the most part, we assume here that we have reached the stage of running a program which we want to terminate but for which there is no guarantee that it does. We further assume that during the course of testing the program we observe behaviour that makes us suspect, amongst a range of possible explanations, that we might have a non-terminating program.

Error	Unexpected	Unexpected Failure to Produce	Wrong
Side Effect			
Error Message			
Termination			
Instantiated Variable			

Table 1: The Symptom Description Level

We observe that this issue has received comparatively little attention outwith the recommendation of providing a standard run-time loop detection system. Certainly few of the researchers interested in developing Shapiro's approach to diagnosis have done more than provide such loop detection.

2   The Debugging Framework

We describe a four level Bug Description Framework as outlined in [4]. The classification and listing of bugs and debugging strategies is of fundamental importance: to give a foundation for motivating new, or improved, tools; and to provide a framework for integrating tools in a conceptually coherent way.

The particular framework which we have been developing is intended to account primarily for the bugs that are related to the program being developed. This excludes any consideration of bugs that lie outwith a good understanding of Prolog. We illustrate the framework rather than provide a formal definition:

Symptom Description If a programmer believes that something has gone wrong during the execution of some Prolog program then there are a limited number of ways of directly describing such evidence. In our framework, the description of the symptom which indicates a buggy program must be an entry in Table 1.

Note that the description of *Unexpected Failure to Produce Termination* in the above table is used for the purposes of uniformity. We regard this as synonymous with *(Apparent) Non-Termination*. *Wrong Termination*, although it looks like an unusual description, covers the cases of *Unexpected Failure of Goal* and *Unexpected Success of Goal*.[1]

We provide some simple examples.

- Exit with a Prolog error message such as, for example, one caused by an uninstantiated variable in an arithmetic expression. This is an *Unexpected Error Message*.

- Exit to the Prolog top level from an editor (written in Prolog). This is a case of *Unexpected Termination*.

- A Prolog goal succeeds without pretty printing a result — a case of *Unexpected Failure to Produce a Side Effect*.

- A Prolog goal unexpectedly fails — a case of *Wrong Termination*.

- A Prolog goal fails to bind a variable to the desired result — a case of *Unexpected Failure to Produce an Instantiation*.

Program Misbehaviour Description The explanation that is offered for a symptom. The language used is in terms of the flow of control and relates, therefore, to run-time behaviour. At the *Symptom* level, a program is a 'black box'. At the *Program Misbehaviour* level, it is a series of black boxes. Therefore, the detailed analysis of the nature of the *Program Misbehaviour* description level includes the *Symptom* level.

The *Program Misbehaviour* description level also includes a dimension that reflects expectations about control flow and another connected with the granularity of the program — viz. whether we look at the program as a set of black box modules, predicates, or clauses. We illustrate with the following three dimensional table. We also outline the detail present at this level.

- A case of *Wrong Termination* for a specific subgoal of the toplevel query. This illustrates a situation where we can make use of the *Symptom* level descriptions at some finer level of detail. In this case, we have used a level of granularity based on predicates.

- The unexpected failure to make use of some particular clause — perhaps caused by a failure to unify its head with the current, expected goal. This requires a clause-based level of granularity

---

[1]We admit that some items are less likely to occur than others. The relative frequency of these bugs is somewhat application-dependent.

Clause Error	Unexpected	Unexpected Failure to produce	Wrong
Predicate Error	Unexpected	Unexpected Failure to produce	Wrong
Module Error	Unexpected	Unexpected Failure to Produce	Wrong
Side Effect			
Error message			
Termination			
Instantiated Variable			
Transition			

Table 2: The Program Misbehaviour Description Level

```
factorial(N,Ans):-
        N1 is N-1,
        factorial(N1,Ans1),
        Ans is N*Ans1.
```

The series of goals

```
factorial(2,Ans1)
factorial(1,Ans2)
factorial(0,Ans3)
factorial(-1,Ans4)
...
```

Figure 1: A Buggy Version of `factorial/2`

for the description of the problem at the *Program Misbehaviour*
level.

- An unexpected sequence of goals — e.g. when it is expected that
  a recursive call of some predicate will terminate only to find that
  it does not do so. Consider the program for `factorial/2` found
  in Figure 1. This suggests that we have an unexpected sequence
  of goals (we have to move to the *Program Code Error description*
  level to provide the standard 'missing base case' explanation for
  this error).

Program Code Error Description The explanation offered in terms of
the code itself. Such a description may suggest what fix might cure the
program misbehaviour — e.g.

- There is a missing base case.
- There is a clause that should have been deleted.
- A test is needed to detect an unusual case.

Note that the explanation might be in terms of syntactical construc-
tions — such as 'a missing clause' — or some higher level description
such as 'missing base case' which makes an informal reference to the
description of some recursive technique.

We regard such techniques as distinct from algorithms: they have a
parallel with the notion of programming plan as used by Spohrer *et
al.* [21]. We give a simple schema (specialised for lists) of the kind of

code that is repeated again and again — here, **CDCH** stands for *Constructing Datastructures in the Clause Head*, **ChangeH** indicates the mapping between individual elements of the list datastructure and ... indicates an arbitrary number of further arguments. Both **CDCH** and **ChangeH** are capitalised to indicate that these are variables ranging over predicates.

```
:- mode(CDCH,...+, ...-).
:- mode(ChangeH, ...+, ...-, ...).

CDCH(...[], ...[]).
CDCH(...[H1|T1], ...[H2|T2]):-
        .........
        ChangeH(...H1, ...H2, ...),
        .........
        CDCH(...T1, ...T2).
```

We believe such techniques are important because a) there is a great deal of anecdotal evidence that Prolog programmers make use of such informal notions (both in debugging programs and in writing programs), b) we can go some way to defining a number of useful techniques ([2],[13]), and c) there is some leverage to be had by making information obtained from the program creation stage available to the Prolog debugging system.

Underlying Misconception Description Those fundamental misunderstandings and false beliefs that the programmer may have to overcome in order to maintain a consistent meaning for the program being developed. We can distinguish a number of different levels at which there might be misconceptions.

- Computation in general
- The underlying operating system
- The specification of the problem
- The Prolog language
- The nature of code which allows for efficient execution
- Program semantics

All these issues are important aspects of the programming process.

We restrict our attention mainly to the problems associated with the step from (assumed) correct specification to correct Prolog code. This simplification is driven by our interest in supporting the activities of experienced programmers. Consequently, we assume that the programmer has no fundamental conceptual difficulties with any of Prolog's features. Therefore, we have mainly considered the problems associated with how the intended semantics may have changed during program development.

We can identify a number of classes of misconception:

- Removing a constraint (possibly partially)
- Imposing an additional constraint
- Maintaining the 'degree of constraint' but swapping (at least) one constraint for another

The kind of constraints to which we refer include: mode information; type information; user-defined operator declarations; and information obtained from the program construction stage. As an illustration, consider the following program for `factorial/2` which has been written with the intention that the mode of `factorial/2` is given by `factorial(+,-)`:

```
factorial(0,1):- !.
factorial(N,Ans):-
        N1 is N-1,
        factorial(N1,Ans1),
        Ans is N*Ans1.
```

A modified Byrd box model trace for the query `factorial(0,0)` provides us with:

```
call: factorial(0,Ans1)
call: factorial(-1,Ans2)
call: factorial(-2,Ans3)
...
```

The *Program Code Error* featured in this program can be seen as arising, in part, from the belief that the mode is really `factorial(+,?)`. One possible explanation for this is that the programmer has assumed that the mode could be generalised.

Although we have mainly focussed on the problems facing programmers who have a good model of Prolog execution, we ought to extend the framework to allow for misunderstandings about Prolog. This is because even relatively experienced programmers possess some subtle misunderstandings about Prolog execution. For example, many have problems with how to write code to obtain increased efficiency. This is an important issue which needs further attention.

The approach we are advocating is mainly a descriptive one. However, we also hold a weak hypothesis that states that programmers will progress from a *Symptom* description through to the *Program Code Error* description via the *Program Misbehaviour* description and then, if necessary, on to the *Underlying Misconception* level.

For example, using the program listed in Figure 1, we start by obtaining a *Symptom* of *(Apparent) Non-Termination*, we explore the behaviour with the help of a debugger and, perhaps, obtain the *Program Misbehaviour* of *Unexpected Transition* in that we did not expect to find the subgoal factorial(-1,Ans4). Analysing the code results in a *Program Code Error* of, say, *Missing Base Case* in the application of the technique of *Primitive Recursion*. We do not pursue this error to the level of *Underlying Misconception* — except to say that such an error, if not due to some slip (such as forgetfulness), suggests that the programmer has some problem with the nature of computation in general.

Note that, for this paper, we are mainly concerned with the move from the *Symptom* of *(Apparent) Non-Termination* to the level of *Program Misbehaviour*.

3 The Analysis of (Apparent) Non-Termination

Our *Bug Description Framework* provides the framework within which we can develop various debugging strategies to help the programmer move from symptom to cause. We now set out to show how the framework helps us sift through the various possibilities. We have chosen to illustrate how, given the *Symptom* of *(Apparent) Non-Termination*, we can provide some guidance about how we proceed in our search for the root cause of the problem.

First, we remark that the basic symptom can be seen as arising from causes that can either be reduced to *Program Misbehaviour* descriptions or to factors outwith the correct behaviour of the Prolog system[2] — such as a bug in the Prolog interpreter or in the operating system. We will do no in-depth

---

[2] *Prolog Misbehaviour* descriptions? Also, *inter alia*, *Operating System Misbehaviour* and *Network Misbehaviour* descriptions.

exploration of the problems associated with an incorrect Prolog interpreter, an incorrect operating system or some bug in the interface. Consequently, the *Program Misbehaviour* descriptions can be seen as concerning the expected behaviour of some program relative to Prolog. We can consider them as relating to various *internal* factors. The other causes can be seen as relating to *external* factors. Our emphasis here is on the *internal* factors.

Given that we have decided to ignore *external* factors, we can turn to consider how we use the information about the symptom that we have detected to drive the search for a description at the *Program Misbehaviour* level.

We show how this search leads to a consideration of the activities of the Prolog Interpreter in building the execution tree. We will take this tree to be an extended AND/OR tree — and, since it therefore makes sense to see the programmer as working with the Transparent Prolog Machine (TPM), we assume the same notation [12]. We also assume that the programmer examines any side effects and results over a finite period of time via a single window for I/O.[3] Note that the TPM captures some notion of backtracking as further annotations to the tree.

We start from the *Symptom* of *(Apparent) Non-Termination* for some procedure call. Suppose that we now 'pursue' this symptom, with the help of a debugger, through the AND/OR execution tree until we can go no further. We assume that we use a top-down approach: we skip over a call. If we decide that we have a bug symptom then we retry and creep into the body of the procedure.

Let us assume also that the programmer believes that the length of time that he/she has waited is long enough to trigger the necessary description of *(Apparent) Non-Termination*.[4]

Scenario 1 We keep on finding a subgoal of the query under current investigation which has the *Program Misbehaviour* of *(Apparent) Non-Termination* but we eventually cannot creep into the body of the procedure.

We have reached a leaf of the execution tree.[5]

We call this *Suspended Building*.

---

[3]This situation is only a crude approximation to the circumstances under which debugging takes place.

[4]It is always possible, of course, that the programmer was wrong in ascribing *(Apparent) Non-Termination*.

[5]If a Prolog system made use of modules that were compiled in such a way as to be untraceable then calls to externally visible procedures would, in effect, be system predicates.

Scenario 2 We keep on finding a subgoal of the query under current investigation which has the *Program Misbehaviour* of *(Apparent) Non-Termination* and, though we don't know it without some further analysis, we will continue to find this to be the case.

We call this *Malignant Endless Building*.

Scenario 3 We keep on finding a subgoal of the query under current investigation which has the *Program Misbehaviour* of *(Apparent) Non-Termination* and, though we don't know it without some further analysis, this process will eventually terminate.

We call this *Slow Building*.[6]

Scenario 4 We find one subgoal of the query under current investigation fails and, on backtracking, a previous subgoal succeeds. This pattern continues and, though we don't know it without further analysis, will continue forever because the subgoal that failed will always do so and the subgoal that succeeded on redoing will always do so too.

The subgoal that always succeeds is a case of *Benign Endless Building*.

Scenario 5 We find one subgoal of the query under current investigation has a *Program Misbehaviour* of *Unexpected Failure to Produce a Side Effect*. On further investigation, we note that the side effect was produced but we had not looked in the right place for this.

This is termed *Hidden Building*.

In Section 4, we show how these notions are of help in debugging programs featuring *(Apparent) Non-Termination*.

From this partial analysis, we can distinguish two states of affairs concerning the execution tree during the programmer's observations: it can be in the same state throughout; or it can have changed state. We can also distinguish two related states in connection with side effects: they may or may not have occurred as expected.

Note that we should include an aspect that derives from our framework in connection with error messages. We get a modified analysis by considering, for example, whether we get a single error message when we skip a procedure call and derive a *Program Misbehaviour* of *(Apparent) Non-Termination* or whether we get an apparently endless stream of such messages when we skip the procedure call. We are in the process of extending our analysis to meet this deficiency in the near future.

---

[6]This is not to say that the call succeeds — it may fail. Also, another subgoal of the top level query might suffer from *Malignant Endless Building*.

We have structured this analysis in terms of three categories of low level behaviour: *Suspended Building, Hidden Building* and *Unfinished Building*. We have sketched how the various explanations for these kinds of behaviour are derived by considering the *Program Misbehaviour* involved and shown how they are a refinement of our previous classification.

Although we are mainly interested here in the *internal* factors as it is these that we wish to link up to the *Program Misbehaviour* description, we also provide some indication as to how the same basic scheme can be used in terms of the *external* factors. First, however, we consider the *internal* factors and give a more formal description:

Suspended Building The execution tree is not being extended and neither is backtracking taking place. Consequently, no side effect activity is visible. This can only occur when some system primitive is being executed and has not terminated — e.g. waiting for keyboard input via read/1.

Hidden Building The execution tree is being built but some side effect is not visible in the expected place — e.g. some use of write/1 is expected to produce output on the terminal's screen but the output is being redirected to a file.

Unfinished Building The execution tree is being built but Prolog has not finished executing the program in the time during which the program has been observed. All associated side effects are as expected. Common description of this might include looping (endless building) or building very complex data structures (slow building).

Note that the category of *Unfinished Building* permits two subcategories — those of *Endless Building* and of *Slow Building*. If the programmer can show that the program terminates and if we have a case that is definitely that of *Unfinished Building* then we must have a case of *Slow Building*. Unfortunately, the programmer may have high confidence in the program's termination but not be 100% sure. Consequently, a major problem (but, in practice, by no means the only one) is to discriminate between *Slow Building* and *Endless Building*.

Endless Building itself can be further divided in terms of *Malignant Endless Building* and *Benign Endless Building*: we shall discuss this issue further in Section 3.4.

There are equivalents for these in terms of external factors:

Investigate for External Factors
Check for Suspended Building
Check for Hidden Building
Investigate for Slow Building
Investigate for Endless Building

Figure 2: Different Strategies Available

Suspended Building Since the factors are now external ones, we seek explanations in terms that lie outwith Prolog — e.g. the system is dead, or the terminal has been set to take no input.

Hidden Building Again, we can find a corresponding situation in terms of external factors — e.g. the terminal has been set to redirect/flush all output.

Unfinished Building This could be due to a variety of causes. The system is heavily laden (sometimes producing an effect equivalent to slow building), or even that there is a bug in the Prolog interpreter (perhaps endless building).

It might be thought that we could construct a decision tree that could be used to guide us through the debugging process. We know, however, that the debugging strategy chosen will depend on contextual information that is not captured by the framework. Consequently, the programmer should be able to choose from a number of *checks* and *investigations* — a subset of which are shown in Figure 2.[7] A *check* has a fairly definite test associated with it while an *investigation* is a more open-ended sequence of activities. For example, the check for *Suspended Building* is relatively straightforward but investigating whether or not we have a case of *Endless Building* is much harder.

As we do not explore the *external* factors in great detail, we note briefly that the check for whether the problem is connected with external factors would require us to formulate an approach which includes checks to see that the computer is still functioning, that the loading is adequately low, that the terminal is functioning properly and so on.

---

[7]This can only be a subset because we have not yet extended our analysis to other symptoms.

3.1   Suspended Building

The case of *Suspended Building* due to internal factors can be reduced to the
Program Misbehaviour of *(Apparent) Non-Termination* for a system predicate.

An example would be a use of skip/1 which might be waiting for a particular
character to be input before terminating — but this has not happened. A
pathological case occurs (in several well-known Prolog systems) with the
built-in predicate length/2 when it is used to evaluate the length of a circular
list — e.g.:

```
?- X=[a,b,c|X],length(X,Y).
```

Although the *occurs* check should spot the circularity in the unification as-
sociated with X=[a,b,c|X], report this and fail (possibly reporting this as
an error), many Prolog systems do not do this. A call to length/2 then has
to evaluate a list which is of infinite length. Therefore, the behaviour of the
system predicate can be described as a *Program Misbehaviour* of *(Apparent)
Non-Termination*.

The check as to whether we are waiting on the successful termination of a
built-in predicate ought to be straightforward — assuming we have ruled out
a possible external factor. If we are using the TPM, it is simply a matter of
inspecting the display.

3.2   Hidden Building

If we have the *Symptom* of *(Apparent) Non-Termination* then we presumably
were not expecting to see any side effects. If we had been expecting to see
evidence of side effects then we would have derived the *Symptom* of *Unexpected Failure to Produce a Side Effect* — and we are not directly addressing
the issue as to how to debug programs with this symptom.

On the other hand, when we are searching for an explanation for *(Apparent)
Non-Termination* then we might be about to examine a procedure that we
do associate with side effects. If we look for these and they do not occur
where we expect them to occur then we have a *Program Misbehaviour* of
Unexpected Failure to Produce a Side Effect. We have already pointed out
how this can be seen as *Hidden Building* due to *internal* factors.

This would suggest that the programmer did not expect some particular
program control choice to be made — e.g. the program may either produce

a side-effect (or go off and do something else which does not produce a side-effect).

We might think that only a very few system predicates can ultimately be responsible for this. Unfortunately, the predicates that can achieve this effect include many of the side effecting ones — e.g. assert/1, record/3, retract/1, tell/1 etc.

3.3 Unfinished Building

We have already pointed out that this can be seen as either *Slow Building* or *Endless Building*. Discriminating between these two cases is a major problem: if we have a case of *Slow Building* then we may want to know which aspect of the computation is producing the problem.

The main point about *Slow Building* is that the computation will terminate but it is taking a longer time to do so than anticipated. Given that there are no unusual *external* factors, we might have simply failed to appreciate that the datastructures being manipulated would be as complex as they actually are. This raises issues about the anticipated computational complexity of the code.

When we turn to the case of *Endless Building* then we ask whether we want to distinguish between different forms of this. We obtain a natural distinction if we remember that our execution tree is an augmented AND/OR tree. In particular, the annotations which we attach to the tree skeleton allow us to capture the program's backtracking behaviour.

We can distinguish between two extreme cases of *Endless Building*: one case in which the fundamental tree structure is being extended; and another case in which the tree structure is not being extended but further annotations are being added. A purely deterministic program suffering from *Endless Building* would feature the first of these behaviours.

As an example, consider this buggy version of factorial/2:

```
factorial(N,Ans):-
        N1 is N-1,
        factorial(N1,Ans1),
        Ans is N*Ans1.
```

If we pose the query factorial(2,X) then the execution tree built is infinite and no backtracking takes place.

Now consider a very artificial example that makes use of a failure driven loop:

```
echo:-
        repeat,
        read(X),
        write(X),
        nl,
        fail.
```

This program is not necessarily buggy — but if the programmer intended to insert a test for some input term then the program is buggy. We might ascribe a *Program Code Error* of *Missing Test* in the implementation of a *Generate and Test* technique.

A call to echo/0 does not terminate. We can regard this call as doing no building of the execution tree skeleton after the call to fail/0.[8] This is subject to the proviso that repeat/0 is a system primitive.

This is a specific instance of a much more general scenario which we informally describe by the metaphoric description of 'bouncing around'. Basically we have a recursively defined procedure that terminates but, later, is redone as a consequence of backtracking. The call terminates and the computation eventually backtracks to redo the call whereupon the call terminates — and so on.

This raises an issue as to how many "kinds" of non-termination we really want to distinguish.

3.4   Kinds of Endless Building

The fundamental case is that in which the flow of control enters the Byrd box associated with this procedure and never exits. We could informally regard this as *Malignant Endless Building.*

Another interesting case arises when the program contains a procedure call that always generates a further solution on demand (i.e. an infinite generator), and if, for each such solution, there is some later call that will (finitely) fail for that solution. Again, we have *Endless Building* — but this time we will informally call this *Benign Endless Building*. We can see this situation as corresponding to a generalisation of the failure-driven loop technique which, if unintended, has resulted in a bug.

---

[8]We appreciate that it is possible to see this differently.

There is a third option: we have a procedure call that follows the *Benign Endless Building* behaviour for a few (or even very many) calls but then, eventually, turns into *Malignant Endless Building*.

In short, there are two fundamental ways in which a call can turn out to produce *Endless Building*. Any other non-terminating behaviour may result from the combination of these two fundamental causes.

4 Debugging an (Apparently) Non-Terminating Program

We now apply a simple top-down debugging strategy which copes with several different *Symptoms* other than the one in which we are interested here — namely, the *Symptom* of *(Apparent) Non-Termination*. The basic schema is to:

Turn on the trace

Issue the goal

creep to examine the subgoals

skip over each subgoal

If an incorrect result is detected, **retry** the last subgoal

creep to examine the behaviour of the defective subgoal's subgoals

Repeat the process for the new set of subgoals

This approach is related to the partially automated approach to finding missing answers suggested by Shapiro [20] and the approach for tracking down wrong answers outlined by Lloyd [14]. We explore debugging strategies for programs exhibiting the *Symptom* of *(Apparent) Non-Termination* using a similar top-down approach. This is of interest as other attempts to track down the causes of non-termination have generally examined the goal stack after some arbitrary depth bound has been exceeded.

Our method of presentation is to describe an idealised situation and then relate this to the actual facilities usually provided.

4.1   Suspended Building

If we are using a graphical debugger that shows the execution tree as it is being grown then detecting *(Apparent) Non-Termination* caused by *Suspended Building* is trivial since no tree building activity will be visible — so it will be clear where the execution has stopped.

Note that the graphical debugger must not be a post-mortem one for this to work. The TPM is able to make use of either a post-mortem mode or a run-time mode. Consequently, the TPM is ideal for this problem.

Now consider how we might locate this problem using a standard DEC-10 style debugger. During the execution of the top-level goal, we can apply the following strategy for the standard debugger:

Raise an interrupt;

Switch on tracing;

If no trace output, raise another interrupt; and

Abort

and we have a *Program Misbehaviour* of *(Apparent) Non-Termination* for a system predicate. Now we have to track down exactly where in the program this is happening as the debugger gives no help either with identifying the system predicate causing the offence or with the context in which this predicate is called!

Although using the simple top-down approach with the standard debugger does work, the process is extremely slow. This is roughly how it works out: using the top-down approach, we spot which subgoal of the top-level goal caused the problem. We then have to start again as the debugger doesn't offer the normal range of choices (since we are stuck 'inside' a box). Now we go one level deeper to spot the subgoal of the subgoal that causes the problem — and so on. We can keep going but this is really painful.

How can the standard debugger be improved so that we can avoid this tedious problem? In principle, the Prolog system knows which system primitives can cause *Suspended Building*. We need the Prolog system to tell us which is the last 'box' that has been entered. On interrupting execution, we should be able to request this information.

An alternative approach which is more in tune with the top-down approach requires that the debugger can determine that the execution of some of the subgoals of a goal cannot be involved in causing *Suspended Building*. The system could then safely skip over them — otherwise, we should require the system to recommend the programmer to creep 'into the body' of the relevant goal. Note that this suggests that a programmer should be able to communicate which hypothesis is being followed up.

4.2 Hidden Building

As pointed out above, if we seek an explanation for *(Apparent) Non-Termination* then we would probably not expect *Hidden Building* due to internal factors. This is because *Hidden Building* carries with it the idea that we are dealing with some form of *Unexpected Failure to Produce a Side Effect*.

On the other hand, the check that something is going on would be cheap so that we can at least determine whether or not we are in this situation *if we had the right tools*.

This class of tools is one which we might expect Prolog to possess in order to handle this type of problem. We have already suggested that a view onto the program database is essential for the basic story of how Prolog works [7] and have shown how this is necessary for extending the story to cope with side-effects such as those caused by assert/1 and record/3 [3]. We also need to consider views onto all side-effects caused by write/1.

The desired approach is to be able to view activity on any output (or input) channel. This would allow the programmer to inspect a window for each open channel (to see what is going on) and to monitor activity on the channel. We can then expect the programmer to be alerted to a channel wanting/receiving data — it is up to the programmer to know which channels should carry which items of data.

Although it is possible to cobble together some partial remedy for this situation, few environments really handle this well. As far as we are aware, Eisenstadt and Brayshaw's TPM does not possess these tools either [1]. The best we can do is to inspect various aspects of the environment for these side effects — e.g. using tail -f filename (in the Unix-like environment) to see how some file is being processed or looking for side effects associated with built-in predicates such as write/1. Although the separate I/O window (such as that provided by MacProlog) is an improvement over the standard debugger, we do not see why the programmer should not be provided with monitoring of all channel activity as a default.

4.3   Unfinished Building

We now consider the case of *Unfinished Building* by considering the ways in which we might detect that we have a case of *Slow Building*.

Now, if we have ruled out all but the case of *Unfinished Building* then finding positive evidence in favour of *Slow Building* is negative evidence in favour of *Endless Building* and vice versa. The check for *Suspended Building* provides very strong positive evidence — as does the check for *Hidden Building*. The investigations that can now be done are theoretically impossible to turn into a completely general decision procedure (*c.f.* the halting problem).

The main point about *Slow Building* is that the computation will terminate but it is taking a longer time to do so than anticipated. Given that there are no unusual *external* factors, we might have simply failed to appreciate that the datastructures being manipulated would be as complex as they actually are. This raises issues about the anticipated computational complexity of the code.

There are various checks that we might do on the computation in order to provide us with some positive evidence in favour of *Slow Building*. Many of these checks can be done during program construction. If we can do these checks within the environment in which program construction is done then so much the better. If the guarantees provided by the checks can be passed reliably to the program execution stage and, therefore, to the debugger, then we should have an easier task in debugging our program. Here, we assume that we have not obtained the necessary guarantees for at least some of the predicates found within the program.

- For some procedures that are recursing, check that some input structures are the anticipated ones: this is connected with type checking

- For some procedures which are recursing, check that the recursion arguments are 'decreasing' in anticipated ways

- For some procedures that are recursing, check that some output structures are being built in the anticipated ways

- For some procedure(s) which is recursing, check that the inputs and outputs are sufficiently well instantiated: this is connected with the expected modes but can be carried further than the standard description (i.e. not just +, - and ? but also describing the positions of variables in arbitrary terms)

```
perms(X,Y):-
        perms(X,[],Y).

perms(Inlist,Acc,Outlist):-
        perm(Inlist,Perm),
        \+ memberchk(Perm,Acc),!,
        perms(Inlist,[Perm|Acc],Outlist).
perms(X,Acc,Acc).

perm([],[]).
perm(X,[A|Y]):-
        extract(A,X,B),
        perm(B,Y).

extract(A,[A|Tail],Tail).
extract(A,[H|T],[H|Ans]):-
        extract(A,T,Ans).
```

Figure 3: Code Featuring 'Slow' Building

- For some procedures that are recursing, check that the depth of the recursion is no larger than expected: this is connected to complexity analysis

In the absence of any guarantees that the program will terminate these checks will not provide completely reliable evidence.

We will also briefly examine the basic techniques for looking for positive evidence of *Endless Building*. The received wisdom is to examine the ancestors and look for a repeated goal. The main suggestion here (that we have made before) is to automate the search for these repeated goals. If none are found, then continue. From our point of view this is, however, not quite sufficient as a strategy. This is partly because several different accounts can be given in terms of the *Program Misbehaviour*.

Input Terms are OK We use an example of a very slow sorting program — perms/3 — as shown in Figure 3.

For example, we can examine the growth of the *accumulator argument* used in perms/3 using the advice package (as shown below).

The advice package was written by Richard O'Keefe in 1984 to provide Interlisp-like advice package facilities. The intention is that it should

```
?- advise(perms(_,X,_),call,(write('Call: '),write(X),nl)).
?- advise(perms(_,X,_),exit,(write('Exit: '),write(X),nl)).
?- advise(perms(_,X,_),fail,(write('Fail: '),write(X),nl)).
?- advise(perms(_,X,_),redo,(write('Redo: '),write(X),nl)).

?- perms([a,b,c,d,e,f],X).

Call: []
Call: [[a,b,c,d,e,f]]
Call: [[a,b,c,d,f,e],[a,b,c,d,e,f]]
Call: [[a,b,c,e,d,f],[a,b,c,d,f,e],[a,b,c,d,e,f]]
Call: [[a,b,c,e,f,d],[a,b,c,e,d,f],[a,b,c,d,f,e],[a,b,c,d,e,f]]
Call: [[a,b,c,f,d,e],[a,b,c,e,f,d],[a,b,c,e,d,f],[a,b,c,d,f,e],
    [a,b,c,d,e,f]]
```

Figure 4: Watching the Accumulator Grow

be used to implement a trace package. It allows the programmer to attach output commands and checking commands to the various ports defined by the Byrd box model [16]. We show how this can be done in Figure 4. We can see how the *accumulator* is growing: as there are no exits, fails or redos we can be sure that the datastructure is being built recursively.[9] Here, we are fairly sure that the structure is being built correctly as we can see that each addition is added at the head of the list and that each is a permutation of the input list and that there are no repetitions — i.e. we can check additions against a set of expectations that we have. We can think of this as checking the type we have implicitly assigned to the accumulator.

In general, if we give the accumulator argument a type and we arrange for this type to be checked at run-time then we cannot guarantee that the lack of a type error means that all is going well. All we can guarantee is that if our type description of the *accumulator* argument is broken then we will be told.

In this case, we have some hope of spotting a problem but, in general, we have no hope of looking at some very complex term and reliably saying "yes, that is exactly what the program should produce".

Recursion Argument 'Decreasing' Healthily Examining the recursion

---

[9]We can also see how clumsy it is to provide the necessary specification of what is wanted.

```
intersect([],_ , []).
intersect([Element|Residue], Set, Result):-
      member(Element, Set), !,
      Result = [Element|Intersection],
      intersect(Residue, Set, Intersection).
intersect([_|Rest], Set, Intersection):-
      intersect(Rest, Set, Intersection).
```

Figure 5: Code Featuring a Recursion Argument

argument of **perms/3** cannot be done because there isn't one. Instead, let us consider the program found in Figure 5.

The predicate `intersect/3` is considered to have mode `intersect(+,+,-)` and the first argument position is the recursion argument. Let us assume that we are finding the intersection of two fairly large sets. Then we might want to engage in a dialogue with Prolog such as found in Figure 6. With this trace, we can spot all is well as the numbers output indicate the number of elements in the list which is the input in the recursive argument position.

As long as the programmer has some expectation of how the recursion is supposed to progress, such a tool is very useful. Although we have given a fairly trivial example, the basic idea is useful and can be generalised to constructor functions other than [...|...]. Of course, there are other measures but the commonest ones can be catered for. Another extension would provide for cases where there are two recursion arguments and so on.

Output Structures 'Growing' Well When we know that an argument of some predicate is going to be instantiated more fully then we may want to examine this argument position to see how the growth is going. Unfortunately, this is a hard thing to do using the advice package.

Essentially, we want to accumulate a record from information that is not available at call time but is

- Sometimes available after unification of the goal with the head of a clause
- Sometimes only available at the time when the next recursive call is made

We will consider a desirable scenario for the program in Figure 7 with the goal:

```
?- advise(intersect(X,_,_),call,
   (length(X,Y),write('Call: '),write(Y),nl)).
?- advise(intersect(X,_,_),exit,
   (length(X,Y),write('Exit: '),write(Y),nl)).
?- advise(intersect(X,_,_),fail,
   (length(X,Y),write('Fail: '),write(Y),nl)).
?- advise(intersect(X,_,_),redo,
   (length(X,Y),write('Redo: '),write(Y),nl)).

?- intersect([a,b,c,d,e,f],[s,e,r,t,a,g,a,z,s,e],X).

Call:   6
Call:   5
Call:   4
Call:   3
Call:   2
Call:   1
Call:   0
Exit:   1
...
```

Figure 6: Watching the Recursion Argument Decrease

```
delete(El,[],[]).
delete(El,[El|Rest],Ans):-
        delete(El,Rest,Ans),!.
delete(El,[H|Rest],[H|Ans]):-
        delete(El,Rest,Ans).
```

Figure 7: Code Featuring Output Structures

```
?- watch_grow(delete(_,_,X)).
?- delete(a,[a,s,w,e,r,s,a,a,a,e,r,t,q],X).

[s|_]
[s,w|_]
[s,w,e|_]
[s,w,e,r|_]
[s,w,e,r,s|_]
[s,w,e,r,s|_]
[s,w,e,r,s|_]
[s,w,e,r,s|_]
[s,w,e,r,s,e|_]
[s,w,e,r,s,e,r|_]
[s,w,e,r,s,e,r,t|_]
[s,w,e,r,s,e,r,t,q|_]
```

Figure 8: Watching Output Structures Grow

```
delete(a,[a,s,w,e,r,s,a,a,a,e,r,t,q],X)
```

The output is found in Figure 8.

There are many problems with this kind of output. If backtracking causes some structure building to be undone this can be hard to follow. On the other hand, if we can move away from the teletype model for output to a window model we could at least watch the dynamic growth and contraction of the structure as it is built. In many cases, however, it will not be easy to say that a datastructure is being built correctly.

Groundness of Input and Output Arguments We will not look at an example of this case now. There is a strong parallel with the type checking situation anyway.

Checking the Depth of Recursion Dec-10 Prolog had a feature which allowed the programmer to set an arbitrary number of calls as the maximum allowed before interrupting the computation.[10] This is a very crude way of managing affairs. A less crude method would be to have user-definable bounds on all recursive predicates. This would allow the programmer to represent intuitions about the complexity of the computation. An ambitious extension would be to try to infer the

---

[10]Other Prolog implementations have taken up this idea. This includes Quintus Prolog and MProlog.

expected depth of the recursion for each recursive predicate and for each combination of inputs. The check, therefore, is to be warned (e.g. dumped in the debugger) whenever some threshold is crossed.

Looking for Benign Endless Building If we suspect that we have a case of *Benign Endless Building* then the best solution is a graphical debugger — based on the TPM — with which we are able to watch control 'bouncing around'. This is, however, not ideal because we would see too much behaviour — so we would prefer much of the irrelevant information to be suppressed.

Turning to the standard debugger, we would like to use the top-down approach to quickly find the lowest root that contains both the over generating procedure call and the goal that keeps on failing.

This can be done by a variant of the standard top-down method (we know here we will have trouble in trying to skip over some predicate): switch on the trace, issue the query, creep to examine the subgoals, skip over each subgoal, if it looks like *(Apparent) Non-Termination* then switch tracing on and go back to the call port of the problematic skipped call, creep to examine the subgoals, skip over each subgoal until the failing subgoal found and then backup to the last succeeding subgoal.

Now the backup command should go back to the call port of the most recent box *at the same level in the execution tree* whose call has outstanding alternatives to try. This is, however, still not exactly what we want.

Between the infinite generator and the subgoal that keeps on failing there may be several subgoals that are non-deterministic for the particular inputs provided. Unless we have some intuition about which subgoal is infinitely generating we cannot say whether a given subgoal is the cause of the problem.[11]

This still does not guarantee that we have found the first 'wall'[12] of the two between which the 'control' ball might be bouncing[13]. So we

---

[11]Note that we can expect that only a limited number of such predicates need to be investigated. We can also expect that some will have been subjected to analysis so that we can be given guarantees that they do terminate. Also, an intelligent debugger could cut out any subgoals that are not defined recursively *for this particular command*. We would like to be able to tell the debugger that we should keep on going back (if there is another subgoal left to go back to).

[12]i.e. the infinitely generating procedure call.

[13]The second of these 'walls', the procedure call that keeps on failing, is found inside that failing subgoal but we don't know exactly where yet and, taking the top-down approach, we don't need to know for now.

should be able to set up markers which say effectively "unleash the trace for a bit but only report 'bounces' between this subgoal and the failing subgoal. If a bounce doesn't occur then report this as I will want to set up new 'walls'".

We may suspect that we are in this situation — locked forever into the cycle represented informally as "a ball bouncing between two walls" — but we don't know for certain. It may turn out, for example, that there are other 'walls' awaiting being 'set up' once the current 'walls' are breached[14]. For example, suppose we suspect that we have the following situation:

goal :-

        subgoal1,
        subgoal2,   **wall1**
        subgoal3,
        subgoal4,   **wall2**
        subgoal5.

We assume that we suspect that `subgoal2` is an infinite generator and `subgoal4` is a call that always fails. This may be incorrect in both respects and it may well be that the real combination of infinite generator and failing subgoal is as in:

goal:-

        subgoal1,   **wall1**
        subgoal2,
        subgoal3,
        subgoal4,
        subgoal5.   **wall2**

This does not settle the matter because there may be other walls awaiting being 'set up'. Things can be even worse in that we might have a number of different failing goals and a number of different procedures that are over-generating. Consequently, we need efficient ways of extracting the desired information automatically under programmer control.

Looking for Malignant Endless Building If, on the other hand, we are looking for evidence of a procedure that produces the behaviour of *Malignant Endless Building*, then we can find the offending call much

---

[14]For example, we might only suspect an infinitely generating predicate — and this suspicion is not well founded.

more easily using the standard debugger. We can keep on **skipping**, **retrying** and **interrupting** by hand but we would like to be able to automate this and/or be able to attach print statements to the apparent cause of the problem as discussed previously. The graphical debugger again promises much if some way can be found to suppress detail automatically.

If we have a program that possesses a predicate which will at first, generate solutions that keep on being rejected by some call that always fails then things can fall out in one of two main ways (all other things being equal). If we interrupt too early, then there is a hope that we can detect the 'walls' between which the 'control ball' is bouncing. If we wait long enough then we can use a similar method as for detecting the predicate featuring *Malignant Endless Building*.

5   The Bug Description Framework Revisited

We have discussed the debugging of apparently non-terminating programs in terms of the execution tree. This has allowed us to move towards the description of various possible and hypothetical debugging tactics.

We now briefly discuss how our description of *Program Misbehaviours* takes into account the various inputs to a procedure. For instance, suppose we provide a top-level query that has an incorrect parameter value[15]. Alternatively, suppose that a subgoal is provided with an input through the success of a previous subgoal. This suggests that one of three possible events has taken place:

- We have made a mistake in the 'bolting' together of the various parts of the program — i.e. the subgoal-about-to-executed is correctly written and everything that has taken place previously is correct but the programmer never intended this sequence of goals to occur in the code. Consequently, we have a *Program Code Error* description.

- We have suddenly realised that our specification for the subgoal-about-to-be-executed is misconceived. This suggests one of the kinds of error that are made at the *Underlying Misconception* level.

- If the subgoal-about-to-be-executed is correct in that no mistake has been made about what sorts of input the procedure should work on

---

[15]Pereira and Calejo call such a goal inadmissible [18]

then a previous subgoal may have produced some *Program Misbehaviour* connected with instantiation (unexpected instantiation, unexpected failure to instantiate or a wrong instantiation).

Alternatively, we have taken a wrong path through the search space which could be due to a variety of causes — including a previously undetected case of a procedure being called with the wrong inputs. This might be characterised as an *Unexpected Transition* which is one of the possible *Program Misbehaviour* descriptions.

As we can see, encountering such a problem, may lead us to investigate for the cause in terms of *Program Misbehaviour*, *Program Code Error* or *Underlying Misconception*. Yet, on the surface, we have what can be regarded as a type error.

We also point out how the behaviour of recursively defined procedures fits into our framework. There are two types of information considered here: the recursion argument(s) and the expected depth of recursion for some recursive procedure(s).

Knowledge about how the recursion argument should decrease is a consequence of the intentions of the programmer at the code writing stage. Knowing that a certain recursion argument should decrease during execution places an expectation on an argument of the recursive call. This appears in our framework at the *Program Misbehaviour* level in roughly the same way that type errors appear.

At first sight, knowing about the expected depth does not appear to fit into our framework at all. It imposes an expectation on some particular recursive call not being found after the expected number of recursive calls. If we are examining the execution of a program that results in a recursive program exceeding the anticipated depth then the occurrence of such a call results in a *Program Misbehaviour* description of an *Unexpected Transition* in that (presumably) the expectation is that termination should have been achieved through calling some different procedure.

6 Other Approaches

We restrict ourselves here to some brief remarks.

- The graphics-based debuggers such as TPM do win in the case of *(Apparent) Non-Termination* of a system predicate but it is extremely painful to use the standard debugger to localise the fault.

- No systems provide much direct support for watching channel activity in order to detect errors described as *Unexpected Failure to Produce a Side Effect*. This includes TPM as well.

- There are few tools that help programmers monitor potential problems connected to the *Slow Building/Endless Building* scenarios. The spy package built by Richard O'Keefe and distributed with the Prolog library is flexible — but is not flexible enough. Dichev and du Boulay's data tracing system is too primitive and aimed at novices [9]. We are not aware of how we could handle this problem in Opium$^+$. The retrospective approaches advocated by Shapiro and many others can only be regarded as a partial solution. As far as we know, TPM cannot easily handle this situation either.

- Watching out for (what is, in effect, unintended) endless failure-driven loops is not supported directly by any system of which we are aware. Again, it may be that Opium+ can be used to construct a useful tool. The TPM is partly useful here.

We note that often systems fail to provide the right 'handles' for debugging: programmers are not able to manipulate debuggers in terms of the strategies that they are following. Instead, programmers are required to encode their strategies to fit the low level facilities provided. We would like to see a more positive approach to controlling debugging within a good conceptual structure.

The work of Shapiro suggests that communicating expectations to the debugger (i.e. pursuing wrong answers or missing answers) pays off. Calejo and Pereira have developed a much friendlier dialogue with the programmer allowing for a greater range of expectations to be communicated [19]. Other work, such as that by Ducassè [11] may yet provide the groundwork for building a far more powerful system for communicating expectations about programs at a level closer to the one at which a programmer is currently working. We have shown here the need both to extend the scope of such work and to take into account the various different levels at which debugging takes place.

7   Conclusions

We summarise our observations about the needs for debugging Prolog programs.

- Debugging Prolog programs requires a high level framework which can be used by the programmer to guide his/her debugging. For example, there is a need for a high level interface to O'Keefe's advise package.

- By using the framework, we can reduce some debugging strategies to a level at which the Prolog system ought to be able to offer considerably more help than is typically the case. This required us to introduce the notions of *Suspended Building* etc.

- We have pointed out the problem with finding the root cause of *Suspended Building* and indicated how the standard debugger can be improved at low cost.

- We have indicated how the problem of dealing with *Hidden Building* can be eased by automatically providing each I/O channel with a monitor.

- We have stressed the need for tools: to watch the growth of terms; to watch the behaviour of a term associated with a recursion argument; and to watch the growth of output terms.

- We have suggested an elaboration on the simple idea of a depth limit on the computation by annotating predicates with an expression that provides some notion of the expected computational complexity.

- We have motivated the need for tools to watch for patterns associated with a buggy version of the failure-driven loop — the infinite generate-always fail loop.

In short, we have made a contribution to the methodology of debugging programs and illustrated this with respect to programs that do not appear to terminate. We have also suggested a strategy for debugging based on: seeking to discriminate between *internal* and *external* factors; checking for *Suspended Building* and *Hidden Building*, and discriminating between *Slow Building* and *Endless Building*.

- We have analysed the *Symptom* of *(Apparent) Non-Termination* in terms of a number of factors related to the behaviour of Prolog.

- We have pointed out that, although distinguishing between *Slow Building* and *Endless Building* is a major problem, there are other, non-trivial causes that need methods for debugging them.

- We have indicated a number of debugging tools useful to monitor the execution in ways which are not currently supported in Prolog environments.

- We have sought to show how the four level bug description framework motivates this analysis.

We believe that work on improving the debugging of Prolog programs must be based on more than a collection of low level programming tools. It is essential that we have a principled framework into which the various tools can be located.

References

[1] M. Brayshaw and M. Eisenstadt. A practical tracer for Prolog. Technical Report 42, Human Cognition Research Laboratory, The Open University, 1989.

[2] P. Brna, A. Bundy, A. Dodd, M. Eisenstadt, C.K. Looi, H. Pain, D. Robertson, B. Smith, and M. van Someren. Prolog programming techniques. *Instructional Science*, 20(2/3):111–133, 1991.

[3] P. Brna, A. Bundy, H. Pain, and L. Lynch. Impurities and the proposed Prolog story. Working Paper 212, Department of Artificial Intelligence, Edinburgh, 1987.

[4] P. Brna, A. Bundy, H. Pain, and L. Lynch. Programming tools for Prolog environments. In J. Hallam and C. Mellish, editors, *Advances in Artificial Intelligence*, pages 251–264. John Wiley, 1987. Formerly DAI Research Paper no. 302.

[5] D. R. Brough and C. J. Hogger. The treatment of loops in logic programming. Research Report DoC 86/16, Department of Computing, Imperial College of Science and Technology, 1986.

[6] A. Bundy, G. Grosse, and P.A. Brna. A recursive techniques editor for Prolog. Technical Report 2/3, 1991.

[7] A. Bundy, H. Pain, P. Brna, and L. Lynch. A proposed Prolog story. Research Paper 283, Department of Artificial Intelligence, Edinburgh, 1985.

[8] M. A. Covington. Eliminating unwanted loops in Prolog. *SIGPLAN Notices*, 20(1), 1985.

[9] C. Dichev and B. du Boulay. A data tracing system for Prolog novices. Technical Report CSRP 113, School of Cognitive Studies, University of Sussex, 1988.

[10] W. Drabent, S. Nadjm-Tehrani, and J. Maluszynski. Algorithmic debugging with assertions. In J. W. Lloyd, editor, *Proceedings of the workshop on Meta-programming in Logic Programming*, Bristol, 1989. MIT Press.

[11] M. Ducassè. Opium⁺, a meta-interpreter for Prolog. In Y. Kodratoff, editor, *ECAI-88: Proceedings of the 8th European Conference on Artificial Intelligence*, pages 272–277. Pitman, 1988.

[12] M. Eisenstadt and M. Brayshaw. TPM revisited. Technical Report 21a, Human Cognition Research Laboratory, The Open University, 1987. An extended version of technical report 21 to appear in the Journal of Logic Programming.

[13] T. S. Gegg-Harrison. Basic Prolog schemata. Technical Report CS-1989-20, Department of Computer Science, Duke University, 1989.

[14] J. W. Lloyd. Declarative error diagnosis. Technical report 86/3, Department of Computer Science, University of Melbourne, 1986.

[15] L. Naish. Declarative diagnosis of missing answers. Technical Report 88/9, Department of Computer Science, University of Melbourne, 1988.

[16] R. A. O'Keefe. Advice.pl. Documentation and code provided with the Prolog Library — available from the Artificial Intelligence Applications Institute, Edinburgh University, 1984.

[17] L. M. Pereira. Rational debugging in logic programming. In E. Y. Shapiro, editor, *Proc. of 3rd International Logic Programming Conference*, pages 203–210, July 1986.

[18] L. M. Pereira and M. Calejo. A framework for Prolog debugging. In R. A. Kowalski and K. A. Bowen, editors, *Proceedings of the 5th International Conference and Symposium on Logic Programming*, pages 481–495, Seattle, USA, August 1988.

[19] L. M. Pereira and M. Calejo. *ALPES final report*, chapter 10. Universidade Nova de Lisboa, 1989.

[20] E. Y. Shapiro. *Algorithmic Program Debugging*. MIT Press, 1983.

[21] J. C. Spohrer, E. Soloway, and E. Pope. A goal-plan analysis of buggy pascal programs. *Human-Computer Interaction*, 1:163–207, 1985.

[22] A. van Gelder. Efficient loop detection in Prolog using the tortoise-and-hare technique. *Journal of Logic Programming*, 4(1):23–32, March 1987.

Event Abstraction Debuggers for Layered Systems in Prolog

Andrew Casson

Abstract

This paper describes a general architecture for integrated run-time debugging tools for layered programming systems built on Prolog. The method used allows dynamic monitoring and interactive control of all layers, without the need to add code for using and responding to the debugger to any layer but Prolog. This is achieved by using Event Abstraction Rules which describe significant events in one layer in terms of those in lower layers, and Control Refinement Rules which describe how commands for directing control flow in one layer are achieved by giving more basic commands to lower layers.

1 Introduction

1.1 Layered programming

Computer programming consists in writing instructions in a programming language to perform a specified task. Different languages are good for different tasks. For example, Lisp is designed for list processing and general symbolic manipulation, whereas Fortran is ideal for intensive numerical calculations.

In rapidly developing fields like Artificial Intelligence where novel formalisms and algorithms are constantly being developed, the programmer may not always be able to find an entirely suitable language for implementing new ideas. Instead a multi-purpose AI language, such as Lisp or Prolog, may be used to implement an interpreter for a new, higher-level language in which the given task can then be expressed clearly and concisely. This methodology is called *layered programming* (see Figure 1).

In general, any number of intermediate layers may be developed, each written in terms of the one below and more suited than it to expressing the final

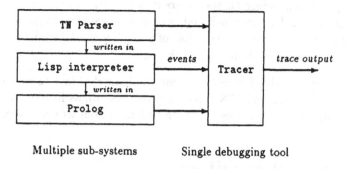

Figure 1: Some layered systems

task. In practice, two-layered systems are by far the most common, e.g. a Parlog interpreter written in Prolog, or a general purpose production system interpreter written in Lisp. However, the work described here applies to layered systems of any depth.

Layered programming can also be useful when a program for a specific task is available but written in a language that is not. For example, suppose you want to run a parser written in Lisp but only have a Prolog interpreter. Instead of porting the parser to Prolog, it might be better to write a Lisp interpreter in Prolog and run the parser directly, since the parser won't then have to be ported again if it is subsequently updated, and the Lisp interpreter can be used elsewhere.

1.2   Debugging requirements for layered systems

Different fields of computing not only use different languages, they also have particular approaches to software development. In AI programming the emphasis is on rapid prototyping. Programs are not fully specified before coding begins, rather the specification develops in directions indicated by the success or failure of programming experiments. This means that an AI programmer constructing a layered system will probably want to get an experimental version up and running as quickly as possible, and then to develop and refine all the layers in parallel.

But debugging a layered system that grows in this way can be difficult. A run-time error that manifests itself as incorrect behaviour in the top layer may in fact be the result of a coding bug at any layer in the hierarchy. Applying conventional debugging tools to each layer in turn in the hope of finding the culprit is clearly an inadequate and inefficient approach, especially if each tool has to be rewritten for each layer. What we need is an integrated debugger that can debug all the layers in a layered system, either one at a time or concurrently, and which makes it easy to see what is going on where. This paper is about the construction of such a multi-layered debugger, for layered systems where Prolog forms the base.

The programs described here have been implemented in Poplog Prolog and tested on a Prolog/Lisp/ATN Parser layered system, as in Figure 1. Simplified excerpts from this are used throughout the paper as examples.

2   The tool architecture

2.1   Event descriptors and the debugging hook

Dynamic debugging tools monitor (and sometimes control) program execution. To do this they need to know when *significant events* [1] occur in the program. An "event" is any conceptually distinct, identifiable piece of a computation, for example calling a Prolog predicate, suspending a Parlog goal, returning from a Lisp function, and so on; "significant" simply means relevant to the functionality of the debugging tools available.

An *event descriptor* (ED) is a Prolog term which describes an event. For instance, to support tracing of Prolog programs, a Prolog system might generate EDs for the *call, exit, redo* and *fail* ports of the Byrd box execution model [2]. It can then pass these to a debugger by calling an interface predicate or *debugging hook*, which takes an ED and feeds it to the tracer and any other run-time tools that are available.

Suppose for example that a Prolog program defines the usual member/2 predicate. During execution of the program, Prolog can keep the debugger informed about the predicate's behaviour by calling the debugging hook debug/1 at each port of a member/2 goal with an ED of the form

        prolog_event(Port,Goal)

That is, just before member/2 is called, the Prolog system may make a call like

        debug(prolog_event(call,member(c,[a,b,X])))

and then later, just after it exits:

        debug(prolog_event(exit,member(c,[a,b,c])))

```
% interpret/1 is the standard pure Prolog interpreter.
interpret(true) :- !.
interpret((G,H)) :- !, interpret(G), interpret(H).
interpret(H) :- cf(H), clause(H,B), interpret(B), er(H).


% cf/1 calls the hook at the "call" and "fail" ports.
cf(G) :- debug(prolog_event(call,G)).
cf(G) :- debug(prolog_event(fail,G)), fail.


% er/1 calls the hook at the "exit" and "redo" ports.
er(G) :- debug(prolog_event(exit,G)).
er(G) :- debug(prolog_event(redo,G)), fail.


% debug/1 passes the event descriptor to the tracer;
% calls to other tools should go in the body here.
debug(ED) :- trace(ED).


% trace/1 displays the ED in a readable format.
trace(prolog_event(Port,Goal)) :-
    write(Port), write(': '), write(Goal), nl.
```

Figure 2: A simple debugging interpreter for Prolog.

How exactly we get Prolog to call debug/1 depends on the flexibility and mutability of the Prolog system concerned. Poplog Prolog[1] makes it very easy, since at each port of a spied predicate it checks to see whether there are any clauses for the user-definable predicate prolog_trace(Port,Goal,I)[2], and if there are then this is called instead of the normal tracing routines. We can then have this predicate call debug/1 by defining it so:

```
prolog_trace(Port,Goal,_) :-
    debug(prolog_event(Port,Goal)).
```

For Prolog systems without such facilities we might directly augment the existing interpreter or compiler with calls to the hook. Alternatively, if this is not possible, or if the type of information we want in the EDs is not actually available to the system, then writing a special debugging interpreter for Prolog in Prolog is probably the best solution. The toy interpreter in Figure 2 demonstrates this. At each of a goal's four ports it calls debug/1 which passes the ED to the simple tracer defined by the predicate trace/1. This is all we need in order to get trace output like the following:

```
?- interpret(member(world,[hello,X])).
call: member(world, [hello, _1])
call: member(world, [_1])
exit: member(world, [world])
exit: member(world, [hello, world])
X = world ? ;
redo: member(world, [hello, world])
redo: member(world, [world])
call: member(world, [])
fail: member(world, [])
fail: member(world, [_1])
fail: member(world, [hello, _1])
no
```

So, by constructing EDs and passing them to debug/1 which displays them, we can do basic tracing of Prolog programs. Note that the information content of the EDs described above is pretty much the minimum for tracing Prolog. More sophisticated tracers may need more information from the Prolog system, which can be packaged into event descriptors as required.

It is interesting to note that EDs can very easily be recorded as they are generated, which makes it simple to repeatedly re-examine the dynamic behaviour

---

[1] Version 14 and later.
[2] The third argument is not important here

of a run through a program, without actually having to re-run it (which can be time-consuming especially if the program is highly interactive). Suppose for example that we redefine the event hook like this:

```
debug(ED) :- assertz(event(ED)), calltools(ED).
calltools(ED) :- trace(ED), ...
```

We can then define a predicate which will take each stored ED and pass it back to the tracer:

```
retrace :- event(ED), calltools(ED), fail.
```

Now we can call `retrace/0` over and over again, and, if we give the tracer the facility to select particular events for display each time, we can get many different views of the same run of the program.

Recording events also makes it very easy to support conditional tracing commands which depend on the calling sequence of Prolog goals, for example, 'trace `append/3` only when called by `nrev/2`', or 'trace non-recursive calls of `member/2`'. This simply requires that when a predicate is called, the debugger adds the ED generated to the head of a list of callers recorded in the database. When the predicate exits the ED is removed from the list. The tracing tool can the inspect this list as necessary to check that the conditions on the calling sequence are satisfied.

So much for Prolog debugging; let us now consider how this basic event hook mechanism can be extended to support the debugging of multi-layered systems.

2.2 Events in layered systems

We have traced Prolog using *call*, *exit*, *redo* and *fail* events. The simplest Lisp tracers, on the other hand, display just two types of occurrence, namely the *call* of a function with some arguments, and the *return* from a function with some result. Tracing our ATN parser, written in Lisp, involves displaying higher-level events such as parsing a syntactic constituent, or reading a word from a sentence. So each layer in a layered system has its own notion of what constitutes a significant event for a given tool.

Figure 3 shows the simplified code for part of a Lisp interpreter written in Prolog. How might we trace Lisp programs run using this interpreter?

```
% lisp_interpret/2 evaluates a Lisp expression;
% note that Lisp lists and atoms are represented as
% Prolog lists and atoms.
lisp_interpret(t,t).
lisp_interpret([],[]).
lisp_interpret([quote,Xpr],Xpr).
lisp_interpret([Fn|Xprs],Result) :-
    interpret_args(Xprs,Args),
    lisp_fncall(Fn,Args,Result).

interpret_args([],[]).
interpret_args([Xpr|Y],[Result|W]) :-
    lisp_interpret(Xpr,Result),
    interpret_args(Y,W).

% lisp_fncall/3 applies a Lisp function.
lisp_fncall(car,[[H|T]],H).
lisp_fncall(cdr,[[H|T]],T).
lisp_fncall(cons,[H,T],[H|T]).
```

Figure 3: Simplified portion of a Lisp interpreter in Prolog.

```
lisp_interpret([Fn|Xprs],Result) :-
   interpret_args(Xprs,Args),
   debug([lisp_event,call,Fn,Args,Result]),
   lisp_fncall(Fn,Args,Result),
   debug([lisp_event,return,Fn,Args,Result]).
```

Figure 4: The last clause of `lisp_interpret/2` redefined to call the hook.

Firstly, because Lisp has different events from Prolog, it ought to have a distinct set of EDs. The basic data structure in Lisp is the list (represented in the interpreter by Prolog lists), so we will express the two basic types of Lisp ED in list form,[3] i.e.

```
[lisp_event,call,Fn,Args,Result]
[lisp_event,return,Fn,Args,Result]
```

Now, one obvious solution is to have the Lisp interpreter call the debugging hook directly, exactly as Prolog does. It should be clear from the code in Figure 3 that it is `lisp_fncall/3` that does the job of applying a named Lisp function to a list of evaluated arguments. So, we can inform the debugger of the Lisp events by adding a couple of calls to `debug/1`, one just before the call to `lisp_fncall/3` inside `lisp_interpret/2`, and one just after — see Figure 4 for the new code. With additions to `trace/1` to tell it how to display Lisp events, this will give us basic Lisp tracing.

Unfortunately there are a few problems with this method. Firstly, and most obviously, adding such code to the Lisp interpreter makes it harder to read and obscures the way it works. The same could perhaps be said of the hook calls in Prolog; however, since Prolog is the base of the layered systems we are considering, i.e. it is a complete, sound layer which the layered systems programmer can build on, then its internal structure is assumed to be unseen and unimportant.

Secondly, the next layer up (if there is one), will of course be written in Lisp, not Prolog, so how can it call the debugging hook predicate? Either the Lisp interpreter will have to include a special built-in function through which the new layer (a production system interpreter, say) can access the hook, or maybe it could offer a means of dropping down through Lisp into Prolog so that the PS interpreter can call `debug/1` directly. Providing such facilities will have to be repeated for all the higher layers in a multi-layered system.

---

[3]This means that Lisp EDs can be processed easily by Lisp programs — see Section 2.3.

The consequence of this is that, during its development, a multi-layered system may have bits of debugging code in various languages dotted about the layers, and this really doesn't help the programmer to produce clear and efficient code for the primary functionality of each layer. Moreover, when all layers are working perfectly, the debugging code will become redundant clutter which the programmer will probably want to take out. But, of course, the tiniest mistake in removing the ability to use the debugger is likely to introduce new bugs, which would then be very difficult to track down.

Another problem with the above method is that when the first call of **debug/1** in **lisp_interpret/2** exits, the Lisp interpreter will obviously carry on and call the Lisp function. This makes it difficult, for instance, to implement a tracer command that lets the user override the result of the function by simply binding the result variable of **lisp_fncall/3** without calling it; the only solution, which is inelegant and probably inefficient, would be for the debugger to temporarily redefine the predicate as simply

```
lisp_fncall(_,_,_).
```

and then restore its previous definition on the next call of the hook.

So, for the sake of clarity, efficiency, safety and general flexibility it would probably be better if all code for using the debugging tools could be kept out of the layered system as much as possible. That is, we want to be able to use the debugger on the higher layers without having to modify them specially for that purpose. In the next section we will see how it is possible to do this, by generating and processing the events in higher layers from descriptions of them in terms of Prolog events. We will then see how this can be extended to support interactive program control flow redirection for all layers, such as the ability to override Lisp function calls as mentioned above.

2.3   Event abstraction rules

In our Lisp interpreter, as we noted above, it is **lisp_fncall/3** that applies functions. In other words, when **lisp_fncall/3** is called (which is a Prolog event), a Lisp function is called (which is a Lisp event). Similarly, when the predicate exits, the function returns. There is thus a simple, one-to-one correspondence between Prolog events and Lisp events. We might think of this in terms of data abstraction — the Prolog ED

```
prolog_event(call,lisp_fncall(car,[[a,b,c]],Result)
```

in some sense represents, at a lower level, the Lisp ED

```
[lisp_event,call,car,[[a,b,c]],Result]
```

Such relations can be expressed as *event abstraction* rules, written as a clauses of the predicate `event_abstraction/2` thus:

```
event_abstraction(prolog_event(call,
                  lisp_fncall(Fn,Args,Result)),
                  [lisp_event,call,Fn,Args,Result]).
event_abstraction(prolog_event(exit,
                  lisp_fncall(Fn,Args,Result)),
                  [lisp_event,return,Fn,Args,Result]).
```

Now, each time the debugger is given an event descriptor, it can first call the individual tools, as before, and then use these rules to see if the event corresponds to an abstract event in a higher layer. If one is found, then the debugger will call itself recursively with the new event descriptor, and the process will be repeated all the way up through the layers. This means that the EDs of any higher layer can be deduced from those of the layer immediately below, not just from Prolog events. For example, our ATN parser has its own EDs for specialised tracing, which are produced by event abstraction rules like:

```
event_abstraction([lisp_event,call,transit,[Net],_],
                  [atn_event,transit,Net]).
event_abstraction([lisp_event,return,transit,_,[]],
                  [atn_event,backtrack]).
```

We can even have "intra-layer" rules such as

```
event_abstraction([lisp_event,call,set,[Var,Value],Result],
                  [lisp_event,assign,Var,Value]).
```

which describes one type of Lisp event in terms of another, so that tracing of variable assignment can be treated as a special case.

An updated version of `debug/1` which does this is shown in Figure 5, which collects together the Prolog interpreter, the Lisp interpreter, and the debugger into one program. With this code we can evaluate a simple Lisp expression, running the Lisp interpreter under the Prolog interpreter, and get mixed Prolog and Lisp tracing, as follows:

```
?- interpret(lisp_interpret([cons,[quote,a],[quote,[b]]],
```

```
% Prolog interpreter with calls to the hook
interpret(true) :- !.
interpret((G,H)) :- !, interpret(G), interpret(H).
interpret(H) :- cf(H), clause(H,B), interpret(B), er(H).

cf(G) :- debug(prolog_event(call,G)).
cf(G) :- debug(prolog_event(fail,G)), fail.
er(G) :- debug(prolog_event(exit,G)).
er(G) :- debug(prolog_event(redo,G)), fail.


% Lisp interpreter without calls to the hook
lisp_interpret(t,t).
lisp_interpret([],[]).
lisp_interpret([quote,Xpr],Xpr).
lisp_interpret([Fn|Xprs],Result) :-
    interpret_args(Xprs,Args),
    lisp_interpret(Fn,Args,Result).

interpret_args([],[]).
interpret_args([Xpr|Y],[Result|W]) :-
    lisp_fncall(Xpr,Result),
    interpret_args(Y,W).

lisp_fncall(car,[[H|T]],H).
lisp_fncall(cdr,[[H|T]],T).
lisp_fncall(cons,[H,T],[H|T]).


% The debugger
event_abstraction(prolog_event(call,
                      lisp_fncall(Fn,Args,Result)),
                  [lisp_event,call,Fn,Args,Result]).
event_abstraction(prolog_event(exit,
                      lisp_fncall(Fn,Args,Result)),
                  [lisp_event,return,Fn,Args,Result]).

debug(ED) :-
    calltools(ED),
    abstract(ED).

abstract(ED) :-
    event_abstraction(ED,X), !,
    debug(X).
```

```
      Result)).
call: lisp_interpret([cons, [quote, a], [quote, [b]]], _1)
call: interpret_args([[quote, a], [quote, [b]]], _2)
call: lisp_interpret([quote, a], _3)
exit: lisp_interpret([quote, a], a)
call: interpret_args([[quote, [b]]], _4)
call: lisp_interpret([quote, [b]], _5)
exit: lisp_interpret([quote, [b]], [b])
call: interpret_args([], _6)
exit: interpret_args([], [])
exit: interpret_args([[quote, [b]]], [[b]])
exit: interpret_args([[quote, a], [quote, [b]]], [a, [b]])
call: lisp_fncall(cons, [a, [b]], _1)
LISP call [cons, [a, [b]], _1]
exit: lisp_fncall(cons, [a, [b]], [a, b])
LISP return [cons, [a, [b]], [a, b]]
exit: lisp_interpret([cons, [quote, a], [quote, [b]]],
      [a, b]))
Result = [a, b] ?
yes
```

Of course, it is unlikely that we should want to trace every event in both Prolog and Lisp at the same time. However, as mentioned in Section 2.1, it is up to the tracer, not the event handler, to sort out events and display them selectively according to the user's instructions.

Also, the Lisp tracing above doesn't look any more like real Lisp than the argument to `lisp_interpret/2` does! However, a more sophisticated Lisp interpreter would provide routines for reading and writing expressions in their normal syntax (round brackets, no commas etc.), and these could be made available to the tracer.

Note that representing Lisp EDs as lists makes it possible to write trace output routines for Lisp events in Lisp (given a sufficiently sophisticated Lisp interpreter): if we have defined a Lisp function `trace-print` to do this then it can be used by changing the second clause of `trace/1` to:

```
trace([lisp_event|X]) :- lisp_interpret(['trace-print',X],_).
```

2.4   Control Flow Redirection

The debugging hook as so far described only supports tools which monitor or test the behaviour of a running layered system in some way. It doesn't

Command	Description
call(G)	Unify the goal with G and call it.
exit(G)	Unify the goal with G and go to its *exit* port.
fail	Go to the goal's *fail* port, causing backtracking
continueto(G)	Proceed normally, ignoring other commands in the control list, up to the *call* port of the next goal in conjunction with the current one that unifies with G.
goto(G)	Skip over goals as far as the *call* port of next goal in conjunction with the current one that unifies with G.
quit	Return successfully to the parent goal.

Figure 6: Prolog control commands at the call port of a goal.

allow any actual control over what the system does next, that is, there is no provision for the layers to respond to commands issued by the debugger.

For example, it is a standard feature of Prolog tracers that at each port of a spied goal the user can give a command, e.g. to force backtracking or failure. In Lisp, as mentioned above, we might wish to trap a function call and cause it to return immediately with a given value as its result, or perhaps quit a conditional loop early. When debugging a production system it would be useful to be able to override the choice of rule made by the PS interpreter. How can we achieve this *control flow redirection* (CFR), still without modifying any layer but the Prolog base?

Let us concentrate on Prolog to start with. For it to be able to respond to debugging control, the debugger obviously has to communicate the control information to Prolog somehow. To achieve this we can add an extra argument to the debugging hook, giving

```
debug(ED,Control)
```

The debugger binds the Control variable to some sequence of commands to which the Prolog system then responds. To keep things simple we will assume that Prolog only processes control commands at the call port of a goal. A selection of useful commands it might support is shown in Figure 6. To see how they work, consider a pair of simple predicates like:

```
a(X) :- b(Y), c(Y), d(X,Y).
```

```
c(Z) :- p(Z), q, r.
```

and suppose we have called a/1 and control is currently at the *call* port of b/1. The Prolog system calls:

```
debug(prolog_event(call,b(Y)),Control)
```

and the debugger binds Control to a Prolog list of commands from Figure 6. Here are some examples of the behaviour resulting from different values of Control:

- Control = []

  Proceed as normal, i.e. call b(Y).

- Control = [call(b(3))]

  Bind Y=3 and call b(3).

- Control = [continueto(d(3,_))]

  Call b(Y) and c(Y), then bind X=3 and wait for the next command at the call port of d(3,Y).

- Control = [goto(c(3)),call(_),continueto(r),quit]

  Skip over b(Y), bind Y=3, and call c(3). Call p(3) and q, then return to a(X) without calling r. Wait for the next command at the *call* port of d(X,3).

Control commands may be supplied interactively, by a tracer prompting the user for instructions at each port. Alternatively, they might be set before a program is run, e.g. by a debugging tool which allows CFR to be triggered by specific events in the program, so that, for instance, a buggy section of code could be temporarily ignored by jumping over it, or screen output suppressed by causing all calls of write/1 to exit immediately.

Adding the necessary facilities to a Prolog system to support CFR is not likely to be a trivial task. Poplog Prolog [5], for instance, cannot easily be extended to provide goto(G), continueto(G) and quit because the information these commands require about goal continuations and callers is not readily available to its present debugger. However, writing a continuation-based Prolog interpreter in Prolog that can support CFR is not too difficult, once it has been worked out in detail what kind of commands are needed in Prolog, and how they interact with backtracking, cuts and so on. We have implemented such an interpreter to test our ideas, and all subsequent examples in this paper will simply assume that the Prolog system used supports CFR.

```
% This clause is added to lisp_interpret/2.
lisp_interpret([loop|Body],Result) :-
    loop(next,Body,Result).

% loop/2 does the body of the loop until Status=quit,
% then evaluates the result expression
loop(next,Body,Result) :-
    doloop(Body,Status),
    loop(Status,Body,Result).
loop(quit,Body,Result) :- quitloop(Body,Result).

doloop([[do,Xpr1],[until,Xpr2],_]) :-
    lisp_interpret(Xpr1,_),
    (lisp_interpret(Xpr2,t), !, Status=quit ; Status=next).

quitloop([_,_,[result,Xpr3]],Result) :-
    lisp_interpret(Xpr3,Result).
```

Figure 7: Adding conditional loops to the Lisp interpreter.

2.5 CFR in Layered Systems

Having seen how CFR works in Prolog, we will now return to layered systems
to consider how we can integrate the concepts of CFR and event abstraction
in order that the dynamic behaviour of higher layers can be controlled interactively without modifying their code.

In Section 2.3 we noted that when the predicate lisp_fncall/3 in the Lisp
interpreter is called, a Lisp function is called, and when it exits, the function
returns. A consequence of this is that when a Lisp function is about to be
called, we can cause it to return immediately with a given result by using the
exit(G) command to instruct lisp_fncall/3 to exit with its third argument
bound to that result. This fact can be expressed in a *control refinement* rule,
which is a Prolog clause describing how one debugging command can be
broken down into a sequence of others. So we might have:

```
control_refinement(lisp_return(R),
    [exit(lisp_fncall(_,_,R))]).
```

This is a very simple example, because one Lisp command can be implemented by just one Prolog command. For a slightly more complicated example, consider the code in Figure 7 which adds a simple conditional loop

construct based on that in [3] to the Lisp interpreter. This allows expressions
of the form:

$$[\text{loop},[\text{do},<\textit{expr-1}>],[\text{until},<\textit{expr-2}>],[\text{result},<\textit{expr-3}>]]$$

in which *<expr-1>* and *<expr-2>* are evaluated repeatedly until *<expr-2>* returns t, whereupon *<expr-3>* is evaluated to get the final result of the loop.
These loops might be traced with the aid of an event abstraction rule which
states that calling loop/2 with next as its first argument corresponds to the
beginning of each pass round the loop:

```
event_abstraction(prolog_event(call,loop(next,_,_)),
    [lisp_event,loop]).
```

Now suppose that when the tracer displays a "loop" ED, we want to give it
a lisp_quitloop command which will quit the loop immediately, not doing
the body but still evaluating the result expression to determine the loop's
value. This is done by calling loop/2, skipping over the call to doloop/2 and
then doing the recursive call of loop/2 with Status bound to quit. Hence
we can write a control refinement rule for lisp_quitloop as follows:

```
control_refinement(lisp_quitloop,
    [call(_),goto(loop(quit,_,_))]).
```

The control refinement method extends naturally to higher layers in the
system. So, for instance, commands for guiding our ATN parser can be
written in terms of Lisp commands, which are in turn built up from the
basic Prolog actions. Figure 8 shows a simplified Prolog program for using
CFR and control refinement rules in layered systems, assuming that the
Prolog system used can call debug/2 and execute CFR commands. There
are a couple of things to note about the program. Firstly, the tracer is the
only tool called by the debugger. With more tools the debugger would need
to deal with the possibility of more than one tool issuing CFR commands.
Secondly, every ED generated gets printed, and a command is requested
every time this happens. A more sophisticated tracer would allow the user
to control which events are shown, and when input should be requested. It
would also, as mentioned in Section 2.3, tailor input and output to the layer
concerned, so that for example Lisp expressions could be read and written
in standard Lisp format.

```
% debug/2 calls the tools on each ED as before, but
% only tries the EA rules if no CFR commands are given.
debug(ED,Control) :-
    calltools(ED,C),
    (C=[], !, abstract(ED,Control) ; Control=C).


% abstract/2 calls the hook recursively if it can,
% then refines any CFR commands returned into
% commands appropriate to the current layer.
abstract(ED,Control) :-
    event_abstraction(ED,X),
    debug(X,C),
    refine(C,Control).
abstract(_,[]).


% refine/2 applies the control refinement rules
% where possible to each item in the control list.
refine([],[]).
refine([C|Cs],Z) :-
    control_refinement(C,X), !,
    refine(Cs,Y),
    append(X,Y,Z).
refine([C|Cs],[C|Y]) :- refine(Cs,Y).


% calltools/2 just calls a tracer; calls to other tools
% should be added here.
calltools(ED,Control) :- trace(ED,Control).


% trace/2 displays the ED and inputs a command.
trace(ED,[Command]) :- write(ED), read(Command).
```

Figure 8: An Event Abstraction Debugger with Control Flow Redirection.

3   Conclusions and future directions

The incorporation of a debugging hook into Prolog, through which Prolog event descriptors can be passed to the debugger and commands for directing control flow can be received, provides a neat way of monitoring and guiding the dynamic behaviour of programs, and thereby supports the implementation of a range of run-time debugging tools, tracers being just one example. With the addition of event abstraction and control refinement rules, such tools can be used for debugging any layer in a layered system built on Prolog, without the need for a separate interface between each layer and the debugger.

The basic ideas presented here have been thoroughly tested by implementing a multi-level tracer for a reasonably sophisticated layered system incorporating a CFR Prolog Interpreter, a Lisp interpreter in Prolog, and an ATN parser in Lisp. Future work will include trying out the ideas on different layered systems, and implementing other dynamic debugging tools. For example, the flex^{TM} expert system tool [6] has recently been ported to Poplog Prolog, and work on using E.A. debugging techniques in a "serious" system like this should be very helpful.

We have assumed throughout this paper that Prolog is the base language of a layered system, and indeed Prolog's unification greatly simplifies the formulation of event abstraction and control refinement rules. However, though the elegance of the method might be lost, there is no theoretical reason why Event Abstraction debuggers should not be provided for procedural languages. Also, we have concentrated on systems built solely from interpreters, but the methods used should extend fairly easily to systems including compilers whose target language is the language they are themselves written in, e.g. a Prolog program which compiles Lisp into Prolog. Experiments in both these areas are needed.

Finally, this work will benefit from integration with other results of the LPE project. In particular, a reimplementation within the LOS framework [4], with its ability to view events as logical objects, may well provide a useful new theoretical angle on the techniques used. For example, the debugging events of each layer might be objects of a layer-specific class, from which they would inherit methods for tracing and typechecking themselves, and so on.

References

[1] A. W. Bowles and P. F. Wilk. Tracing requirements for multi-layered

meta-programming. Technical report, Artificial Intelligence Applications Institute, University of Edinburgh, 1988.

[2] L. Byrd. Understanding the control flow of Prolog programs. In S.-A. Tarnlund, editor, *Proceedings of the Logic Programming workshop*, pages 127–138, Debrecen, Hungary, July 1980.

[3] E. Charniak and D. McDermott. *Introduction to Artificial Intelligence*, pages 39–41. Addison Wesley, 1985.

[4] F. G. McCabe. Logic and objects (part one: The language). Research Report DOC 86/9, Dept. of Computing, Imperial College, 1988.

[5] C. S. Mellish and S. Hardy. Integrating Prolog in the Poplog programming environment. In J. A. Campbell, editor, *Implementations of Prolog*. Ellis Horwood, 1984.

[6] P. Vasey. *The flex Expert System Toolkit*. Logic Programming Associates Ltd., 1988.

Extending the Integrity Maintenance Capability in Deductive Databases

Subrata Kumar Das   M.H.Williams

Abstract

The methods proposed so far for checking integrity in deductive databases suffer from two major drawbacks. The first is that they deal with (integrity) constraints which are restricted closed first-order formulae and confining constraints to this form they exclude some important kinds of constraints from consideration. The second is that the methods are only applicable to definite databases and are unable to check integrity in indefinite databases. To take account of the first problem, extensions of some of the existing methods are proposed in the context of definite databases which allow a set of *aggregate predicates* to be included within formulae representing constraints. To overcome the second problem, the paper proposes extensions of the methods in another direction to handle constraints imposed on indefinite databases. This is based on a new definition of constraint satisfiability in indefinite databases. The constraint verification program, based on this concept of constraint satisfiability, uses a query evaluator which works on the principle of *negation as possible failure* for inferring negative information from indefinite databases.

1   Introduction

In a database an *integrity constraint* [9],[24], [11] (or simply a constraint) is a formal representation of a property which the data in the database must satisfy to be consistent with some model of the real world from which it comes. In a logic programming context, a constraint can be defined as a closed formula. Different ways of maintaining integrity in deductive databases have been proposed in several papers, e.g. generalisations of the simplification method [21] by Lloyd and Topor [17] , Decker [10] , and Bry *et al.* [3] , a general theorem-proving technique by Sadri and Kowalski [22] , using Prolog not-predicate by Ling [14] , consistency proof method and a modified program method by Asirelli et al. [2] , a path finding method by Das and Williams [7], etc. The following two major shortcomings have been observed [8] in the methods proposed so far:

1. The methods only allow a subset of the set of all closed first-order formulae as constraints [8]. Confining constraints to this form excludes some important kinds of constraints from consideration. For example, constraints of the form

   the total number of employees in a particular department may not exceed 100, or

   a student obtaining the highest marks in a particular course receives an award, or

   a student obtaining an average mark greater than or equal to 50, passes the examination, etc.

   cannot be expressed conveniently as first-order formulae and it is not possible to evaluate them efficiently even if they are expressed as first-order formulae.

2. The underlying database is always *definite*, i.e. the head of each database clause is an atom and the body is a conjunction of literals. When the database becomes *indefinite* by allowing the head of a database clause to be a disjunction of atoms, the methods are unable to handle this.

In response to the first problem, the paper attempts to extend the *simplification method* of Lloyd *et al.* [17] and the *path finding method* [7] in the context of definite databases by allowing a set of aggregate predicates (e.g. *Count*, *Sum*, *Maximum*) to be included within formulae representing constraints. The extended methods can be implemented efficiently in Prolog by using the aggregate predicate `setof`.

In response to the second problem, the paper extends both the simplification and the path finding methods to handle integrity checking in indefinite databases. This is based on a new definition of constraint satisfiability in indefinite databases. This definition is a generalised version of the *theoremhood* [22] view of constraint satisfiability defined in terms of *completion* [4] in the context of definite databases. Following this definition, a constraint is satisfied by an indefinite database if and only if the constraint is satisfied by each *possible form* of the indefinite database.

Although a constraint verification program based on the above concept of constraint satisfiability can work on any query evaluator for the underlying database, the paper considers the semantics of the database based on the *negation as possible failure rule* for inferring negative information from a database. In the declarative semantics of negation as possible failure, a ground atom is taken as false if its negation is true in the completion of each of the possible forms of the database. The procedural semantics is based on two mutually recursive resolution schemes, *definite resolution* and *possible resolution*. These two resolution schemes coincide and reduce to the mechanism of simple SLDNF-resolution when the database is definite.

There is a direct link between the introduced notion of constraint satisfiability and the negation as possible failure rule. If a constraint (in *denial form*) has a *finitely failed possible tree* in a database D, then the constraint is said to be satisfied by D.

The Prolog implementation of the method and a meta interpreter of extended nH-Prolog [19] are described. The extended nH-Prolog which is capable of inferring negative information from the database is based on the idea of negation as possible failure rule. The query evaluator which is required for constraint evaluation operates on this extended nH-Prolog.

The organisation of the paper is as follows. The following section describes some basic concepts. Section 3 considers the extension of integrity mainte- nance for definite databases to include formulae which are not closed first- order, whereas Section 4 looks at constraints which are closed first-order formulae but in indefinite databases. The C-Prolog [5] syntax has been used in the subsections dealing with Prolog implementation.

2 Basic concepts

Definition 1 *A* (first-order) literal *is an atom (referred to as a* positive literal*) or its negation (*negative literal*).*

Definition 2 *A* (database) clause *is a formula of the form*

$$A_1 \vee \cdots \vee A_m \leftarrow L_1 \wedge \cdots \wedge L_n, m \geq 1, n \geq 0$$

where $A_1 \vee \cdots \vee A_m$ is the head *(or conclusion or consequent) of the clause and $L_1 \wedge \cdots \wedge L_n$ the* body *(or condition or antecedent). Each A_i is an atom and each L_j is either an atom (a positive condition) or a negated atom (a negative condition). The $\vee$ symbols in the consequent denote disjunction and the $\wedge$ symbols in the antecedent denote conjunction. Any variables in $A_1, \ldots, A_m, L_1, \ldots, L_n$ are assumed to be universally quantified over the whole clause.*

The different forms of a clause corresponding to different values of m and n are as follows:

1. $m = 1, n = 0$, i.e. the body is empty and the head is a single atom. The clause is called a (*definite*) *fact*.

2. $m > 1, n = 0$, i.e. the body is empty and the head is a disjunction of atoms. The clause is called an *indefinite fact*.

3. $m = 1, n > 0$, i.e. the head is a single atom and the body is non empty. The clause is called a (*definite*) *rule*.

4. $m > 1, n > 0$, i.e. the head is a disjunction of atoms and the body is non empty. The clause is called an *indefinite rule*.

A *definite clause* is either a fact or a rule. An *indefinite clause* is either an indefinite fact or an indefinite rule.

Definition 3 *A* database *is a finite set of clauses. A* definite database *is a finite set of definite clauses.*

Definition 4 *A* (database) query *(or goal or* denial*) is a formula of the form*

$$\leftarrow L_1 \wedge \cdots \wedge L_n, n \geq 1$$

where $L_1, \ldots, L_n$ are literals. Any variables in $L_1 \wedge \ldots \wedge L_n$ are assumed to be universally quantified over the whole goal.

Definition 5 *Let D be a database and G a goal. A clause $A_1 \vee \cdots \vee A_m \leftarrow L_1 \wedge \cdots \wedge L_n$ in D is* allowed *(or* range-restricted *[12]) if every variable that occurs in the clause occurs in a positive literal of the body $L_1 \wedge \cdots \wedge L_n$. The whole database D is* allowed *if each of its clauses is allowed. A goal G is* allowed *if G is $\leftarrow L_1 \wedge \cdots \wedge L_n$ and every variable that occurs in G occurs in a positive literal of the body $\leftarrow L_1 \wedge \cdots \wedge L_n$*

To avoid floundering in the construction of a derivation of $D \cup \{G\}$, where D is a database and G a goal, it has been assumed in the rest of the paper that both D and G are *allowed* [15].

Definition 6 *A* computation rule *is a function which maps a goal to a literal, called the* selected literal, *in that goal. A* safe computation rule *is a function from a set of goals, none of which consists entirely of non-ground negative literals, to a set of literals such that the value of the function for such a goal is either a positive literal or a ground negative literal.*

Unless otherwise stated, computation rules have been assumed to be safe to evaluate a query correctly. Most Prolog systems do not enforce this safeness condition with the result that they will compute a query correctly only if the literals of each query and database clause are ordered in such a way as to meet this condition.

3 Extension using higher order predicates

In this section, the class of databases considered is definite and hence any usage of the terms 'database' will be taken as 'definite database'.

3.1 General formulae and integrity constraints

In extending clauses to include aggregate predicates, the following five have been chosen as an initial set:

$Count$

$Average$

Sum

$Maximum$

$Minimum$

although this set can clearly be enlarged to include other such functions.

Definition 7 *An* aggregate atom *is one of the following forms :*

$Count(W, n)$

$Average(x, W, r)$

$Sum(x, W, r)$

$Maximum(x, W, r)$

$Minimum(x, W, r)$

where W is a conjunction of literals (a goal written without $\leftarrow$) in which some of the variables are free and the remaining variables are assumed to be existentially quantified in front of W. The variable x is one of the bound variables of W, and variables n and r represent the result of the function (as an integer or real number, respectively). The variable x can be replaced by an identifier (e.g. an integer) which will identify uniquely the occurrence of x in W. For the sake of readability, it has been considered as a variable. Thus $Count(W, n)$ is interpreted as counting the number of different answers to the query $\leftarrow W$ which are true in D, and returning this value as n; $Average(x, W, r)$ computes the average of all the values of the variable x obtained from different answers of the query $\leftarrow W$ which are true in D, and return this value as r; and so on. In each case the query $\leftarrow W$ is assumed to be allowed.

An aggregate literal *is either an aggregate atom or the negation of an aggregate atom. A* general atom *(resp.* general literal*) is either an atom (resp. literal) or an aggregate atom (resp. aggregate literal). In each of the above aggregate atoms the formula W will be called the* key *formula.*

Definition 8 *A general formula may now be defined as follows :*

1. *A general literal is a general formula.*

2. *If A and B are general formulae, then so are $\neg A$, $A \vee B$, $A \wedge B$, $A \rightarrow B$ and $A \leftrightarrow B$.*

3. *If A is a general formula and x is a variable, then $\forall x A$ and $\exists x A$ are general formulae.*

4. *Nothing else is a general formula.*

Definition 9 *Given a formula consisting of the single general atom α, the general atom α is said to* occur positively *in the general formula α. If a general atom α occurs positively (resp. negatively) in a general formula A, then α occurs positively (resp. negatively) in $\exists A$ and $A \wedge B$ and $A \vee B$ and $B \rightarrow A$. If a general atom α occurs positively (resp. negatively) in a general formula A, then α occurs negatively (resp. positively) in $\neg A$ and $A \rightarrow B$.*

Definition 10 *Let λ be an aggregate literal occurring in a general formula A. Then all the bound variables of the key formula W of λ are said to be* local *to the aggregate literal λ. Any other variables occurring in λ are said to be* global *variables of A.*

Definition 11 *A* closed general formula Γ *is a general formula with no free occurrences of any global variables.*

Definition 12 *A* first-order constraint *is a closed first-order formula.*

The standard view of constraint satisfiability of a first- order constraint C imposed on a database D, where $comp(D)$ is assumed to be consistent, is defined as follows. D is said to satisfy C if C is a logical consequence of $comp(D)$; otherwise D violates C.

A first-order constraint imposed on a database D can always be assumed to be in the form of a denial. If a first-order constraint is not in the form of a denial then it can be transformed to denial form by suitably extending the database [22]. Let C be a constraint which is an arbitrary closed first order formula such that the database D satisfies C. Then this constraint can be replaced by a new constraint $\leftarrow A$, where A is a predicate symbol of zero arity that does not occur elsewhere in the database or constraints, provided that, to the database D is added a set of rules obtained by transforming

$$A \leftarrow \neg C$$

using the transformation as described in [16]. If D_T is the resulting database, then D_T must be allowed.

Definition 13 *An* aggregate constraint *is a closed general formula Γ of the form*

$$\lambda_1 \wedge \cdots \wedge \lambda_n \rightarrow \alpha_1 \vee \cdots \vee \alpha_m$$

where $\alpha_1 \vee \cdots \vee \alpha_m$ is the conclusion of Γ and $\lambda_1 \wedge \cdots \wedge \lambda_n$ is the condition. Each α_i is a general atom and each λ_j is a general literal and at least one of $\alpha_1, \ldots, \alpha_m, \lambda_1, \ldots \lambda_n$ is an aggregate literal. Variables occurring in the condition are assumed to be universally quantified at the front of Γ. Any variables in the conclusion which do not occur in the condition are assumed to be existentially quantified at the front of the conclusion.

Thus the example of constraints given in the introduction can be expressed using this notation, as follows:

$$Dept(x) \wedge Count(EmpDept(y, x), z) \rightarrow z \leq 100,$$

$$Paper(x) \wedge Maximum(v, Marks(u, x, v), y) \wedge Marks(z, x, y) \rightarrow Award(z, x),$$

and

$$Student(x) \wedge Average(v, Marks(x, u, v), y) \wedge y \geq 50 \rightarrow Pass(x),$$

where x, y, z, u, v are variables and the schema for the predicates *Dept*, *EmpDept*, *Paper*, *Marks*, *Award* are respectively *Dept(department)*, *EmpDept(employee, department)*, *Paper(paper)*, *Marks(student, paper, marks)*, *Award(student, paper)*. According to the definition, the variables x and z in the first constraint are assumed to be universally quantfied in front of the whole constraint, whereas the variable y is assumed to be existentially quantified in front of *EmpDept(y, x)*.

Definition 14 *A constraint is either a first-order constraint or an aggregate constraint.*

In following two subsections, the only aggregate predicate considered will be the predicate *Count*. In Subsection 3.4 this will be generalised to other aggregate predicates from the initial set.

3.2   Aggregate constraint satisfiability

Let D be a database and Q_D be the set of all queries. Consider the second-order function $\chi_D : Q_D \to N$, where N is the set of all non-negative integers, defined in the following way:

$$\text{for} \ \leftarrow W \in Q_D, \chi_D(\leftarrow W) = card\{W\theta : comp(D) \vdash W\theta\}$$

where $cardX$ denotes the cardinality of the set X. Clearly the mapping is well defined, i.e. every query $\leftarrow W$ is mapped into a unique integer which is equal to the number of instances of W which can be derived from $comp(D)$. This asserts that the number of different instances of W which are true in D is $\chi_D(\leftarrow W)$. Thus if a constraint contains the aggregate atom $Count(W, n)$ and all global variables occurring in W are instantiated, $\chi_D(\leftarrow W)$ represents n. In other words, $\chi_D(\leftarrow W)$ is the number of different computed answres of the SLDNF-derivation of $D \cup \{\leftarrow W\}$, provided that it is capable of returning all answres without going into an infinite loop.

Lemma 1 *Let D be a database and $\leftarrow W$ a member of Q_D . Let $x_1, \ldots, x_n$ be all the variables of W and D_T be $D \cup \{\forall x_1 \cdots \forall x_n(P(x_1, \ldots, x_n) \leftarrow W)\}$, where P is a predicate symbol not occurring elsewhere in the database D. If $\chi_D : Q_D \to N$ and $\chi_{D_T} : Q_{D_T} \to N$ are the two mappings defined as above, then $\chi_D(\leftarrow W) = \chi_{D_T}(\leftarrow P(x_1, \ldots, x_n))$.*

Proof : This follows from the fact that $comp(D) \vdash W\theta$ if and only if $comp(D) \vdash P(x_1, \ldots, x_n)\theta$. $\square$

In view of the above lemma, the key formula of an aggregate atom under the predicate $Count$ occurring in a constraint will be assumed to be an atom.

Definition 15 *The first-order equivalent of an aggregate atom $Count(A, n)$ is the first-order atom $Count_A(n, y_1, \ldots, y_g)$ (or simply $Count(n, y_1, \ldots, y_g)$), where n is a variable and $y_1, \ldots, y_g$ are the other attributes of A. The first-order equivalent form of a general formula Γ is obtained from Γ by replacing its aggregate atoms with their first-order equivalent form.*

Definition 16 *Let D be a database and $Count(A, n)$ be an aggregate atom. Suppose, $z_1, \ldots, z_l$ are the local variables of A and $y_1, \ldots, y_g$ are the other attributes of A (some of which may be constants). One can always assume that A has the form $P(z_1, \ldots, z_l, y_1, \ldots, y_g)$, where P is a first-order order predicate. Suppose there are a finite number of constant terms $a_1, \ldots, a_m$ in the language underlying the database. In the context of database D, the expansion of $Count(A, n)$ defining its first-order equivalent, denoted by $Exp_D(Count(A, n))$ (or simply $Exp(Count(A, n))$, when D is clear from the context), is the following set of $m^g + m^l + m^l(m^l - 1)/2 + m^l(m^l - 1)(m^l - 2)/3.2 + \cdots + 1$ first-order clauses:*

m^g clauses:

$$Count(0, y_1, \ldots, y_g) \quad \leftarrow \quad y_1 = a_1^1 \wedge \cdots \wedge y_g = a_g^1 \wedge$$
$$\neg Count(1, y_1, \ldots, y_g) \wedge \cdots$$
$$\wedge \neg Count(m^l, y_1, \ldots, y_g)$$

where each a_i^1 is equal to a_p for some p.

m^l clauses:

$$Count(1, y_1, \ldots, y_g) \quad \leftarrow \quad P(a_1^1, \ldots, a_l^1, y_1, \ldots, y_g) \wedge$$
$$\neg Count(2, y_1, \ldots, y_g) \wedge \cdots$$
$$\wedge \neg Count(m^l, y_1, \ldots, y_g)$$

where each a_i^1 is equal to some a_p for some p.

$m^l(m^l - 1)/2$ clauses:

$$Count(2, y_1, \ldots, y_g) \quad \leftarrow \quad P(a_1^1, \ldots, a_l^1, y_1, \ldots, y_g) \wedge$$
$$P(a_1^2, \ldots, a_l^2, y_1, \ldots, y_g) \wedge$$
$$\neg Count(3, y_1, \ldots, y_g) \wedge \cdots$$
$$\wedge \neg Count(m^l, y_1, \ldots, y_g)$$

where each a_i^k, $k = 1, 2$ is equal to a_p for some p and for $k \neq k'$, $1 \leq k, k' \leq 2$, there exists a p such that $a_p^k \neq a_p^{k'}$.

$m^l(m^l - 1)(m^l - 2)/3, 2$ *clauses:*

$$Count(3, y_1, \ldots, y_g) \leftarrow P(a_1^1, \ldots, a_l^1, y_1, \ldots, y_g) \land$$
$$P(a_1^2, \ldots, a_l^2, y_1, \ldots, y_g) \land$$
$$P(a_1^3, \ldots, a_l^3, y_1, \ldots, y_g) \land$$
$$\neg Count(4, y_1, \ldots, y_g) \land \cdots$$
$$\land \neg Count(m^l, y_1, \ldots, y_g)$$

where each a_i^k, $k = 1, 2, 3$ *is equal to* a_p *for some p and for* $k \neq k'$, $1 \leq k, k' \leq 3$, *there exists a p such that* $a_p^k \neq a_p^{k'}$.

$\vdots$

1 clause:

$$Count(m^l, y_1, \ldots, y_g) \leftarrow P(a_1^1, \ldots, a_l^1, y_1, \ldots, y_g) \land \cdots$$
$$\land P(a_1^{m^l}, \ldots, a_l^{m^l}, y_1, \ldots, y_g)$$

where each a_i^k, $k = 1, 2, \ldots, m^l$ *is equal to some* a_p *for some p and for* $k \neq k'$, $1 \leq k, k' \leq m^l$ *there exists a p such that* $a_p^k \neq a_p^{k'}$.

When the above set of clauses has been added to the database, it would be said that the *database is expanded wrt the aggregate literal Count(A, n)* and the expanded database would be denoted as $Exp(D, Count(A, n))$.

Lemma 2 *For all ground substitutions θ of the variables in $\{y_1, \ldots, y_g\}$, at most one of $Count(1, y_1, \ldots, y_g)\theta, \ldots, Count(m^l, y_1, \ldots, y_g)\theta$ can be derived at a time from $comp(Exp(D, Count(A, gn)))$.*

Proof : Assume that both $Count(M, y_1, \ldots, y_g)\theta$ and $Count(N, y_1, \ldots, y_g)\theta$ can be derived from $comp(Exp(D, Count(A, n)))$, for $N \neq M$. Without any loss of generality one can assume $0 \leq M < N \leq m^l$. Since $Count(M, y_1, \ldots, y_g)\theta$ is derivable from $comp(Exp(D, Count(A, n)))$, from the clauses defining $Count(M, y_1, \ldots, y_g)$ one can say that none of $Count(M + 1, y_1, \ldots, y_g)\theta, \ldots, Count(N, y_1, \ldots, y_g)\theta$, $\ldots, Count(m^l, y_1, \ldots, y_g)\theta$ is derivable from $comp(Exp(D, Count(A, n)))$. This contradicts the initial assumption. Hence the lemma. $\square$

Lemma 3 *For all ground substitutions θ of the variables in $\{y_1, \ldots, y_g\}$, $\chi_D(\leftarrow A\theta) = N$, where $Count(N, y_1, \ldots, y_g)\theta$ is derivable from $comp(Exp(D, Count(A, n)))$.*

Proof : Suppose that only M different instances of θ are derivable from $comp(D)$ (i.e. $\chi_D(\leftarrow A\theta) = M$). The instances of $A\theta$ which are derivable from $comp(D)$ occur in the body of $U\theta$, where U is a clause in $Exp(D, Count(A, n))$. The head of U is $Count(M, y_1, \ldots, y_g))$ and $Count(M, y_1, \ldots, y_g)\theta$ is derivable from $comp(Exp(D, Count(A, n)))$. Hence, by Lemma 2, $M = N$. □

Definition 17 *Let D be a database and Γ an aggregate constraint and suppose $Count(A_1, n_1), \ldots, Count(A_p, n_p)$ are the only aggregate literals occurring in Γ. The expansion of D wrt Γ, denoted by $Exp(D, \Gamma)$, is the set $D \cup Exp(Count(A_1, n_1)) \cup \cdots \cup Exp(Count(A_p, n_p))$. Let I be a set of constraints and $\Gamma_1, \ldots, \Gamma_p$ be the only aggregate constraints in I. The expansion of D wrt I, denoted by $Exp(D, I)$, is the set $D \cup Exp(D, \Gamma_1) \cup \cdots \cup Exp(D, \Gamma_p)$.*

Lemma 4 *Let D be a database and I be a set of constraints with occurrences of aggregate literals $Count(A_1, n_1), \ldots, Count(A_p, n_p)$. If $comp(D)$ is consistent then $comp(Exp(D, I))$ is also consistent.*

Proof : For each integer n, suppose that $Count(n, y_1, \ldots, y_g)$ corresponding to $Count(P_i, n_i)$ for some $i = 1, 2, \ldots, p$ is replaced by another atom $Countn_i(y_1, \ldots, y_g)$, where $Countn_i$ does not appear elsewhere in the database. Then the clauses added to D to obtain $comp(Exp(D, I))$ can be taken as satisfying the hierarchical constraint. Because of the hierarchical nature of the clauses added to D and because added clauses define predicates which are not already defined in D, $comp(D)$ is consistent. □

Suppose Γ is an aggregate constraint and G is its first-order equivalent. In view of Lemma 3, D can be said to satisfy Γ if G is a logical consequence of $comp(Exp(D, \Gamma))$; otherwise D violates Γ. D is said to satisfy I, where I is a set of constraints, if D satisfies each constraint in I; otherwise D violates I.

An aggregate constraint Γ is transformed to its *first-order equivalent denial form* $\leftarrow G_d$ through the following steps:

1. Each first-order atom A which occurs in the conclusion and which contains at least one existentially quantified variable of the conclusion, is replaced by $P(x_1, \ldots, x_n)$. D is expanded by adding the clause $P(x_1, \ldots, x_n) \leftarrow A$ to it, where $x_1, \ldots, x_n$ are the variables of A also occurring in the condition and the predicate symbol P does not occur elsewhere in the database. Let D_T be the transformed database and G_T be the transformed aggregate constraint.

2. Convert G_T to its first-order equivalent form G_f .

3. G_f is transformed to its equivalent denial form $\leftarrow G_d$ by simply adding the negated form of each atom A, occurring in the conclusion, as a conjunct of the condition.

When a first-order constraint $\leftarrow W$ in denial form is considered, the standard method of determining whether a database satisfies or violates the constraint is by evaluating the query $\leftarrow W$ in the context of the database. If there is an SLDNF-refutation of $D \cup \{\leftarrow W\}$ via a safe selection then D violates $\leftarrow W$. If $D \cup \{\leftarrow W\}$ has a finitely failed SLDNF-tree, then D satisfies W. When an aggregate constraint Γ is considered, it is transformed to its equivalent first-order denial form $\leftarrow G_d$ in the above way by transforming the database D to $Exp(D_T, \Gamma)$. Then one can have the following syntactic definition of aggregate constraint satisfiability of C.

Lemma 5 *Let D be a database, Γ an aggregate constraint and R a safe selection rule. The terms D_T and $\leftarrow G_d$ are defined as above. Suppose $comp(D)$ is consistent. If there is an SLDNF-refutation of $Exp(D_T, \Gamma) \cup \{\leftarrow G_d\}$ via R then D violates Γ. If $Exp(D_T, \Gamma) \cup \{\leftarrow G_d\}$ has a T-finitely failed SLDNF-tree via R, then D satisfies Γ.*

Proof : Similar to the case of first-order constraint. □

3.3   The extended simplification theorem

An important task of the simplification method proposed by Lloyd *et al.* in [17] is to capture the difference between a model for $comp(D')$ and a model for $comp(D)$, where D and D' are databases and D' is obtained from D by the application of a transaction t to D. This is done by treating the transaction t as a sequence of deletions followed by a sequence of insertions where the application of the sequence of deletions to D produce the intermediate database D''. By using only rules of the database and updates, the method computes in stages the four sets of partially instantiated atoms $Pos_{D'',D'}$, $Neg_{D'',D'}$, $Pos_{D'',D}$ and $Neg_{D'',D}$, where the two sets $Pos_{D'',D'} \cup Neg_{D'',D}$ and $Neg_{D'',D} \cup Pos_{D'',D}$ represent respectively the part that is added to the model for $comp(D)$ when passing from D to D' due to a transaction and the part that is deleted. To preserve the consistency of the updated database, constraints are instantiated appropriately with these two sets of atoms and only affected constraints are evaluated. Instantiated constraints are evaluated using the SLDNF [4] proof procedure. The formulae for deriving the above two sets of atoms are inductively defined as follows :

$$Pos_{D,D'}^0 = \{A : A \leftarrow W \in D' \setminus D\}$$

$$Neg_{D,D'}^0 = \{\}$$

$$Pos_{D,D'}^{n+1} = \{A\theta : A \leftarrow W \in D, B \text{ occurs positively in } W,$$
$$C \in Pos_{D,D'}^n, \text{ and } \theta \text{ is an mgu of } B \text{ and } C\} \cup$$
$$\{A\theta : A \leftarrow W \in D, B \text{ occurs negatively in } W,$$
$$C \in Neg_{D,D'}^n, \text{ and } \theta \text{ is an mgu of } B \text{ and } C\}$$

$$Neg_{D,D'}^{n+1} = \{A\theta : A \leftarrow W \in D, B \text{ occurs positively in } W,$$
$$C \in Neg_{D,D'}^n, \text{ and } \theta \text{ is an mgu of } B \text{ and } C\} \cup$$
$$\{A\theta : A \leftarrow W \in D, B \text{ occurs negatively in } W,$$
$$C \in Pos_{D,D'}^n, \text{ and } \theta \text{ is an mgu of } B \text{ and } C\}$$

$$Pos_{D,D'} = \cup_{n \geq 0} Pos_{D,D'}^n$$

$$Neg_{D,D'} = \cup_{n \geq 0} Neg_{D,D'}^n$$

The generalised simplification method for the case of an aggregate constraint is as follows:

Theorem 1 *Let D be a databases and Γ an aggregate constraint such that D satisifies Γ. Suppose that t is a transaction consisting of a sequence of deletions followed by a sequence of insertions such that when the sequence of deletions is applied to D, it produces the intermediate database D'', and when the sequence of insertions is applied to this, it produces the database D'. Suppose that the completion of each of D and D' are consistent (this is guaranteed when each of D and D' is stratified [1]). If $x_1, \ldots, x_m$ are the global variables of Γ, the following three sets can be defined:*

$$\Theta = \{\theta : \theta \text{ is the restriction to } x_1, \ldots, x_m \text{ of an mgu of the atom } A,$$
$$\text{where } Count(A, n) \text{ is an aggregate atom occuring in } \Gamma,$$
$$\text{and an atom } in Pos_{D'',D'} \cup Neg_{D'',D'} \cup Pos_{D'',D} \cup Neg_{D'',D}\}$$

$$\Phi = \{\phi : \phi \text{ is the restriction to } x_1, \ldots, x_m \text{ of an mgu of a first-order}$$
$$\text{atom occurring negatively in } \Gamma (i.e. \text{ in the condition of } \Gamma)$$
$$\text{and an atom in } Pos_{D'',D'} \cup Neg_{D'',D}\}$$

$$\Psi = \{\psi : \psi \text{ is the restriction to } x_1, \ldots, x_m \text{ of an mgu of a first-order}$$
$$\text{atom occurring positively in } \Gamma (i.e. \text{ in the conclusion of } \Gamma)$$
$$\text{and an atom in } Neg_{D'',D'} \cup Pos_{D'',D}\}.$$

Then D' satisfies Γ if and only if D' satisfies $\Gamma\mu$, for all $\mu \in \Theta \cup \Phi \cup \Psi$.

Proof: Let E denote $Exp(D, \Gamma)$. If $comp(D)$ is consistent, then by Lemma 4, $comp(E)$ is also consistent. Suppose that the transaction t produces E' when it is applied to E and produces the intermediate database E''. Recall that $Count(n, y_1, \ldots, y_g)$ is the first-order equivalent of an aggregate atom $Count(A, n)$, where $y_1, \ldots, y_g$ are the attributes other than the bound variables of A. Suppose G is the first-order equivalent of Γ. Consider the following two sets:

$$\Omega_1 = \{\omega : \omega \text{ is the restriction to } y_1, \ldots, y_g \text{ of an mgu of an atom}$$
$$Count(n, y_1, \ldots, y_g) \text{ occurring in the condition of } G$$
$$\text{and an atom in } Pos_{E'',E'} \cup Neg_{E'',E}\},$$

and

$$\Omega_2 = \{\omega : \omega \text{ is the restriction to } y_1, \ldots, y_g \text{ of an mgu of an atom}$$
$$Count(n, y_1, \ldots, y_g) \text{ occurring in the conclusion of } G$$
$$\text{and an atom in } Neg_{E'',E'} \cup Pos_{E'',E}\}.$$

Suppose $\theta \in \Theta$ and $A' \in Pos_{D'',D} \cup Neg_{D'',D}$ such that A' unifies A, where A has the form $P(z_1, \ldots, z_l, y_1, \ldots, y_g)$. Each y_j is equal to x_k, for some k, $1 \le k \le m$. Whatever the bindings to the variables $z_1, \ldots, z_l$ corresponding to θ, $Count(1, y_1, \ldots, y_g)\theta, \ldots, Count(m^l, y_1, \ldots, y_g)\theta$ are members of $Pos_{E'',E'} \cup Neg_{E'',E}$, and $Count(0, y_1, \ldots, y_g)\theta, \ldots, Count(m^l - 1, y_1, \ldots, y_g)\theta$ are members of $Neg_{E'',E'} \cup Pos_{E'',E}$.

Again, suppose $\omega \in \Omega_1$. This implies that $P(a_1^i, \ldots, a_l^i, y_1, \ldots, y_g)\omega$ is a member of $Pos_{E'',E'} \cup Neg_{E'',E}$, i.e. $P(a_1^i, \ldots, a_l^i, y_1, \ldots, y_g)\omega$ is a member of $Pos_{D'',D'} \cup Neg_{D'',D}$.

The above two paragraphs prove that, in the case of the addition of a fact, the satisfiability of $\Gamma\theta$ in D' is equivalent to the satisfiability of $\Gamma\omega$ in E. Similarly, in the case of deletion. Hence,

$$E' \text{ satisfies } \Gamma\omega, \text{ for all } \omega \in \Omega_1 \cup \Omega_2 \cup \Phi \cup \Psi$$
$$\Leftrightarrow \quad E' \text{ satisfies } \Gamma\mu, \text{ for all } \mu \in \Theta \cup \Phi \cup \Psi.$$

Again,

$$D' \text{ satisfies } \Gamma$$
$$\Leftrightarrow \quad E' \text{ satisfies } G \text{(by definition)}$$
$$\Leftrightarrow \quad E' \text{ satisfies } G\omega, \text{ for all } \omega \in \Omega_1 \cup \Omega_2 \cup \Phi \cup \Psi$$
$$\text{(by simplification theorem for first-order constraints)}$$
$$\Leftrightarrow \quad E' \text{ satisfies } G\mu, \text{ for all } \mu \in \Theta \cup \Phi \cup \Psi$$
$$\Leftrightarrow \quad D' \text{ satisfies } G\theta, \text{ for all } \theta \in \Theta \cup \Phi \cup \Psi.$$

$\square$

3.4 Generalisation to other aggregate predicates

If an aggregate atom involving the predicate Sum occurs in a constraint, then the lemmas in the previous section as well as the above simplification theorem still hold since an occurrence of an aggregate atom of the form $Sum(z, A, r)$ in a constraint can be replaced by $Sum(r, y_1, \ldots, y_g)$ by adding the following clauses to the database (assuming that A has the form $P(z_1, \ldots, z_l, y_1, \ldots, y_g)$ and without any loss of generality z has been taken as z_1) :

1 clause

$$Sum(x, y_1, \ldots, y_g) \leftarrow Sum(\_, x, y_1, \ldots, y_g)$$

$m^l(m^l - 1) \cdots (m^l - k + 1)/k(k - 1) \cdots 2.1$ clauses, for each $k = 1, \ldots, m^l$:

$$
\begin{aligned}
Sum(k, x, y_1, \ldots, y_g) \leftarrow\ & P(a_1^1, \ldots, a_l^1, y_1, \ldots, y_g) \wedge \cdots \\
& \wedge P(a_1^k, \ldots, a_l^k, y_1, \ldots, y_g) \wedge \\
& x = a_1^1 + \cdots + a_1^k \wedge \\
& \neg Sum(k + 1, \_, y_1, \ldots, y_g) \wedge \cdots \\
& \wedge \neg Sum(m^l, \_, y_1, \ldots, y_g)
\end{aligned}
$$

where each a_i^p, $p = 1, \ldots, k$ is equal to a_q, for some q' and for $q \neq q'$, $1 \leq q, q' \leq k$, there exists an i such that $a_i^q \neq a_i^{q'}$.

For an occurrence of the aggregate predicate $Maximum$, the set of clauses added is the following:

1 clause :

$$Maximum(x, y_1, \ldots, y_g) \leftarrow Maximum(\_, x, y_1, \ldots, y_g)$$

For each $k = 1, \ldots, m^l$, $km^l(m^l - 1) \cdots (m^l - k + 1)/k(k - 1) \cdots 2.1$ clauses:

$$
\begin{aligned}
Maximum(k, x, y_1, \ldots, y_g) \leftarrow\ & P(a_1^1, \ldots, a_l^1, y_1, \ldots, y_g) \wedge \cdots \\
& \wedge P(a_1^k, \ldots, a_l^k, y_1, \ldots, y_g) \wedge \\
& a_1^j > a_1^1 \wedge a_1^j > a_1^{j-1} \wedge \cdots \\
& \wedge a_1^j > a_1^{j+1} \wedge \cdots \wedge a_1^j > a_1^k \\
& \wedge \neg Maximum(k + 1, \_, y_1, \ldots, y_g) \wedge \\
& \cdots \wedge \neg Maximum(m^l, \_, y_1, \ldots, y_g)
\end{aligned}
$$

where each a_i^p, $p = 1, \ldots, k$ is equal to a_q for some q, and for $q \neq q'$, $1 \leq q, q' \leq k$, there exists an i such that $a_i^q \neq a_i^{q'}$.

The case of an aggregate atom involving the predicate $Minimum$ is similar to the above case for $Maximum$. The aggregate predicate $Average$ can be defined as an extension of the predicate Sum.

3.5   Prolog implementation

Let D be a database and Γ an aggregate constraint. Lemma 5 and Theorem 1 state that the simplified first-order equivalent denial form of Γ would have to be evaluated in the updated database E' to preserve consistency, where E' is obtained by applying the transaction to $E(= Exp(D, \Gamma))$, assuming that the existentially quantified variables have already been resolved). However, in the Prolog implementation, the effect of the resolution in E' of a selected literal $Count(x, y_1, \ldots, y_g)$ from a goal which is the first-order equivalent of an aggregate literal $Count(P(z_1, \ldots, z_l, y_1, \ldots, y_g), n)$, can be achieved by evaluating the Prolog goal $? - setof([Z_1, \ldots, Z_l], p(Z_1, \ldots, Z_l, Y_1, \ldots, Y_g), N)$ in D'. Hence, one does not need to expand the underlying database D to E. In Prolog, the aggregate predicate $Count(A, N)$ is represented by $count(p([Z_1, \ldots, Z_l], [Y_1, \ldots, Y_g]), N)$, and defined as

```
count(P, N):-
    P=..[_|[Z|_]],
    setof(Z, P, ZL),
    length(ZL, N).
```

where the procedure length(ZL, N) returns the length of the list ZL into N. To get the correct intended meaning of an aggregate constraint Γ, it is necessary to follow a generalised computation rule, called *generalised safe*, which selects

1. a first-order negative literal, only when it is ground, and

2. an aggregate positive literal, only when its key formula is ground wrt to its free variables, and

3. an aggregate negative literal, only when it is ground wrt its global variables.

In Prolog's leftmost literal selection strategy, to get the effect of a generalised safe computation rule an aggregate literal λ (resp. negative literal L) can be placed after all the positive literals containing all the occurrences of global variables of λ (resp. variables of L). The other aggregate predicates can be implemented efficiently using a similar mechanism.

4 Extension to indefinite databases

In this section, the class of databases considered is indefinite and hence any usage of the term 'database' will be interpreted as 'indefinite database'.

4.1 Possible forms of a database

The definition of an indefinite database given in Section 2 is slightly different from that given in [12]. The definition adopted in this paper does not allow a negative fact to be explicitly represented in the database. Instead, a special rule is introduced to infer negative facts from the database. This is somewhat similar to the closed world assumption or negation as failure in the case of definite databases.

Consider the following example of an indefinite database.

Example 1 *Database D*1:

Rules: Definite rules:

$$Postgraduate(x) \leftarrow MSc(x)$$

$$Postgraduate(x) \leftarrow PhD(x)$$

$$Student(x) \leftarrow Undergraduate(x)$$

Indefinite rule:

$$MSc(x) \vee PhD(x) \leftarrow Student(x) \wedge \neg Undergraduate(x)$$

Facts: Definite facts:

$$Student(Subrata)$$

$$Supervisor(Howard, Subrata)$$

Indefinite fact:

$$Undergraduate(Choux) \vee MSc(Choux)$$

Definition 18 *Let D be a database and R be a clause in D. Let A be an atom occurring in the head of R. The* possible form *of R with respect to A denoted by pos(R, A) is the clause obtained from R by replacing its head by A.*

According to this definition, the possible form of a definite rule R with respect to the only atom in its head is the rule R and the possible form of a definite or indefinite fact with respect to the atom A appearing in it, is the fact A. The set of clauses comprising at least one possible form of each of the clauses of D is called a *possible form* of the database D. For example, database $D1$ has nine possible forms, each of which is the union of the set of all definite clauses of $D1$ with different possible forms arising from the two indefinite clauses of $D1$.

A query relating to the database $D1$ is

Who are the postgraduate students ?

which can be expressed as

$$\leftarrow Postgraduate(x).$$

In the context of both relational and definite databases, a substitution for the variables of a query makes the bound body of the query either true or false in the database. If the bound body is true in the database then the corresponding substitution is called an answer substitution. By contrast, an indefinite database may represent several possible worlds and in the context of this kind of database, a substitution for the variables of a query can make the bound body of the query neither true nor false in the database. A substitution which makes the query true in every possible form of the database is called a *definite answer* (e.g. for the query $\leftarrow Postgraduate(x)$ the substitution $\{x/Das\}$ is a definite answer) whereas one which makes the query true in at least one possible form of the database (e.g. $\{x/Choux\}$) is called a *possible answer*.

4.2   The declarative semantics for negative information

Let D be a database and $HB(D)$ its Herband base. Let $\{D_1, \ldots, D_n\}$ be the set of all possible forms of D such that the completion of each D_i is consistent. Then the Herband base $HB(D)$ can be partitioned into three subsets:

$$
\begin{aligned}
Def\_true(D) &= \cap_{i=1}^{n}\{A : A \in HB(D) \text{ and } comp(D_i) \vdash A\} \\
Def\_false(D) &= \cap_{i=1}^{n}\{A : A \in HB(D) \text{ and } comp(D_i) \vdash \neg A\} \\
Unknown(D) &= HB(D) \setminus (Def\_true(D) \cup Def\_false(D))
\end{aligned}
$$

where the symbol \ denotes set difference. The set of facts in $Def\_true(D)$ can be taken as definitely true in D whereas the set of facts in $Def\_false(D)$ are definitely false in D. The facts in $Unknown(D)$ are possibly true in D.

Clearly, when the database is definite the above definition of semantics reduces to Clark's idea of a completed database. When the database is definite and hierarchical the set $Unknown$ is empty and the Herband base is divided between the two sets Def_true and Def_false. The SLDNF-resolution mechanism suffices to determine any element of the set Def_true and hence any element of the set Def_false. When all three subsets are non-empty, the situation is more complex. In this case the definite resolution mechanism determines the elements of the set Def_true. The possible resolution mechanism will be able to determine the set of elements which are either in the set $Unknown$ or in the set Def_true. An element of the Herband base which is not generated by the possible resolution mechanism can be taken to be false and hence is a member of Def_false.

4.3 The procedural semantics for negative information

The procedural semantics is based on two mutually recursive resolution schemes, one for possible resolution and the other for definite resolution.

4.3.1 Possible Resolution

Let D be a database, G a goal, and R a computation rule. Initially, none of the clauses in D is marked as used possibly with respect to atoms occurring in their heads. A *possible derivation* for $D \cup \{G\}$ via R consists of a sequence $D_0^+ = D, D_1^+, D_2^+, \ldots$ of positive databases, a sequence $D_0^- = \{\}, D_1^-, D_2^-, \ldots$ of negative databases, a sequence $G_0 = G, G_1, G_2, \ldots$ of goals, a sequence $C_1, C_2, \ldots$ of variants of ground negative literals or program clauses from the possible forms of D, and a sequence $\theta_1, \theta_2, \ldots$ of substitutions satisfying the following:

1. For each i, G_i is $\leftarrow L_1 \wedge \cdots \wedge L_m \wedge \cdots \wedge L_p$, the selected literal L_m in G_i is

   (a) a positive literal and L_m unifies with

       i. A definite fact A in D_i^+ with an mgu θ_{i+1}. Then C_{i+1} is A, D_{i+1}^+ and D_{i+1}^- are respectively D_i^+ and D_i^-, and G_{i+1} is $\leftarrow (L_1 \wedge \cdots \wedge L_{m-1} \wedge L_{m+1} \wedge \cdots \wedge L_p)\theta_{i+1}$.

ii. The head of a definite rule $H \leftarrow B$ in D_i^+ with an mgu θ_{i+1}. Then C_{i+1} is $H \leftarrow B$, D_{i+1}^+ and D_{i+1}^- are respectively D_i^+ and D_i^-, and G_{i+1} is $\leftarrow (L_1 \wedge \cdots \wedge L_{m-1} \wedge B \wedge L_{m+1} \wedge \cdots \wedge L_p)\theta_{i+1}$.

iii. An atom A occurring in an indefinite fact F of D_i^+ with an mgu θ_{i+1} and F has not been used possibly with respect to A. If none of the literals of D_i^- has a definite refutation in $D_i^+ \cup \{pos(F, A)\}$ then C_{i+1} is $pos(F, A)$, D_{i+1}^+ is $D_i^+ \cup \{A\}$, D_{i+1}^- is D_i^-, and G_{i+1} is $\leftarrow (L_1 \wedge \cdots \wedge L_{m-1} \wedge L_{m+1} \wedge \cdots \wedge L_p)\theta_{i+1}$. Finally, F is marked as used possibly with respect to A.

iv. An atom A occurring in the head of an indefinite rule $R : F \leftarrow B$ of D_i^+ with an mgu θ_{i+1} and R has not been used possibly with respect to A. If none of the literals of D_i^- has a definite refutation in $D_i^+ \cup \{pos(R, A)\}$ then C_{i+1} is $pos(R, A)$, D_{i+1}^+ and D_{i+1}^- are respectively $D_i^+ \cup \{pos(R, A)\}$ and D_i^-, and G_{i+1} is $\leftarrow (L_1 \wedge \cdots \wedge L_{m-1} \wedge B \wedge L_{m+1} \wedge \cdots \wedge L_p)\theta_{i+1}$. Again, R is marked as used possibly with respect to A.

(b) a ground negative literal $\neg A$ and there is no definite refutation (introduced in the next section) for $D_i^+ \cup \{\leftarrow A\}$. In this case, θ_{i+1} is an identity substitution, C_i is $\neg A$, D_{i+1}^+ and D_{i+1}^- are respectively D_i^+ and $D_i^- \cup \{A\}$, and G_{i+1} is $\leftarrow L_1 \wedge \cdots \wedge L_{m-1} \wedge L_{m+1} \wedge \cdots \wedge L_p$.

2. If the sequence $G_0, G_1, \ldots$ of goals is finite, then the last goal G_n of the sequence is either empty or has the form $\leftarrow L_1 \wedge \cdots \wedge L_m \wedge \cdots \wedge L_p$, where L_p is selected and

(a) L_m is an atom and there is no program clause in D_n^+ for which any of the literals occurring in its head unifies with L_m, or

(b) L_m is an atom and there are program clauses $\{R^1, \ldots, R^l\}$ in D_n^+ such that for each j, one of the atoms A occurring in the head H^j of R^j unifies with L_m. But, for each j, there exists a literal A' in D_n^- such that $D_n^+ \cup \{pos(R^j, A)\} \cup \{\leftarrow A'\}$ has a definite refutation, or

(c) L_m is a ground negative literal of the form $\neg A$ and $D_n^+ \cup \{\leftarrow A\}$ has a definite refutation.

Each derivation of a possible resolution constructs a sequence of positive databases and a sequence of negative databases. When a goal is refuted by a possible resolution with an answer substitution θ, it can be said that the goal bound with the answer substitution θ is true in the last database of the sequence of positive databases. The sequence of negative databases keeps track of the ground negative atoms occurring in goals and which have been inferred false by step 1.1b. Thus, a member of D_i^- is false in D_i^+, for every i.

Steps 1(a)i and 1(a)ii formalise the SLD-resolution principle for definite clauses and hence in these two cases both positive and negative database remain fixed. Step 1.1b is a negation as failure which is concerned with keeping track of the inferred negative literal by adding it to the literal to the latest negative database. The process of marking clauses in steps 1(a)iii and 1(a)iv is necessary to avoid redundant answers.

A possible derivation is *finite* if it consists of a finite sequence of goals; otherwise, it is *infinite*. A possible derivation is *successful* if it is finite and the last goal is the empty goal. A successful possible derivation is called a *possible refutation*. A possible derivation is *failed* if it is finite and the last goal is not the empty goal.

From the definition of possible derivation, a *possible tree* for $D \cup \{G\}$ via R is defined in the usual way where each branch of the possible tree corresponds to a possible derivation. A branch of a possible tree for which the terminating node is an empty goal is called a *success branch*, a branch which does not terminate is called an *infinite branch* and a branch for which the terminating node is other than an empty goal is called a *failure branch*. A possible tree for which every branch is a failure branch is a *finitely failed possible tree*.

If each possible form of a database D is hierarchical, then the possible resolution in D terminates, provided that the definite resolution of step 1.1b for resolving negative literals terminates.

Definition 19 *Let D be a database and G be a goal $\leftarrow W$. An* answer substitution *for $D \cup \{G\}$ is a substitution for the variables of G. A possible computation of $D \cup \{G\}$ is an attempt to construct a possible derivation of $D \cup \{G\}$. A possible computed answer θ for $D \cup \{G\}$ is the substitution obtained by restricting the composition $\theta_1 \cdots \theta_n$ to the variables of G, where $\theta_1, \ldots, \theta_n$ is the sequence of substitutions used in a possible-refutation of $D \cup \{G\}$. When G is allowed, every possible computed answer for $D \cup \{G\}$ is a ground substitution for variables in G. A possible computed answer for $D \cup \{G\}$ will also be referred to as a* possible answer substitution *for the possible-refutation of $D \cup \{G\}$.*

4.3.2 Definite resolution

The formal definition of a resolution principle to obtain a definite answer substitution of a query can be adopted from either the definite resolution introduced in [6] or the proof procedure like SLGNF [18] or nH-Prolog [19],[23] (by extending the capability of inferring negative information). In this paper, an nH-Prolog-like resolution has been considered to define a *definite derivation*,

definite refutation, etc. From the implementation considered these terms can
be defined easily.

4.3.3   Negation as possible failure

Based on the two resolution strategies discussed in the previous two sections,
the rule (procedural semantics) for inferring negative information denoted by
negation as possible failure, is defined as follows. The negation of a fact A
is taken as true in a database D if $D \cup \{\leftarrow A\}$ has a finitely failed possible
tree.

See [6] for more details about the two resolution schemes and the equivalence between declarative and procedural concepts of negative information
semantics.

4.4   Constraint satisfiability in indefinite databases

In this subsection and the remainder of Section 4, a constraint is taken to be
a closed first order formula. In the context of database $D1$ the constraint

> every postgraduate student has a supervisor

can be expressed as the first order formula

$$\forall x(Postgraduate(x) \rightarrow \exists y\, Supervisor(y, x)).$$

Definition 20 *(Declarative definition of constraint satisfiability) A database
D is said to satisfy a constraint C if C is a logical consequence of the completion of each of the possible forms of D. The database D is said to satisfy
a set of constraints I if D satisfies each of the constraints of I; otherwise, D
violates I.*

From the above definition of constraint satisfiability if one wants to impose
the above constraint on the database $D1$ the integrity of the database would
be violated as *Choux* can be proved to be a postgraduate student in one of
the possible forms of $D1$ without having a supervisor in that possible form.

For the method introduced in the next section for checking integrity in a
database, each constraint is an allowed formula expressed in denial form. If
a constraint W is not in denial form then it can be transformed to denial
form by the same process described in Section 3.1. When the database D

is indefinite, the constraint W is a logical consequence of the completion of each of the possible forms of D if and only if the transformed constraint $\leftarrow A$ is a logical consequence of the completion of each of the possible forms of D_T. This is true because the difference between D_T and D is only a set of definite clauses and they are part of each and every possible form of D_T. This justifies the transformation of a constraint to a denial. As an example, the *Postgraduate* $-$ *Supervisor* constraint can be transformed to a denial of the form $\leftarrow A$ by adding the rules

$$
\begin{aligned}
A &\leftarrow Postgraduate(x) \wedge \neg B(x) \\
B(x) &\leftarrow Supervisor(y, x)
\end{aligned}
$$

to the database, where the two predicates A and B are not used elsewhere in the database.

Let I be a set of constraints. Then I_d will represent the transformed set of clauses of the form

$$IC(No) \leftarrow B$$

from I, where $\leftarrow B$ is a constraint from I and No is a unique identification of the constraint. $IC(No)$ will be called the *head* of the constraint $\leftarrow B$.

The declarative definition of constraint satisfiability in the context of a database D can be related to the declarative semantics of D as follows. The constraint $\leftarrow B$ violates the database D if a ground instance of B can be made true in $Def\_true(D) \cup Unknown(D)$. Accordingly, the syntactic definition of constraint satisfiability, which is equivalent to the declarative definition, is as follows:

Definition 21 *(Syntactic definition of constraint satisfiability) Let D be a database and $\leftarrow B$ a constraint in denial form.*

1. *If $D \cup \{\leftarrow B\}$ has a finitely failed possible tree then $\leftarrow B$ is said to satisfy D*

2. *If $D \cup \{\leftarrow B\}$ has a possible refutation, then $\leftarrow B$ violates D.*

4.5   The extended path finding method

This method for checking integrity, introduced in [7] for the case of definite databases, is now generalised for checking integrity in indefinite databases. In the case of definite databases the method calculates a set of facts implicitly added to the database and a set of partially instantiated atoms whose

instances are likely to be deleted from the database due to an update. These
two sets of atoms are determined through the computation of all possible
paths from update literals. If a success path is found then the integrity is
said to be violated in the database. In the case of indefinite databases, the
method has been generalised by determining the following two sets:

1. the set of facts implicitly added to the database and possibly true in
   the updated database, and

2. the set of atoms whose instances are likely to be deleted from the
   database.

These two sets are computed through all possible path calculations. The
formal definition of a path is as follows.

Definition 22 *Let D be a database. A (possible) path in D is defined as a
chain of literals*

$$L_0 \overset{R_1}{\twoheadrightarrow} L_1 \overset{R_2}{\twoheadrightarrow} \cdots \overset{R_n}{\twoheadrightarrow} L_n$$

where L_0 is called the source *of the path, L_n its* destination, *n its* length
*and $R_1, \ldots, R_n$ are clauses from the union of the possible forms of D used
to construct the path from L_0 to L_n . If the source L_0 is positive then it is
ground and $D \cup \{\leftarrow L_0\}$ has a possible-refutation. For any two consecutive
literals L_i and L_{i+1} , L_{i+1} is called the* successor *of L_i in the path, and is
obtained from L_i in one of the following ways:*

1. If

   (a) L_i is positive, and

   (b) L_i unifies with a positive literal L occurring in the body of the
       clause $R : A_1 \vee \cdots \vee A_m \leftarrow B$, and

   (c) α is an mgu of L_i and L, and

   (d) θ is a possible computed answer for $D \cup \{G\}$, where G is the goal
       $\leftarrow B\alpha$

   then L_{i+1} is the term $A_j \alpha \theta$, $1 \leq j \leq m$, and R_{i+1} is $pos(R, A_j)$.

2. If

   (a) L_i is positive, and

   (b) the negative literal $\neg L$ occurs in the body of the clause $R_i : A_1 \vee
       \cdots \vee A_m \leftarrow B$ such that L_i unifies with L, and

(c) α is an mgu of L_i and L, and

(d) $\neg A_j \alpha, 1 \leq j \leq m$, is not an instance of any one of the L_k 's, where $0 \leq k \leq i$

then L_{i+1} is the term $\neg A_j \alpha, 1 \leq j \leq m$, and R_{i+1} is $pos(R, A_j)$.

3. If

    (a) L_i is negative, and

    (b) L_i unifies with a negative literal L occurring in the body of the clause $R : A_1 \vee \cdots \vee A_m \leftarrow B$, and

    (c) α is an mgu of L_i and L, and

    (d) θ is a possible computed answer for $D \cup \{G\}$, where G is the goal $\leftarrow B\alpha$

then L_{i+1} is the term $A_j \alpha \theta, 1 \leq j \leq m$, and R_{i+1} is $pos(R, A_j)$.

4. If

    (a) L_i is negative and has the form $\neg M$, and

    (b) M unifies with a positive literal L occurring in the body of the clause $R : A_1 \vee \cdots \vee A_m \leftarrow B$, and

    (c) θ is an mgu of M and L, and

    (d) $\neg A_j \alpha, 1 \leq j \leq m$, is not an instance of any one of the L_k 's, where $0 \leq k \leq i$

then L_{i+1} is the term $\neg A_j \alpha, 1 \leq j \leq m$, and R_{i+1} is $pos(R, A_j)$.

From this definition, it is possible to construct more than one path starting from the same literal. Furthermore, a positive literal on a path is always ground and possibly true in the database. For simplicity, a path will sometimes be written without showing the clauses used to construct the path. In the path $L_0 \rightarrow L_1 \rightarrow \cdots \rightarrow L_n$, the *distance* of L_p from L_q $(0 \leq q \leq p \leq n)$ is $p - q$ and L_p is said to be at a *distance $p - q$ from L_q* .

Definition 23 *Let D be a database and L a literal such that if L is positive then it is ground and $D \cup \{\leftarrow L\}$ has a possible-refutation. Let S be the set of all paths with L as the source. The (possible) path space rooted at the literal L is a tree defined as follows :*

1. Each node of the tree is a literal.

2. The root node is L.

3. If N is a node of the tree, then the set of all successors of N in the paths of S are the only descendants of N in the tree.

Each branch of the path space corresponds to a path in the database with the root node as the source and vice-versa. A path which ends at the head $IC(No)$ of a constraint will be called a *(possible) success path*; otherwise, it will be called a *failure path*. A path space containing at least one branch which corresponds to a success path is referred to as a *(possible) success path space*.

To check integrity in a database when a new constraint is added, the database is queried directly to make sure that the constraint is a logical consequence of the completion of each of the possible forms of the database. If a constraint is deleted then this cannot cause any inconsistency. To check integrity in the updated database D' as a result of the transaction t applied to D, the source is taken as an update literal. An *update literal* of the transaction t applied to a database D may be one of the following :

1. An atom occurring in a fact of t which is to be added to D.

2. The negation of an atom occurring in a fact of t which is to be deleted from D.

3. If an indefinite rule $R : A_1 \vee \cdots \vee A_m \leftarrow B$ in t is to be added to D then for a possible computed answer θ for $D' \cup \{\leftarrow B\}$, the corresponding instance of an atom occurring in the head of the rule R, i.e. $A_i\theta$, $1 \leq i \leq m$, which is possibly implicitly added to D due to the transaction.

4. If a rule $R : A_1 \vee \cdots \vee A_m \leftarrow B$ in t is to be deleted from D then the negation of an atom occurring in the head of the rule R, i.e. $\neg A_i$, $1 \leq i \leq m$, whose instances are likely to be deleted from D due to the transaction.

To preserve integrity one must ensure that a success path space does not exist with source as an update literal in the updated database. The algorithm tries to construct a success path through backtracking.

It has been assumed that the transaction does not add and delete the same clause. A transaction is valid if all of its update literals can be computed successfully without going into an infinite derivation. Equally, a transaction is rejected if a success path is found in the updated database. Modification can be considered as being accomplished by a deletion followed by an addition.

The method is illustrated by means of the following few examples.

Example 2 *Database D2:*

Rules: R1. $P(x,y) \leftarrow Q(x,y) \wedge R(x)$

     R2. $Q(x,y) \leftarrow S(x,y) \wedge \neg M(x)$

     R3. $R(x) \leftarrow U(x)$

     R4. $R(x) \leftarrow V(x)$

     R5. $U(x) \vee V(x) \leftarrow T(x) \wedge \neg W(x)$

     R6. $M(x) \leftarrow R(x) \wedge N(x)$

Facts: $N(A)$

     $S(A,C)$

     $S(B,C)$

Integrity constraints *I*2: IC1. $IC(1) \leftarrow P(x,y) \wedge \neg O(x)$

Update: insertfact $T(A) \vee T(B)$

where x,y are variables and A,B,C are constants. As each of the possible forms of $D2$ is hierarchical in nature, their completions are consistent. Before the update is applied, database $D2$ satisfies the constraint $I2$. Let $D2'$ be the updated database.

As the update is the insertion of an indefinite fact $T(A) \vee T(B)$, the set of update literals is $\{T(A), T(B)\}$. Taking $T(A)$ as a source one can have, with the help of **R5**, either of $U(A)$ or $V(A)$ as the next literal of the source. Considering $U(A)$ first, the next literal of the path is $R(A)$. To find a successor of $R(A)$ with the help of **R1**, one has to find a possible computed answer of $D2 \cup \{\leftarrow Q(A,y) \wedge R(A)\}$. The fact $Q(A,C)$ is an instance of $Q(A,y)$ which is true in one of the possible forms of $D2$ provided that $M(A)$ is false in that possible form. $R(A)$ could be taken to be true in that possible form if $M(A)$ was not provable with the help of **R6**. Hence no instance of $Q(A,y) \wedge R(A)$ is true in the constructed database and **R1** fails to generate a successor for $R(A)$. In the process of backtracking when $V(A)$ is considered, the generated path also becomes failed for the same reason. Backtracking further and considering $T(B)$ as the source, one can construct the success path

$$T(B) \stackrel{pos(R_5,U(x))}{\longrightarrow} U(B) \stackrel{R_3}{\longrightarrow} R(B) \stackrel{R_1}{\longrightarrow} P(B,C) \stackrel{IC1}{\longrightarrow} IC(1).$$

The two complete path spaces generated as a result of the update are shown in Figure 1.

S. K. Das and M. H. Williams

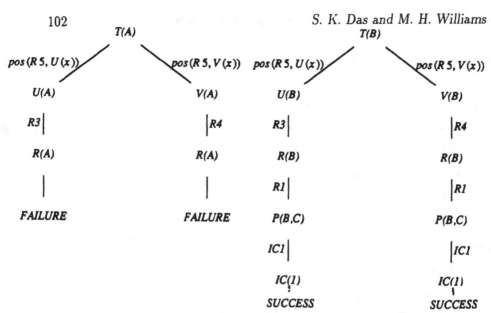

Figure 1: The two complete path spaces in the case of Example 2

4.6 Prolog implementation

This section describes how the integrity checking method described in the previous section and the two resolution strategies described in Section 4 may be implemented in Prolog.

A unique number has been assigned to each newly inserted constraint as an identification. A constraint $\leftarrow B$ numbered No is stored directly as a Prolog rule

$$ic(No) : -B.$$

A rule or a constraint can be retrieved efficiently by using a reference which uniquely identifies the corresponding rule or constraint.

The top level C-Prolog goal for integrity checking ($? - ic\_violated(Tran).$) can be defined as

```
ic_violated(Tran):-
        path(ic(No),Tran,[],P,N),!.
```

where $Tran$ represents an update literal and $path(D, S, NegList, P, N)$ means that a path is to be constructed from the literal S to the literal D and the set comprising the negation of each literal of the list $NegList$ are the only negative literals which have occurred so far in this path construction. Each of P and N is an open-ended structure of the form

$$((\ldots((X, C_1), C_2), \ldots), C_n)$$

where X is variable and each C_i is a structure or an atom which will be described later in this section. This helps to keep information regarding the dynamic construction of a possible form of a database. With this convention if the database becomes inconsistent due to the transaction $Tran$, then the first inconsistency is reported at a constraint numbered No.

The path can be computed efficiently by maintaining additional information for each rule and constraint in the database. For each literal L occurring in the body of a rule $R : A_1 \vee \cdots \vee A_m \leftarrow B$ and for each i, $1 \leq i \leq m$, clauses of the form

$$depend(Ref, A_i, L)$$

$$depend(Ref, \neg A_i, CompL)$$

have been maintained, where Ref is the reference which uniquely identifies the clause R and $CompL$, called the complement of L, is defined as follows. When L is positive, $CompL$ is $\neg L$; otherwise, when L is $\neg A$, then $CompL$ is A. For each literal L occurring in a constraint $\leftarrow B$, a clause of the form

$$depend(Ref, ic(No), L).$$

has been maintained, where $ic(No)$ is the head of the constraint and Ref is the reference which uniquely identifies the clause $ic(No) \leftarrow B$.

The task of finding a path from a source literal S to a destination literal D can be achieved in Prolog with the help of the following meta-interpreter:

```
path(D,S,_,P,N):-
    depend(Ref,D,S),
    cl(Ref,Hs,B),
    simplify(B,S,SB),
    simplify(Hs,D,_),
    pos(SB,P,N).

path(D,S,NegList,P,N):-
    depend(_,Via,S),
    Via=(not A),
    not instance_list(A,NegList),
    path(D,Via,[A|NegList],P,N).

path(D,S,NegList,P,N):-
    depend(Ref,Via,S),
    not Via=(not _),
    cl(Ref,Hs,B),
    simplify(B,S,SB),
```

```
simplify(Hs,Via,_),
pos(SB,P,N),
path(D,Via,NegList,P,N).
```

$clause(H, B, Ref)$ means H and B are unified respectively with the head
and body of a clause which is uniquely identified by the reference Ref. The
interpretation of $simplify(B, S, SB)$ is that SB is an instance of B obtained
by unifying one of B's body literals with S. $instance(A, NegList)$ means
that A is not an instance of any of the atoms occurring in the list $NegList$.
This corresponds to conditions 2(d) and 4(d) in the definition of a path and
prevents a possible generation of an infinite path from a negative literal in
the presence of recursive rules. The goal $pos(SB)$ is satisfied if there is a
possible refutation of the goal SB in the underlying database modified by P
and N.

In the implementation of a query evaluation system, nH-Prolog [19],[23] has
been selected and extended with the capability of deriving negative information from the database according to the semantics of negation as possible
failure. In this case the format used for storing a definite clause [23] using a
predicate nH is

$$nH(Head, Body)$$

whereas an indefinite clause is stored under the same predicate as

$$nH(ChosenHead, AuxiliaryHeads, Body, AncestorList).$$

Beside these a separate clause of the form

$$nH\_index(Functor, Arity, RefList)$$

has been maintained to store all the references to clauses containing an occurrence of a particular user-defined predicate in their heads, where the predicate is identified by $Functor$ and $Arity$. In a database the number of clauses
defining a predicate could be very high and in such a situation maintaining
the above set of clauses would be both inefficient and wasteful of storage.
Instead, definite clauses have been stored under the predicate cl as

$$cl(StartRef, NextRef, Goal, Body)$$

and an indefinite clause as

$$cl(IndRef, Posn, StartRef, NextRef, Goal, AuxHeads, Body, NewAnc),$$

where $StartRef$ is the unique reference (1,2,...etc) to the clause among
the set of clauses containing an occurrence in their heads the user defined

predicate P for *Goal* with specific arity; $NextRef$ is the same for the next clause defining P with the same arity and this is represented by a unique reference (zero) when there is no next clause. For indefinite clauses the two parameters $IndRef$ and *Posn* denote respectively a unique indefinite clause reference ($i1, i2, \ldots$ etc) and a unique position ($p1, p2, \ldots$ etc) of *Goal* in the head of the indefinite clause. Under the above convention the database $D1$ can be represented as follows :

$cl(1, 2, postgraduate(X), msc(X))$

$cl(2, 0, postgraduate(X), phd(X))$

$cl(1, 2, student(X), undergraduate(X))$

$cl(2, 0, student(X), true)$

$cl(1, 0, supervisor(howard, subrata), true)$

$cl(i1, p1, 1, 2, msc(X), [dh(phd(X), Y)],$
$(student(X), not\ undergraduate(X)), Y)$

$cl(i1, p2, 1, 0, phd(X), [dh(msc(X), Y)],$
$(student(X), not\ undergraduate(X)), Y)$

$cl(i2, p1, 1, 0, undergraduate(choux), [dh(msc(choux), X)], true, X)$

$cl(i2, p2, 2, 0, msc(choux), [dh(undergraduate(choux), X)], true, X)$

The two mutually recursive top-level procedures *def* and *pos* corresponding to the two resolution strategies in Section 2 have been defined in the following way.

```
def(Goal,P,N):-
    copy_query(Goal,OldGoal),
    def_init((X,Goal),OldGoal,P,N),
    var(X).

pos(Goal,_,_):-
    reserve(Goal),
    call(Goal).

pos(not Goal,P,N):-
    not def(Goal,P,N),
    append_left(Goal,N).

pos((A,B),P,N):-
    pos(A,P,N),
    pos(B,P,N).
```

```
pos(Goal,P,N):-
    cl(_,_,Goal,Body),
    pos(Body,P,N).

pos(Goal,P,N):-
    generator(Goal,Gen),
    cl(IndRef,Posn,_,_,Gen,_,Body,_),
    not in_clause(defcl(IndRef,Posn),P),
    in_clause(NegL,N),
    link(NegL,H,[]),
    def(NegL,P,N),
    !,fail.

pos(Goal,P,N):-
    cl(IndRef,Posn,_,_,Goal,_,Body,_),
    append_left(defcl(IndRef,Posn),P),
    pos(Body,P,N).
```

where the procedure *copy_query(Goal, OldGoal)* means *OldGoal* is a copy of the query *Goal* and *generator(Goal, Gen)* means the generator of the goal *Goal* is *Gen*. Also, *append_left* is a procedure which appends its first argument to its open-ended structure second argument and is defined as follows.

```
append_left(X,Y):-
    var(Y),!,
    Y=(_,X).
append_left(X,(_,X)):-!.
append_left(X,(Y,_)):-
    append_left(X,Y).
```

The following four procedures *def_init*, *def_solve*, *def_restart* and *def_restart_goal* are respectively the modified forms of *nH_init*, *nH_solve*, *nH_restart* and *nH_restart_goal* in [23].

```
def_init(AnsList,OldGoal,P,N):-
    AnsList = (_,Goal),
    def_solve(Goal,1,[anc(q,[])],_,[],DH,init,P,N),
    ( DH = [_|_]
      -> def_restart(AnsList,OldGoal,DH,P,N);
      true).
```

```
    def_solve(Goal,_,_,_,DH,DH,_,_,_):-
        reserve(Goal),
        call(Goal).

    def_solve(not Goal,_,_,_,DH,DH,_,P,N):-
        not pos(Goal,P,N).

    def_solve((A,B),_,Anc,AH,DH1,DH3,Can,P,N):-
        def_solve(A,1,Anc,AH,DH1,DH2,Can,P,N),
        def_solve(B,1,Anc,AH,DH2,DH3,Can,P,N).

    def_solve(Goal,_,_,Goal,DH,DH,yes,_,_).

    def_solve(Goal,StartRef,Anc,AH,DH1,DH3,Cancel,P,N):-
        get_cl(IndRef,Posn,StartRef,NextRef,Goal,AuxHeads,
            Body,NewAnc),
        NewAnc = [anc(Goal,NextRef)|Anc],
        ( (var(IndRef) ; in_clause(defcl(IndRef,Posn),P))
          -> def_solve(Body,1,NewAnc,AH,DH1,DH3,Cancel,P,N);
          append(AuxHeads,DH1,DH2),
          def_solve(Body,1,NewAnc,AH,DH2,DH3,Cancel,P,N) ).

    def_restart(AnsList,OldGoal,DH,P,N):-
        DH = [dh(AH,Anc)|DH1],
        member(anc(ResGoal,StartRef),[anc(not,_)|Anc]),
        def_restart_goal(AnsList,OldGoal,ResGoal,
                         StartRef,Anc,AH,DH1,DH2,Cancel,P,N),
        ( (DH2 = [_|_], Cancel == yes)
          -> def_restart(AnsList,OldGoal,DH2,P,N);
          (DH2 = [], Cancel == yes)
          -> true;
          fail).

    def_restart_goal(_,_,not,_,_,AH,DH,DH,yes,_,N):-
        in_clause(AH,N).

    def_restart_goal(_,_,Goal,StartRef,Anc,AH,DH1,DH2,
            Cancel,P,N):-
        def_solve(Goal,StartRef,Anc,AH,DH1,DH2,Cancel,P,N).

    def_restart_goal(AnsList,OldGoal,q,_,Anc,AH,DH1,DH2,
            Cancel,P,N):-
        copy_query(OldGoal,Query),
```

```
         append_left(Query,AnsList),
         def_solve(Query,1,Anc,AH,DH1,DH2,Cancel,P,N).
```

The first seven parameters of the procedure *def_solve* are defined in the same way as in [23]. The last two parameters P and N are open-ended structures. Each element in P has the form

$$defcl(IndRef, Posn)$$

where the possible form of an indefinite clause identified by $IndRef$ with respect to the head at the position $Posn$ has been used for a possible resolution and the *def_solve* routine will consider those clauses as definite clauses. Each element in N is an atom representing a negative fact true in the database constructed dynamically.

In the new internal representation of clauses, a clause is retrieved with the help of the following routine *get_cl*

```
    get_cl(_,_,0,_,_,_,_,_):-!,fail.   % No more clauses

    get_cl(_,_,StartRef,NextRef,Goal,_,Body,_):-
                        % Retrieve a definite clause
        cl(StartRef,NextRef,Goal,Body).

    get_cl(IndRef,Posn,StartRef,NextRef,Goal,
            AuxHeads,Body,NewAnc) :-     % Retrieve an
        cl(IndRef,Posn,StartRef,NextRef,Goal,
            AuxHeads,Body,NewAnc).        % ind clause

    get_cl(IndRef,Posn,StartRef,NextRef,Goal,
            AuxHeads,Body,NewAnc):-       % Retrieve
        generator(Goal,Gen),             % next clause
        (cl(StartRef,Via,Gen,_);
            cl(_,_,StartRef,Via,Gen,_,_,_)),
        get_cl(IndRef,Posn,Via,NextRef,Goal,
            AuxHeads,Body,NewAnc).
```

5   Conclusion

This paper aims at generalising the approach to handling integrity constraints in deductive databases in two ways. Firstly, closed general formulae have been introduced to represent constraints involving aggregate operations and

Lloyd *et al.*'s simplification method has been extended for checking integrity in definite databases in the presence of such constraints. Secondly, a new definition of constraint satisfiability has been introduced in the case of indefinite databases and the path finding method has been generalised to cope with integrity checking in indefinite databases. An appropriate extension seems possible to maintain integrity in an environment where both the database is indefinite and the imposed constraints are beyond first-order.

The definition of constraint satisfiability in indefinite databases which has been proposed here may seem restricted in the sense that each constraint has to be a theorem of the completion of each of the possible form of the database. An alternative view, which is more relaxed, can be defined as follows. A set of constraints I is said to be satisfied by a database D, if there exists at least one possible form D_i of D such that each constraint in I is a theorem of $comp(D_i)$. While this will permit more flexibility in what is stored, it may produce other problems in terms of inconsistent possible forms unless these can be limited by a more general inference mechanism.

The path finding method for definite databases can also be extended for checking integrity in definite databases in the presence of aggregate constraints as follows. Suppose, at the time of calculating a path P, a fact A' (or a negative literal $\neg A'$) occurring in it, unifies with the key formula A of an aggregate atom $Count(A, n)$ occurring in a constraint Γ. Let θ be an mgu of A and A'. Then, $\Gamma\theta'$ is evaluated in the updated database, where θ' is a unifier obtained from θ by excluding any bindings to the local variables of $Count(A, n)$. For efficiency purpose, all θ's are stored to avoid redundant evaluation of constraints. Lloyd *et al.*'s simplification method can also be extended for checking integrity in indefinite databases, as in the case of definite databases, by calculating a set of partially instantiated atoms whose instances are likely to be deleted from different possible forms of the database.

References

[1] K. R. Apt, H. A. Blair, and A. Walker. Towards a theory of declarative knowledge. In Minker [20], pages 89–148.

[2] P. Asirelli, M. D. Santis, and M. Martelli. Integrity constraint in logic databases. *Journal of Logic Programming*, 3:221–232, 1985.

[3] F. Bry, H. Decker, and R. Manthey. A uniform approach to constraint satisfaction and constraint satisfiability in deductive databases. In *Proceedings of Extending Database Technology*, pages 488–505, Venice, 1988.

[4] K. L. Clark. Negation as failure. In H.Gallaire and J.Minker, editors, *Logic and Databases*, pages 293–322. Plenum Press, New York, 1978.

[5] W. F. Clocksin and C. S. Mellish. *Programming in Prolog.* Springer International, 1984.

[6] S. K. Das. *Integrity Constraints in Deductive Databases.* PhD thesis, Department of Computer Science, Heriot Watt University, 1990.

[7] S. K. Das and M. H. Williams. A path finding method for checking integrity in deductive databases. *Data and Knowledge Engineering*, 4:223–244, 1988.

[8] S. K. Das and M. H. Williams. Integrity checking methods in deductive databases: A comparative evaluation. In M.H.Williams, editor, *Proceedings of the 7th British National Conference on Databases*, pages 85–116. Cambridge University Press, 1989.

[9] C. J. Date. *An Introduction to Database Systems*, volume 2. Addison Wesley, 1985.

[10] H. Decker. Integrity enforcements on deductive databases. In L.Kerschberg, editor, *Proceedings of the First International Conference on Expert Database Systems*, pages 271–285, Charleston, South Carolina, April 1986.

[11] E. B. Fernandez, R. C. Summers, and C. Wood. *Database Security and Integrity.* Addison Wesley, 1981.

[12] H. Gallaire, J. Minker, and J.-M. Nicolas. Logic and databases — a deductive approach. *ACM Computing Surveys*, 16(2):153–185, 1984.

[13] R. A. Kowalski and K. A. Bowen, editors. *Proceedings of the 5th International Conference and Symposium on Logic Programming*, Seattle, USA, August 1988.

[14] T.-W. Ling. Integrity constraint checking in deductive databases using the Prolog not-predicate. *Data and Knowledge Engineering*, 2:145–168, 1987.

[15] J. W. Lloyd. *Foundations of Logic Programming.* Symbolic Computation Series. Springer Verlag, 2nd, extended edition edition, 1984.

[16] J. W. Lloyd and R. W .Topor. Making Prolog more expressive. *Journal of Logic Programming*, 1(3):225–240, 1984.

[17] J. W. Lloyd and R. W. Topor. A basis for deductive database systems. *Journal of Logic Programming*, 2(2):93–109, 1985.

[18] A. Lobo, J. Minker, and A. Rajasekhar. Weak completion theory for non-Horn logic programs. In Kowalski and Bowen [13].

[19] D. W. Loveland. Near-Horn Prolog. In E.Wada, editor, *Proceedings of the 4th International Conference on Logic Programming*, pages 456–469, Tokyo, Japan, July 1987. Springer Verlag.

[20] J. Minker, editor. *Foundation of Deductive Databases and Logic Programming*. Morgan Kaufman Publishers, Inc, 1988.

[21] J.-M. Nicolas. Logic for improving integrity checking in relational databases. *Acta Informatica*, 18:227–253, 1982.

[22] F. Sadri and R. A. Kowalski. An application of general purpose theorem-proving to database integrity. In Minker [20].

[23] B. T. Smith and D. W. Loveland. A simple near-Horn Prolog interpreter. In Kowalski and Bowen [13], pages 794–809.

[24] J. D. Ullman. *Principles of Database Systems*. Computer Science Press International, Inc, Maryland, USA, 2nd edition edition, 1984.

Construction of CLP Programs

Yves Deville   Pascal van Hentenryck

Abstract

This paper is a first attempt to set up the basis for a methodological development of CLP programs. The starting point is an existing methodology for standard Prolog programs which we try to adapt to the specific class of CLP programs. The methodology consists of several steps (Specification, Logic Description, Logic Programs) exploiting the logical foundations of Logic Programming. The specificities introduced by CLP programs at all stages of the methodology are presented and serve as a basis to suggest refinements to the methodology or to explain some of the optimizations specific to CLP programming. The new framework is applied to a real example which we reconstruct entirely. We conclude by stressing that the existing methodology can serve as a basis for CLP program construction and by making explicit some of the assumptions underlying CLP problem-solving.

1   Introduction

Existing approaches in logic program construction can be divided in two classes depending on their logical bases. In the first class, logic programs are constructed by means of the only procedural semantics. There is thus no logical aspect in the construction process. This approach is taken in most Prolog textbooks (e.g. [3], [1], [7]). The development of logic programs by stepwise enhancement is also an example of the procedural based approach [13].

Within the logical based approaches to logic program construction, a first family of methods synthesize programs from formal specifications. This can be seen as a deductive synthesis from a given set of axioms specifying the problem. Examples of this approach are [2], [8], [10], [11], [4], [12] [14]. The synthesis of logic programs can also be done from a set of given examples. This approach, imported from functional programming, is mostly inductive [18], [6].

Within the logical based approach, logic programs can also be constructed from a non formal specification. Our work is based on this approach. A complete presentation of the underlying methodology can be found in [5]. While not as systematic, a similar conception already appears in [20].

Constraint Logic Programming (CLP) is a new class of logic programming languages especially suited to tackle combinatorial problems. Its main motivation is to provide suitable abstractions for this class of problems in order to shorten the development time and to allow the user to focus on the main issues and not on low-level implementation considerations. The abstractions support paradigms coming from various fields of Computer Science including Operations Research, Symbolic Computation, and Artificial Intelligence. CLP languages have only been developed recently and little research has been devoted to the construction of programs in these languages. However there is clearly a need for a methodology for various reasons. First the computation model of CLP programs is more sophisticated than for standard Prolog and might involve data-driven computations in addition to the goal-driven computations of Prolog. Also some aspects of CLP programming are very much related to the operational semantics (although they can be given a clear logical meaning) and are not easily understood by users. Finally, efficiency is very much an issue and experience can be shared among the user community in order to write more efficient programs.

In this paper, we consider the problem of adapting an existing methodology for standard Prolog programs to CLP programs. Section 2 starts by reviewing the methodology (Section 2). Section 3 presents a framework for constructing CLP programs based on the methodology. Section 4 applies the framework to a real example.

2 Overview of the Methodological Framework

In [5], a methodology, referred to as the underlying methodology in the following sections, is proposed for the systematic construction of logic programs. Before presenting its possible extension to tackle the construction of CLP programs solving combinatorial problems, we give here a quick overview of this underlying methodology.

The contention of the approach is that the logic programming paradigm is very powerful and can be used advantageously when programming in Prolog. In order to use the logical framework for constructing Prolog programs, the development of a program is decomposed in several steps. As usual, the first one is the elaboration of a specification of the problem. The second step consists of constructing a logic description in pure logic from the specification, independently of any programming language or procedural semantics. The last step deals with the derivation of a logic program (in Prolog) from the logic description. This step handles the issues that make programming in Prolog different from programming in logic. Note that only the last step deals with a particular logic programming language.

Let us underline the basic choices made in the design of the methodology. In the elaboration of a specification, no particular specification language is imposed. The specification is basically a description of a relation. Type information is added as well as the directionalities, that is the forms of the parameters (ground, variables or other) for which the program has to be correct.

The second step consists of constructing from the specification what is called a logic description. A *logic description* is a formula in typeless first-order logic. More precisely, it is an *if and only if* definition of a predicate. With this form of logic descriptions, the completion of the derived logic programs will be logically equivalent to the logic descriptions. This approach allows the negation as failure rule to be seen as real negation at the logic description level. This construction is independent of the chosen programming language as well as of the procedural semantics. It is based on the declarative semantics of pure logic. This simplifies the construction process. The construction is performed from the description of the relation and the type information stated in the specification.

The last step deals with the derivation of a logic program (in Prolog) from the logic description. This starts with the translation of the logic description into program clauses. In order to get a correct Prolog program, one has to perform an abstract interpretation or a dataflow analysis (using the type and directionality information of the specification) to determine a permutation of the clauses and of the literals such that incompleteness, unfairness, unsoundness and negation problems do not occur. An independent termination proof must sometimes be performed. This step has thus to solve all the problems that make the procedural semantics different from the declarative one used at the logic description level. The Prolog code can finally be transformed by introduction of control information and by optimizations based on Prolog's execution mechanism.

3 A Framework for CLP Program Construction

3.1 Specification of the Problem

3.1.1 Definition of the Problem

Any computer problem is originally given in an informal statement. The first step in the construction of a CLP program always amounts to making this description precise and unambiguous using a formal or semi-formal language. The main steps of this process are

- a choice of the objects considered as significant in the problem statement;

- a definition of the problem in terms of the chosen objects;

- a choice of representation for the objects in the CLP language.

Note that this process is not neutral wrt the final program. It is often the case that particular choices here imply a particular vision of the problem and therefore encourage a particular solution. It is also worth mentioning that the constraints appearing in the specification do not need to be primitives of the target CLP language.

3.1.2 Specification of the Procedure

Once the problem has been specified, it is associated to a procedure which needs to be specified. The underlying methodology requires the specification of a number of features which include a logical relation, directionalities, as well as the number of solutions. CLP procedures share essentially the same properties as standard logic procedures; hence most of framework is inherited directly. However CLP programs have also some unique specificities. One of the specificities of combinatorial problems in general, and CLP programs in particular, is the absence of the completeness requirement. The user is basically interested in one solution to its problem, be it an arbitrary one (in decision problems) or an optimal one (in optimization problems). This is of critical importance when the procedural semantics is taken into account because it allows some optimizations to be carried out which would not be possible otherwise. Another specificity arises with respect to the directionalities of the procedure. Although CLP might allow for more multidirectional procedures, usual CLP procedures are intended to be used in a fixed directionality. Some parameters are supposed to be given (i.e. ground) and will be called *input variables*. The other parameters are variables which will be instantiated by the procedure. They are called *output variables*. Depending of the desired degree of generality of the procedure, some input variables could be considered as constants within the program. Finally CLP procedures might impose some constraints that the constraint-solver might not be able to satisfy when the procedure is called. This information should be provided as part of the specification to prevent incorrect transformations.

3.2   Construction of a Logic Description

Now that we have a specification of the procedure, we turn to its actual construction. The first step towards that goal amounts to constructing a logic description. Once again most of the underlying methodology can be inherited here by CLP programs. However CLP programs have a number of features that make them specific.

First, CLP programs work on richer computation domains. Therefore we have to assume, when reasoning, the presence of a number of axioms characterizing the domain theories we are working with. This will influence the correctness criteria of CLP programs.

Second, CLP programs usually contains some parts that are not easily explained in terms of logic (although they could be given a logical meaning). We basically think of the labelling procedure (used to generate values for the variables) as well as the optimization requirement. Both are very much connected with the computation model and are best left out of this level.

Consequently the logic description is split into two parts:

1. a domain part stating the domain constraints on the variables;

2. a constraint part stating the problem constraints in terms of the variables.

The definition of domains for the variables can be seen as the definition of constraints over the possible values of the variables. Domains and constraints have thus the same logical effect. They form two distinct parts only for reasoning purposes. In addition, if we face an optimization problem, the logic description contains as well a description of the objective function in term of the variables. Program schematas are given in Figures 1 and 2. Note that, for optimization problems, Obj is often among the Out parameters.

```
prob(In,Out) ⟺
            domains(In,Out)
       &    constraints(In,Out)
```

Figure 1: Logic Description Schemata for Decision Problems

```
prob(In,Out) ⟺
            domains(In,Out)
       &    constraints(In,Out)
       &    obj_function(In,Out,Obj)
```

Figure 2: Logic Description Schemata for Optimization Problems

3.2.1 Domains

The logic description for the domain part amounts to specifying the domains of the *output* variables using the primitives of the underlying CLP language. This step does not raise any serious difficulty. A practical issue is that some domains might not be known precisely and hence they have to be overestimated.

3.2.2 Constraints

The logic description of the constraint part is much more critical and amounts to specifying0 the problem constraints as given in the specification in terms of the primitive constraints of the underlying CLP language. Some constraints might not be primitives of the CLP language and we have to find a suitable way to state them using the logic framework. Basically a non-primitive constraints can be expressed either

- as a conjunction of primitive constraints or

- as a disjunction of primitive constraints or

- as a general constraint [21].

The second option should be avoided as much as possible, for instance by using general constraints, as it will introduce choice points and therefore increases the computational complexity. The first two alternatives can be constructed in a natural way while general constraints encourages a *collect and state* approach [21].

3.2.3 Objective Function

For optimization problems, when the objective function is not straightforward (e.g. one of the output variables), it has to be constructed explicitly.

3.2.4 Correctness Criteria

The correctness criteria of standard logic description scales up naturally to CLP programs.

Definition 1 (Correctness of CLP programs) *If* in *is a ground term belonging to the specified type, then* prob(in,out) *is a* $\mathcal{H}(\mathcal{D})$*-logical consequence iff* out *is a solution for* in *and* out *belongs to the specified type, where an* $\mathcal{H}(\mathcal{D})$*-interpretation is a Herbrand interpretation that is a model of the computation domain* $\mathcal{D}$.

The different status for input and output variables comes from the restricted directionality in the specification of this class of problems.

3.2.5 Complexity Analysis

At this stage, it is already possible to compare different designs wrt to their expected complexity. Of course the complexity measures available at this point are necessarily very loose but they can give an initial feeling about the appropriateness of the approach. One measure which experimentally turned out to be useful is the *potential search space* to explore. Assuming the computation domain is *finite domains* and that there is no constraints creating choice points, the potential search space is given by the size of the Cartesian product of the domain of all, or a subset[1] of the, *output* variables. If the computation is *rational linear arithmetics*, the potential search space is probably defined by the constraints used to create choice points. Comparing different designs or creating new designs following the potential search space metrics is a useful activity.

---

[1]In that case, it means that some variables can be given values automatically once some other variables have been instantiated.

3.3   Derivation of a CLP Program

We now have a logic description and would like to transform it into an actual CLP program. This process is best viewed as the following sequence:

1. translation of the description into a CLP clausal form;

2. introduction of control information;

3. introduction of a labelling procedure;

4. analysis of pruning;

5. analysis of redundancy;

6. Prolog optimizations.

Each of these steps will be studied in the following. Note however that steps 2,3, and 4 are specific to CLP programs while steps 1 and 6 are also parts of the underlying methodology.

3.3.1   Translation to CLP Program Form

The constructed logic description is turned into Horn clauses by means of classical and straightforward translation rules such as described in [16, 5]. It amounts to replacing equivalences by implications and to achieve a conjunctive normal form.

3.3.2   Control Information

In the logic description, we describe the logic behind the constraints but no information is given to the underlying CLP language with regard to how to use them. In this step, control information is provided to specify the intended use of constraints and logic procedures. This might take the form of *delay* declarations on logic procedures as well as *forward* and *lookahead* declarations on user-defined constraints.

3.3.3   Introduction of the Labelling

The logic description expresses the logical aspects of the problem. This alone might not be sufficient to solve our problem. The constraint-solver

```
prob(In,Out) ←
     domain(In,Out),
     constraints(In,Out),
     labelling(Out)
```

Figure 3: Logic Program Schemata for Decision Problems

```
prob(In,Out) ←
     domain(In,Out),
     constraints(In,Out),
     obj_function(In,Out,Obj),
     minimize(labelling(Out),Obj).
```

Figure 4: Logic Program Schemata for Optimization Problems

might be too weak to solve all constraints (e.g., non linear constraints in CLP($\mathcal{R}$) or finite domains constraints) or the constraint-solver might yield the most general solution while we are interested in a specific one. A *labelling* procedure is therefore necessary to actually compute solutions and its purpose is to generate values for the variables. This step simply amounts to building the *labelling* procedure and including it inside the logic description. The program schematas after this step are given in Figures 3 and 4.

3.3.4   Analysis of the Pruning

Complexity Analysis   At this point there are many different ways of evaluating the quality of the resulting algorithms.

One possibility to consider is the kind of pruning achieved at each node of the search tree together with its cost. The idea is to find out a suitable trade-off between the time spent in pruning and the time spent in searching.

Another possibility is to analyse the shape of the search tree by identifying how many nodes are expected at different levels of the search tree. Of course the most valuable information at this point would be a statistical analysis of the search procedure (see for instance [9, 17]) but these techniques are too sophisticated as soon as many constraints of different types are involved.

The information gained during this analysis might suggest refinements, that can be included at the constraint or labelling level.

Constraint Level So far only the constraints necessary to formalize correctly the problem have been included. However, in practice, it is often very useful to add constraints that express properties shared by all solutions (decision problems) or all optimal solutions (optimization problems). These constraints can help the constraint-solver to discover failures sooner and reduce the generation of values. These constraints have been given the name *surrogate* constraints in Operations Research. It is a creative process to identify good surrogate constraints.

Labelling Level The labelling process is the place where choices are made. A good labelling may also dramatically speed up search in combinatorial problems and is complementary to a good pruning. The basic choices you face at this level are the following.

- Is instantiation or domain-splitting more appropriate?

- What variable to instantiate (or to split on) next ?

- What value to give to the variable ?

The heuristics to decide on these matters might be very dependent on the problem at hand. However there are a number of guidelines that can be helpful in this matter. Stefik [19] recommends the use of the *least commitment* principle. This principle amounts to postponing decisions as late as possible and, when forced to choose, to restricting oneself the least possible. This principle seems to recommend the use of domain-splitting but the user should also take into account that domain-splitting might not bring enough information for the pruning to be effective. Haralick and Elliot [9] recommends the *first-fail* principle in order to choose the next variable to instantiate. This choice means that we are trying first where we are the most likely to fail. This leads to an early detection of failures and a small growth in the size of the search space. In optimization problems, the *maximal regret* heuristics (e.g. [15]) is also very useful. It amounts to choosing the variable which, if not assigned a particular value, would make the evaluation function grow the most. Finally, the value to assign first could be the one appearing in the smallest number of other domains so that we avoid failures as much as we can. It should be stressed as well that these heuristics are dynamic and hence very much related to the operational semantics.

3.3.5 Analysis of Redundancy

The above refinements do not remove any solution to the problem at hand.
The one we are about to present will remove solutions and is only possible
because we gave up the completeness requirement in the specification. The
idea is that, in these problems, there might be a lot of symmetries and redun-
dancies. Removing them can substantially speed up the search. Symmetries
can be removed in various ways. They can induce the statement of new constraints or the modification of the labelling. In both cases, they can logically
be seen as a filter after the labelling but have been moved before or inside
the labelling to speed up the search.

3.3.6 Prolog Optimizations

Final optimization of the resulting CLP program can be achieved by application of transformations such as described in [5] which include efficient
representation of data, backward unification, and partial evaluation.

4 Example: Graph Coloring

Given a graph, the problem is to find the minimum number of colours necessary to colour the vertices of the graph so that two adjacent vertices are
coloured with different colours. The concept of graph is here supposed to
be well understood. A precise definition is however needed in the following
specification part.

4.1 Specification of the Problem

4.1.1 Definition of the Problem

In the following definition of graph, the edges are undirected and must join
two distinct vertices. Hence we only consider non-reflexive graph here.

Definition 2 *A graph G is a (finite) nonempty set V of vertices or nodes,
and a set E of edges, where each edge is an unordered pair of distinct vertices.
Such pairs of vertices are called adjacent in G.*

Definition 3 *Given a graph G=(V,E) and an integer k, a k-colouring func-
tion of G is a (total) function f from V to a set of colour C (with $|C|=k$),*

such that adjacent vertices are assigned different colours (i.e. $(v_i, v_j) \in E \Rightarrow f(v_i) \neq f(v_j)$).

Definition 4 *A graph G is* minimally k-coloured *(where k is an integer) if there exists a k-colo00ring function of G, and there exists no j-colouring function of G, with $j < k$.*

Although not really important, we assume that the desired output is the number of colours as well as the colouring function. We now turn to the Prolog representation of graphs and colouring functions, where vertices (and colours) will be represented by consecutive integers.

Definition 5 *Let G=(V,E) be a graph, with $V=\{v_1, \ldots, v_n\}$, $C=\{c_1, \ldots, c_k\}$ be a set of colours, and f be a k-colouring function of G.*

- *The graph G is represented by the couple (N, List_Edges), where N is the number n of vertices, and List_Edges is a list of pairs of integers such that $(i, j) \in$ List_Edges iff $(v_i, v_j) \in E$.*

- *The colours $c_1, \ldots, c_k$ are represented by the integers $1 \ldots k$.*

- *The colouring function f is represented by list $[r_1, \ldots, r_n]$, with r_i integers and $f(v_i) = c_{r_i}$. That is r_i is the (representation of the) colour of the node i.*

From now on, we will use the terms *graph, colours* and *colouring function* for these concepts as well as for their representation.

4.1.2 Specification of the Procedure

Procedure colouring(G, Nb_Col, Col_Fct).
Types: G : graph
       Nb_Col : integer
       Col_Fct : list of integers
Relation:
    G is minimally Nb_Col-coloured, and Col_Fct is a Nb_Col-colouring function of G.
Directionality:
    in(ground,var,var) : out(ground,ground,ground) <1-1>

The colouring procedure is specified precisely. The directionality part specifies the form of the parameters before (*in* part) and after (*out* part) the execution of the procedure. In this example, the graph is given as input (input variables) and the procedure will yield Nb_Col and Col_Fct as results (output variables). The multiplicity description (here <1-1> specifies a lower and upper bound to the number of answer substitutions. In this case, we thus know that there will be one and only one answer substitution, even if there exists multiple correct solutions.

4.2   Construction of a Logic Description

We build here the logic description of the colouring problem, but without the minimization requirement. The specification of ld_colouring is the same as colouring, but with the new relation

Col_Fct is a Nb_Col-colouring function of G.

There is no need here to explicitly have the obj_function predicate since the objective function is given by Nb_Col.

The general form of the logic description is given in Figure 5.

4.2.1   Domains

The *output* variables are Col_Fct and Nb_Col. We have to specify their domain. We already know that Nb_Col is an integer. It is however bounded by the number n of vertices of the graph G (because there exist a trivial n-colouring function of G). Hence,

domain Nb_Col :: 1..n

where n is the number of vertices of G.

The result Col_Fct is the list $[X_1, \ldots, X_n]$. We obviously have that X_i is bounded by Nb_Col since it is the size of the set of colours. Hence,

domain Col_Fct=[X1,...,Xn] ::   [1..Nb_Col, ...,1..Nb_Col]

¿From the above specification, a logic description of domain(G, Nb_Col, Col_Fct) can easily be constructed and is given in Figure 6. The predicate sub is the usual substraction. The primitive domain constraint of the underlying CLP language is X in Dom, stating that the domain of X is Dom.

4.2.2 Constraints

The only constraint we should handle is that adjacent vertices have different colours. Let G = graph(n,List_Edges) and Col_Fct=[X1,...,Xn]

$$\text{For all } (\text{I,J}) \in \text{List\_Edges}, X_I \neq X_J$$

The logic description in Figure 7 is a straightforward expression of these constraints. The predicate elem(I, L, XI) states that XI is the Ith element of the list L.

4.3 Derivation of a CLP Program

4.3.1 Translation to CLP Program Form

The translation of the constructed logic description into Horn clauses is here straighforward.

4.3.2 Introduction of the Labelling

The labelling procedure is required to generate all possible values for the output variables Nb_Col and Col_Fct. The specification of the labelling is given in Figure 8.

Figure 9 shows how the labelling is introduced in the colouring procedure through a minimization, as required in the initial specification.

A simple labelling (see Figure 10) can be made via the indomain built-in (specified in Figure 11). The procedure indomain(X) successively instantiates X to the values of its domain. The soundness, completeness and non-redundancy requirements such as described in [5] ensure that a correct implementation of the above specification will instantiate X to all the different values of its domain. In the multiplicity <1-*>, the * specifies that the number of answer substitutions will be finite (but a priori unknown).

In order to understand the specification of indomain, it is worth stating the two following facts.

- The domain of the output variables is finite and is usually restricted during the execution, because of the propagation of constraints.

```
1d_colouring(G, Nb_Col, Col_Fct) ⟺
      domain(G, Nb_Col, Col_Fct)
    & constraint(G, Nb_Col, Col_Fct)
```

Figure 5: The 1d_colouring Logic Description

```
domain(G, Nb_Col, Col_Fct) ⟺
      G = (N, Edges)
    & Nb_Col in 1..N
    & domain_list(Col_Fct, Nb_Col, 1..Nb_Col)

domain_list(List, Nb_Elem, Dom) ⟺
      List = [] & Nb_Elem = 0
    ∨ List = [H|T] & Nb_Elem > 0 & H in Dom
                                 & sub(Nb_Elem, 1, Nb1)
                                 & domain_list(T, Nb1, Dom)
```

Figure 6: The domain Logic Description

```
constraint(G, Nb_Col, Col_Fct) ⟺
      G = (N,Edges)
    & constraint_edges(Edges, Col_Fct)

constraint_edges(Edges, Col_Fct) ⟺
      Edges = []
    ∨ Edges = [(I,J) | TEdges]
        & elem(I, Col_Fct, XI)
        & elem(J, Col_Fct, XJ)
        & XI ≠ XJ
        & constraint_edges(TEdges, Col_Fct)
```

Figure 7: The constraints Logic Description

- At any point during the execution, the following statement is an invariant:
Non-instantiated domain variables have a domain of size ≥ 2.
Procedurally speaking, when a domain variable has a domain of size 1, the variable is immediately instantiated to this value.

4.3.3 Analysis of the Pruning

In this problem, the above simple labelling suggests the following analyses.

- Order of the generated values of the domains.

- Order of the variables to be labelled.

Value Ordering

In the simple labelling, the colour variables are generated in increasing order. This order is the most convenient since we aimed at minimizing Nb_Col.

Labelling Ordering

Col_Fct vs Nb_Col: This reduces to choosing the order of the literals. Such an order is important. It is much more efficient to first find a colouring function and then to minimize the number of colours rather than trying to find a colouring function for every successive values 1,2,3,... of Nb_Col.

Colors within Col_Fct: In the simple labelling, the order of the labelling is made according to the position of the colour variables within the list Col_Fct. Such an order is not effective. In this case a general guideline for the variable choice is the first-fail principle. This principle can be applied here by choosing the colour variable with the smallest domain. Indeed, since fewer values are left in its domain, this variable is likely to be more difficult to instantiate than any other. Giving first some values to the other variables can imply that a failure due to the most constrained variable will be discovered very late in the computation leading to a costly backtracking.

A second heuristics for the first-fail principle is the choice of a variable appearing in the greatest number of constraints. In graph terms it means that

Procedure `labelling`(Nb_Col, Col_Fct).
Types: Nb_Col : integer
          Col_Fct : list of integers
Relation:
    true.
Directionality:
    in(ground or domvar, list(ground or domvar)) :
    out(ground,ground) <1-*>

Figure 8: Specification of `labelling`

```
colouring(G, Nb_Col, Col_Fct) ←
    domain(G, Nb_Col, Col_Fct),
    constraint(G, Nb_Col, Col_Fct),
    minimize( labelling(Col_Fct,Nb_Col), Nb_Col )
```

Figure 9: The `colouring` Procedure

```
labelling(Nb_Col, Col_Fct) ←
    list_indomain(Col_Fct),
    indomain(Nb_Col)

list_indomain(L) ←
    L=[]
list_indomain(L) ←
    L=[H|T],
    indomain(H),
    list_indomain(T)
```

Figure 10: A simple `labelling` Procedure

we choose the variable that has the largest degree. This selection has the advantage of reducing immediately the domain of many other domain variables, pruning the search tree very early.

The choice of a variable within `Col_Fct` is made via `deleteffc(X,L,Rest)`, specified in Figure 12.

The resulting labelling is presented in Figure 13.

4.3.4 Analysis of Redundancy

The objective of the colouring procedure is to find *one* minimal colouring function. However there exist a lot of different minimal colouring functions (e.g. all the permutation of the assigned colours). The labelling process should avoid multiple solutions and take these symmetries as much as possible into account to reduce the size of the search space.

Suppose that all the assigned colours to a partial colouring vary from 1 to k. Which colour to consider for the next chosen vertice? Two alternatives need to be considered.

- Giving an already used colour, that is a colour from 1 to k.

- Giving a new colour, that is a colour $> k$.

While in the first case all the colours need to be considered, in the second case only one needs to be chosen. Indeed, all these colours share the property that they are not used in the partial solution, but none of them has a distinguished feature with respect to the others. They are different conventions for the same choice, and choosing several of them leads to symmetrical solutions and thus to redundancy.

An implementation of the above strategy is given in Figure 14, where an extra parameter specifies the highest colour used in a partial labelling. With this approach, the highest used colour after a successful labelling is the number of colours of the resulting colouring function. Hence, the labelling of `Nb_Col` can be dropped.

This labelling brings an order of magnitude improvement over the naive version. It reduces dramatically the number of different values which can be assigned at each level of the search tree.

Procedure `indomain(X)`.
Relation:
    true.
Directionality:
    in(ground or domvar) : out(ground) <1-*>
    The value of X are given in increasing order.

Figure 11: Specification of `indomain`

Procedure `deleteffc(X, L, Rest)`
Types: `X` : term
       `L` : non empty list $[e_1, \ldots, e_n]$
       `Rest` : list
Relation:
    $X \in L$, and `Rest` is the list L without one occurrence of X.
Directionality:
    in(var, list(ground or domvar), var) :
    out(ground or domvar, list(ground or domvar),
    list(ground or domvar)) <1-1>
Heuristics of the choice:
    A couple (Sd_i, NbC_i) is associated to each e_i,
    with Sd_i the size of the domain of e_i (1 if e_i is ground)
        NbC_i the number of constraints with an occurrence of e_i
        (0 if e_i is ground).
    X is the element of L with the smallest (Sd_i, NbC_i),
    according to the lexical ordering.

Figure 12: Specification of `deleteffc`

```
labelling(Nb_Col, Col_Fct) ←
     choose_var_labelling(Col_Fct),
     indomain(Nb_Col)

choose_var_labelling(L) ←
     L=[]
choose_var_labelling(L) ←
     L=[H|T],
     deleteffc(X, L, Rest),
     indomain(X),
     choose_var_labelling(Rest)
```

Figure 13: A labelling Procedure with Chosen Variables

```
labelling(Nb_Col, Col_Fct) ←
     unsym_labelling(Col_Fct,0,Nb_Col)

unsym_labelling(Col_Fct, UptoNow_Max, Nb_Col) ←
     Col_Fct=[],
     Nb_Col = UptoNow_Max
unsym_labelling(Col_Fct, UptoNow_Max, Nb_Col) ←
     Col_Fct=[H|T],
     deleteffc(C, Col_Fct, Rest),
     C ≤ UptoNow_Max + 1,
     indomain(C),
     New_Max = maximum(C,UptoNow_Max),
     unsym_labelling(Rest, New_Max, Nb_Col)
```

Figure 14: A labelling Procedure Avoiding Symmetries

4.3.5   Prolog Optimizations

Instead of representing the edges of the graph as a list of couples, it is much more convenient to have them represented as a binary relation. The colouring procedure will then receive the name of this relation. The corresponding list of edges is easely obtained trough the **bagof** built-in.

The **constraint** procedure extensively extracts elements of a list from a given position. This is very costly since it requires a scanning of the list. A direct access can be obtained by locally transforming the list in to a term which elements are the elements of the list. The built-in **arg(I,Term,ArgI)** can then be used advantageously.

Finally, usual Prolog optimizations are done. The resulting final program is given in Figure 15.

5   Conclusion

This paper has studied the construction of CLP programs. Starting with the methodology of [5], we have identified which parts of the methodology scaled up to CLP programs, which specificities are introduced by CLP programs, and how the methodology could be extended to take them into account. The specificities of CLP programming wrt the underlying methodology are mainly the following:

- CLP programs are usually intended for some well-defined input-output patterns. This information can lead to specific optimizations;

- CLP programs often drop the completeness requirement. This allows for an analysis of redundancy that might prune significant parts of the search space;

- The labelling and optimization parts of the program are handled at the program (i.e., operational) level.

The advantages of the present approach for CLP programming include

- a simpler construction due to the separation between the declarative and the operational components;

- a more systematic construction process where the role and the goal of each step is clearly defined and separated from the others;

```
colouring((N,Edge_Pred), Nb_Col, Col_Fct) ←
    Nb_Col in 1..N,
    domain_list(Col_Fct, Nb_Col, 1..Nb_Col),
    constraint(G, Nb_Col, Col_Fct),
    minimize( labelling(Col_Fct,Nb_Col), Nb_Col )

domain_list([],0,Dom) ← !
domain_list([H|T], Nb_Elem, Dom) ←
    H in Dom,
    Nb1 is Nb_Elem - 1,
    domain_list(T, Nb1, Dom)

contraint(Edge_Pred, Col_Fct) ←
    Edges =..  [Edge_Pred, X, Y],
    bagof( (X,Y) , Edges, List_Edges),
    Term_Col_Fct =.. [f | Col_Fct],
    constraints_edges(List_Edges, Term_Col_Fct)

constraints_edges([],_) ←
constraints_edges([ (I,J) |T], Term) ←
    arg(I, Term, XI),
    arg(J, Term, XJ),
    XI ≠ XJ,
    constraints_edges(T, Term)

labelling(Nb_Col, Col_Fct) ←
    unsym_labelling(Col_Fct, 0, Nb_Col)

unsym_labelling([], Nb_Col, Nb_Col) ←
unsym_labelling([H|T], UptoNow_Max, Nb_Col) ←
    deleteffc(C, [H|T], Rest),
    C ≤ UptoNow_Max + 1,
    indomain(C),
    New_Max = maximum(C, UptoNow_Max),
    unsym_labelling(Rest, New_Max, Nb_Col)
```

Figure 15: The Complete Program

- an explicit classification of the different opportunities to improve efficiency which makes it possible to carry them in an explicit way.

This paper has also contributed to making clear some of the underlying assumptions in CLP programs. Issues such as relaxation, incrementality, and meta-programming have not been considered yet.

Acknowledgments

The authors were respectively supported by the Belgian National Fund for Scientific Research and by the Belgian National Incentive-Program for Fundamental Research in Artificial Intelligence.

References

[1] I. Bratko. *PROLOG Programming for Artificial Intelligence*. International Computer Science. Addison-Wesley, 1986.

[2] K. L. Clark and F. McCabe. The control facilities of ic-prolog. In D. Mitchie, editor, *Expert systems in the micro electronic Age*, pages 122–149. Edinburgh University Press, 1979.

[3] W. F. Clocksin and C. S. Mellish. *Programming in Prolog*. Springer International, 1984.

[4] G. Dayantis. Logic program derivation for a class of first-order logic relations. In *Proc of the Tenth International Joint Conference on Artificial Intelligence*, pages 9–14. Milano, 1987.

[5] Y. Deville. *Logic Programming: Systematic Program Development*. International Series in Logic Programming. Addison-Wesley, 1990.

[6] P. Flener. Automatic synthesis of logic programs form subsets of their behavior. Technical Report RP-90/7, FUNDP, March 1990.

[7] F. Giannesini, H. Kanoui, R. Passero, and M. van Caneghem. *Prolog*. Addison-Wesley, 1986.

[8] A. Hansson. *A Formal Development of Programs*. PhD thesis, The Royal Institute of Technology and the University of Stockholm, Department of Computer Science, Sweden, 1980.

[9] R.M. Haralick and G.L. Elliot. Increasing tree search efficiency for constraint satisfaction problems. *Artificial Intelligence*, 14:263–313, 1980.

[10] C.J. Hogger. *Introduction to Logic Programming*. Academic Press, 1984.

[11] A-L. Johansson. *Using Symmetry and Substitution in Program Derivation*. PhD thesis, Computer Science Dpt., Uppsala University, Uppsala Sweden, 1985.

[12] A-L. Johansson, A. Erikson-Granskog, and A. Edman. *Prolog versus You*. Springer Verlag, New York, 1989.

[13] A. Lakhotia. *A Workbench for Developing Logic programs by Stepwise Enhancement*. PhD thesis, Dept. of Computer Engineering and Science, CWRU, Cleveland, 1989.

[14] K.K. Lau and S.D. Prestwich. Top-down synthesis of recursive logic procedures from first-order logic specifications. In *Seventh International Conference on Logic Programming*, Jerusalem, June 1990.

[15] J-L. Lauriere. A language and a program for stating and solving combinatorial problems. *Artificial Intelligence*, 10(1):29–127, 1978.

[16] J. W. Lloyd. *Foundations of Logic Programming*. Symbolic Computation Series. Springer Verlag, 2nd, extended edition edition, 1984.

[17] B. Nudel. Consistent labeling problems and their algorithms: Expected-complexities and theory-based heuristics. *Artificial Intelligence*, 21(1,2):135–178, 1983. Special Issue on Search and Heuristics.

[18] E. Y. Shapiro. *Algorithmic Program Debugging*. MIT Press, 1983.

[19] M. Stefik. Planning with constraints (molgen: Part 1). *Artificial Intelligence*, 16:111–139, 1981.

[20] Leon Sterling and Ehud Shapiro. *The Art of Prolog*. MIT Press, 1986.

[21] Pascal van Hentenryck and Y. Deville. The cardinality operator: A new logical connective for constraint logic programming. In Koichi Furukawa, editor, *Eighth International Conference on Logic Programming*, pages 745–759, Paris, June 1991. MIT Press.

Some Control Engineering Applications of Prolog

P. W. Grant   C. P. Jobling   C. Rezvani*

Abstract

The inter-disciplinary Control and Computer Aided Engineering research group at Swansea has been developing Prolog programs to solve a number of problems arising in the study of system descriptions. These form part of a general integrated software system, CES (Control Engineering workStation), which provides the control engineer with access to simulation and analysis tools via a sophisticated graphical interface. Traditionally engineers have used FORTRAN to solve such problems, necessitating the mapping of the system into a matrix representation. Our representation in Prolog, on the other hand, is closer to the graphical description of a system and so in many ways is a more natural approach leading to solutions which are easier to understand.

The two most common ways of describing a system are by the graphical means of a block diagram or signal flow graph (essentially duals of each other). These can be represented in Prolog as a set of assertions (e.g. indicating connections and nodes) and transmittances and signals (usually mathematical expressions) can appear as Prolog terms.

Analysis and manipulation of these graphs can now be carried out at the symbolic level. In this way very general methods may be programmed which are applicable to a variety of types represented by the terms (e.g. scalar, vector or matrix). Only at a later simplification stage may it be necessary to make use of the type of the expression to obtain a simpler result.

We shall illustrate how Prolog has been effectively used in CES. Use is made of rules with heuristics and graph searching which are implemented in Prolog without difficulty. The problems tackled include:-determination of transmittances for linear systems and sampled data systems, general graphic manipulation and aesthetic layout of block

---

*Part of this work was supported by SERC under grant GRE/2960/1

136

diagrams and signal flow graphs, simulation of discrete event systems, translation of discrete event systems to PLC programs, and general dimensional analysis.

1 Introduction

Little seems to have been published in the literature on applications of logic programming to control engineering. There has been some work by Heintze et al. [9] on applying a constraint logic programming language to the analysis of electrical circuits. The only other work we know of, beside our own, has been on the applications of Prolog to build a database environment for Computer Aided Control System Design (CACSD) described by Tan and Maciejowski [17].

The research group at Swansea working on CACSD has made extensive use of Prolog in a number of areas of their work, ranging from general manipulation and analysis of signal flow graphs to simulation and transformation of discrete event dynamic systems. In this paper, we survey some of the work that has been done indicating why logic programming has been useful for these applications. Much of the work was undertaken by the authors, but we also describe some applications which have been developed by our colleagues in the group.

We have been building a general graphical user interface for control engineers, CES (Control Engineering workStation) [2, 3, 5], which gives familiar and natural user interaction with standard simulation or control engineering tools. The engineer is able to describe his problem graphically, by means of one of the diagram editors. In addition a number of special purpose control engineering tools have been constructed and are provided under CES. The current system has now been redesigned and is at present being implemented under X-windows with versions conforming to the OPENLOOK and Motif user interface standards. Prolog has been used for much of the symbolic processing tasks such as calculating and simplifying transmittances and general processing of different sorts of graphical representations used by engineers.

The paper is divided into seven sections, starting with the applications to analysis of signal flow graphs and block diagrams. Section 3 is concerned with system manipulation. Section 4 gives details of algebraic manipulation and dimensional analysis. In Section 5 we sketch the methods for transforming between different system representations and the heuristics used for aesthetic layouts of graphs. In Section 6 we describe some techniques dealing with the transformation of discrete event dynamic systems presented in the

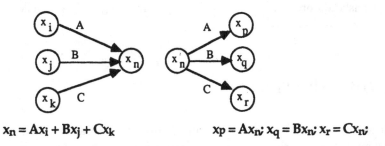

$$x_n = Ax_i + Bx_j + Cx_k \qquad\qquad x_p = Ax_n;\ x_q = Bx_n;\ x_r = Cx_n;$$

Figure 1: Linear Signal Flow Graph Relationship

form of ladder diagrams. We conclude with a summary of our use of logic programming in CACSD.

2 Signal Flow Graph Analysis

Signal flow graphs (SFG's) and block diagrams are the two most common graphical forms of representation for a control system. A SFG consists of nodes and edges which illustrates the flow of signals through a dynamic system. The nodes represent the signals in the system, and the edges categorize the dependencies of each of the signals in the system on the other signals in the system. Control engineers usually work in s-space when the functional dependencies are represented by the Laplace transforms.

In the following, we assume that the signal flow graph is linear so that the edge/node relationships illustrated in Figure 1 apply.

A natural representation in Prolog for a SFG is as a set of assertions stating what are the nodes in the graph and in addition what are the edges and the transmittance or transfer function associated with the edge. The nodes themselves would be represented by atoms and the transmittances by general Prolog terms denoting mathematical expressions. A common form for a transmittance is a rational polynomial in s, but they could be more complex including such types as vectors or matrices if the SFG for example were multi-input multi-output. A simple SFG and its Prolog representation is shown in Figure 2.

One fundamental parameter of a SFG that a control engineer would want to calculate is the *overall transmittance* between two nodes selected in the graph. This gives the relationship between the two signals at the two nodes.

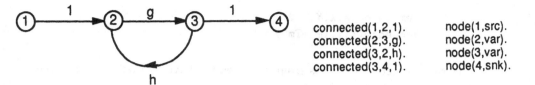

connected(1,2,1).   node(1,src).
connected(2,3,g).   node(2,var).
connected(3,2,h).   node(3,var).
connected(3,4,1).   node(4,snk).

Figure 2: Simple Signal Flow Graph

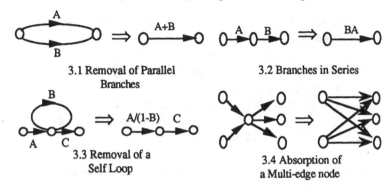

Figure 3: Signal Flow Graph Node Absorption

We have written two different algorithms for this purpose.

The first is a rule-based algorithm which essentially performs a graph reduction by repeatedly applying the rules illustrated in Figure 3, thus removing internal nodes, until only the sources and sinks of the graph remain. This method is often that which is done by hand, but in conventional procedural languages is not so straightforward to implement. In fact a matrix version of the algorithm is usually adopted which was originally developed by Abrahams [1] and extended by Munro and McLeod [15, 14]. These matrix implementations are not as natural or as amenable to modification as the rule based algorithm presented here [11].

The Prolog clause implementing rule 3.1 replaces the parallel edges by one new edge labelled with the updated transmittance.

```
reduce(Srcs,Snks) :-
    clause(connected(X,Y,Tm1),true,Ref1),   % find database
                                             % references of
                                             % two parallel
                                             % edges
    clause(connected(X,Y,Tm2),true,Ref2),
    R1 \== Ref2,                             % Check they are distinct
    remove_edge(X,Y,Tm1),                    % Remove edges and update
```

```
         remove_edge(X,Y,Tm2),
         add_edge(X,Y,Tm1+Tm2).
```

The rule for removing loops from nodes which have one non-looping edge
into a node (see Figure 3.3) is essentially as follows:

```
reduce(Srcs,Snks) :-
         connected(Y,Y,Tm2),     % there is a self loop
         connected(X,Y,Tm1),
         \+ member(Y,Srcs),      % Y is not a source
         in_nodes(Y,2),          % only 2 in edges including loop
         remove_edge(X,Y,Tm1),
         remove_edge(Y,Y,Tm2),   % remove unwanted edges &
                                 % add new transmittance
         add_edge(X,Y,Tm1/(1-Tm2)).
```

There are special forms of the rules for sources and sinks as they must not
be removed. The order of the rules in the database determines the order of
reduction. Alternatively, heuristics can be added to determine a specified
order. This can be useful when the form of the resulting transmittance
becomes complex (which it can very easily do). The order of absorption can
make a difference to the complexity of the final expression and so a good
reduction order can help in the simplification process which normally has to
be carried out after the reduction.

Using the **reduce** predicate, it is recursively applied until no further reductions are possible, at which point the transmittances between each source
and sink will have been obtained.

As indicated earlier one advantage of the using general Prolog terms for transmittances is that they could represent more complex entities than functions.
For example if we suppose our transmittances are vectors of functions, then
we can still carry out the reduction on the symbolic representation of the
vectors. All we need do is to let **simplify** actually manipulate these vectors
in the required manner. The main part of the algorithm remains untouched.

Consider the example in Figure 4. We need to know how to multiply a row
vector by a column vector to give a scalar. If we represent a row vector by a
list then we could represent a column vector by the notation $([x_1, \ldots, x_n])t$
where t (for transpose) has been defined as a postfix operator.

The predicate **simplify** will then have a clause for this type of multiplication

```
         % a ROW vector times a COL vector
```

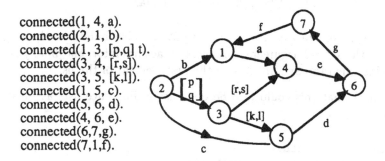

```
connected(1, 4, a).
connected(2, 1, b).
connected(1, 3, [p,q] t).
connected(3, 4, [r,s]).
connected(3, 5, [k,l]).
connected(1, 5, c).
connected(5, 6, d).
connected(4, 6, e).
connected(6,7,g).
connected(7,1,f).
```

Figure 4: Multi-input Multi-output SFG

```
simplify(L1 * (L2)t,DProd) :-
        vector(L1,N),
        vector(L2,N),    % must be vectors
                         % of the same length
        dot_prod(L1,L2,DProd).
```

`vector` just checks that we have a list of length N and `dot_prod` calculates symbolically the scalar product of two vectors.

The first systematic algorithm for calculating transmittances of SFG's was devised by S.J. Mason [12] and is known as *Mason's rule*. However, it is difficult to automate because it requires path finding operations which tend to be inefficient and not so easy to implement in procedural languages.

To use Mason's rule it is necessary to find all the forward paths and closed paths in a SFG and it is just this aspect of the algorithm that we shall illustrate next [8].

First we concentrate on just obtaining the forward paths. The following tail recursive code determines the forward paths in a graph between source Src and sink Snk.

```
path(Src, Snk, Path) :-
        path1(Src, [Snk],  Path).
path1(Src, [Src|Path], [Src|Path] ) .
path1(Src, [Nd2|Path], FinalPath) :-
```

```
connected(Nd1, Nd2, _),
not member(Nd1,[Nd2|Path]),
path1(Src, [Nd1, Nd2|Path], FinalPath) .
```

The `path` predicate uses the auxiliary `path1` which builds up the required paths in the second argument, acting as an accumulator, and finally returns the value when the `Src` appears as the first element of the list.

We remark that this could also be done using difference lists as illustrated below:

```
path(Src, Snk, Path) :-
        path2(Src, Snk,  Path,[]).
path2(Src, Src,  [Src|Path] ,Path) . % forms path from Src
                            % to Snk as a difference list
path2(Src, Nd2,  L,R) :-
        connected(Nd1, Nd2, _),
        path2(Src, Nd1, L,[Nd2|R]) ,
        not_member_dl(Nd2,L,[Nd2|R]).
```

Although straightforward and natural this is however not as efficient because of the tests for non membership occurring at the end of the second clause and so not tail recursive.

The predicate `path(Src,Snk,Path)` will then produce all forward paths from `Src` to `Snk`. We now modify this predicate so that instead of using **member** to prevent paths with loops, we replace it by another predicate that will actual return any cycles it comes across in trying to find a path.

Here is the modified program:

```
path(Src, Snk, Path) :-
        path1(Src, [Snk], Path).
path1(Src, [Src|Path], path([Src|Path]))  .
path1(Src, [Nd2|Path], FinalPath) :-
        connected(Nd1, Nd2, _),
        path2(Src, [Nd1, Nd2|Path], FinalPath) .
path2(_, [Nd1, Nd2|Path], loop([Nd1|Loop])) :-
            split_member(Nd1, [Nd2|Path],Loop, _), !.
path2(Src, [Nd1, Nd2|Path], AccPath) :-
        path1(Src, [Nd1, Nd2|Path], AccPath).
split_member(X, [X|L], [X], L) :- !.
split_member(X, [Y|L], [Y|L1], L2) :-
                split_member(X, L, L1, L2).
```

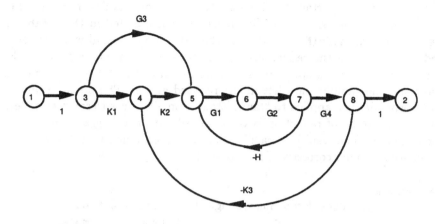

Figure 5: Example Signal Flow Graph

This solution works by not failing and forcing backtracking when a node is found to already occur in the path it is constructing, but instead returns the cycle in the list. `split_member` checks if a node is in the path and if so splits the list at this occurrence.

`path(Src,Snk,PathCycle)` now succeeds with `PathCycle` either a path from Src to Snk or a cycle on a path to Snk. Consider for example this predicate called on the representation of the signal flow graph, shown in Figure 5, with source node 1 and sink node 2.

The solutions of `path(1,2,PathCycle)` are

```
path([1,3,4,5,6,7,8,2]),
path([1,3,5,6,7,8,2]),
loop([8,4,5,6,7,8]),
loop([7,5,6,7])
```

yielding all forward paths from 1 to 2 and cycles on paths to 2.

An extra parameter can be added to path so that as the paths are determined the gains (product of transmittances) are also calculated. These can then be substituted in Mason's formula to arrive at the overall transmittance.

SFG's can be used to deal with sampled signals [16] by allowing sampler nodes and edges which corresponds to taking pulses at some fixed time intervals. Both techniques of using node reduction and an extended version of Mason's rule involving path and cycle creation have been implemented in Prolog. It is important to differentiate the sampled nodes from the continuous in the analysis and so this information is asserted in the database, e.g. in the form **node(Nd,sampler)**. The rule based method is then modified by performing the reductions in two stages. First we repeatedly apply **reduce** leaving any sampler nodes untouched. After this stage only sources, sinks and the samplers are left in the reduced graph. The postfix sampler transform ~ is then applied to transmittances on all inputs to sampler nodes. The second stage of reduction is then carried out on this graph to remove the samplers. The resulting transforms are then obtained with the sampler transforms applied correctly. The top level call is of the form:

```
reduce_sfg :-
        rep_reduce(Srcs,Snks,stage1), % reduce without
                                       % removing samplers
        mark_all_sampler_inputs,       % apply ~ to
                                       % transmittances
                                       % into samplers
        rep_reduce(Srcs,Snks,stage2)   % repeatedly reduce
                                       % as normal
```

The graph searching approach for sampled data systems is similar to the ordinary SFG method above. The essential difference is that we must produce forward paths and cycles but which are separated into type 1 paths, which contain no sampler nodes, and type 2 which do contain sampler nodes. Figure 6 illustrates the two stages of reduction.

Block diagrams are essentially duals of SFG's and can be represented in Prolog in a similar manner. The only difference is that now the data concerning the nodes and the edges of the graph will contain more useful information than in the previous case. Nodes will have extra facts asserted indicating whether they are summers or takeoff points. Edges will have information concerning negative feedbacks, blocks, samplers or unit connections. Figure 7 illustrates a simple block diagram.

This can be represented by the following set of Prolog assertions:

```
block(1,src,r).          blck_conn(1,2,'+').
block(2,sum,_).          blck_conn(2,3,'+').
block(3,fun,f).          blck_conn(3,4,'+').
block(4,fun,h).          blck_conn(4,2,'-').
block(5,snk,c).          blck_conn(3,6,'+').
```

We mention that similar results to those for SFG's presented in this section can be obtained for block diagrams with very little change.

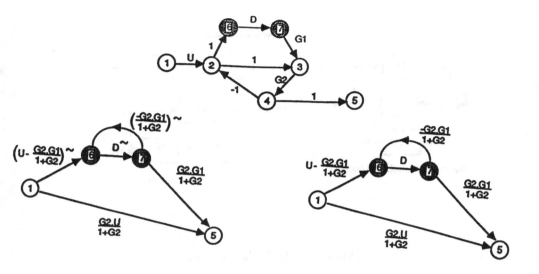

Figure 6: Stages in Reduction for Samplers

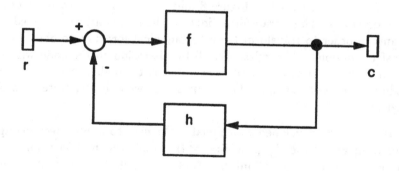

Figure 7: A Simple Block Diagram

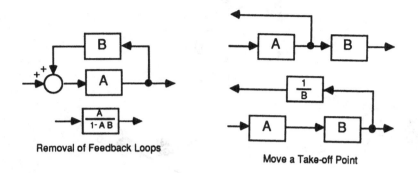

Figure 8: Manipulation Primitives

3   System Manipulation

A novel area of work is the use of symbolic manipulation tools based on the basic graph manipulation rules used for analysis. These provide powerful semantic-preserving operastions on graphical models. Two manipulation primitives are illustrated in Figure 8 and will be familiar to most users of block diagrams. These transformations can be systematically applied to diagrams in order to transform them to canonical forms or to obtain overall transfer functions. The rules, with little alteration to the code will apply to signal flow graphs. All that is required is to modify the type checking predicates to apply to signal flow graphs, but we only illustrate with block diagrams.

Tools have been developed which enable the user to apply these manipulations to diagrams thereby providing editing tools which differ from the normal ones in that the overall input-output relationships of the system remain unchanged. Two manipulations are now illustrated below.

We consider first the *Cascade Combination* of two adjacent blocks into a single block.

```
cascade :-
        blk_conn(Node1, Node2, Trans1),
        blk_conn(Node2, Node3, Trans2),
        cascade_criterion(Node2),
```

```
      assert(blk_conn(Node1,Node3,Trans1*Trans2)).
```

where `cascade_criterion` checks that the node being eliminated is a single input single output node.

Now we give the skeleton code for *Loop Elimination*:

```
loop :-
        blk_conn(Node1, Node2, Trans1),
        blk_conn(Node2, Node1, Trans2),
        loop_criterion(Node1, Node2,SgnTrans2),
        assert(blk_conn(Node1, Node2,Trans1/(1+SgnTrans2))).
```

where `loop_criterion` checks that a summing node is involved, and whether negative feedback must be taken into consideration.

4   Algebraic Manipulation and Dimensional Analysis

Once a transmittance has been obtained invariably some simplification of the result is desirable. We have built a simplifier for this purspose. The basic outline of one the main predicates `eval` is given below in a straightforward recursive descent evaluator. `eval` recursively simplifies arguments of expressions and finally at the top level applies `eval_fun`.

```
eval(AtomicArg, Value) :-
        atomic(AtomicArg), !,
        lookup(AtomicArg,Value).
eval(FnSym(Arg1, ..., Argn), Value) :-
        maplist(eval,[Arg1, ..., Argn],[EvArg1, ..., EvArgn]),
        eval_fun(FnSym(EvArg1, ..., EvArgn),Value) .
% maplist applies eval to each of the elements in the list.
eval_fun(Expr, SimpExpr) :-
        lookup(Expr, Body), !,
        eval(Body, SimpExpr).
eval_fun(Expr, SimpExpr) :-
        arithmetic_expr(Expr), !,
        simplify(Expr,SimpExpr).
% catch all case
eval_fun(Expr, Expr).
```

If the outermost function symbol of the expression is a standard arithmetic operator then an algebraic reduction of the expression is attempted, otherwise if no definition for the function symbol is provided in the data base then the whole expression is treated as a symbol throughout the rest of the program.

This program can be improved in a number of ways. One is by doing some initial simple reduction. This is performed before `eval` is applied.

```
% some basic reduction rules
        init_reduce(Exp*0, 0).
        init_reduce(Exp-Exp, 0).
        init_reduce(Exp+0, x).
        init_reduce(Exp/Exp,1).
% insert following as second clause
eval(Expr, Value) :-
        init_reduce(Expr, ReducedExpr),
        eval(ReducedExpr,Value).
```

As a final improvement, we can avoid evaluating repeated subexpressions by memoing i.e. asserting partial results into the database. The last clause is replaced by:

```
eval(Expr, Value) :- partial(Expr, Value), !.
eval(FnSym(Arg1, ...,Argn), Value) :-
        maplist(eval, [Arg1, ..., Argn], [EvArg1, ...,EvArgn]),
        eval_fun(FnSym(EvArg1,...,EvArgn),Value),
        assert(partial(FnSym(Arg1, ..., Argn), Value)) .
```

Another form of symbolic manipulation of interest to control engineers is dimensional analysis [11]. This can be performed by making use of the simplifier. It enables the units of any signal in the graph to be deduced from the units provided at other signals or transfer functions. It also enables quite useful consistency checking rules to be introduced.

Dimensions are represented by Prolog terms and so can be passed to the algebraic simplifier for possible reduction. This approach greatly reduces the effort of implementation of a dimensional analysis package. An outline of the dimension evaluator appears below.

```
dim(Expr, Dim) :-
        atom(Expr), !,
        fetch_unit(Expr, Dim).
dim(Expr, Dim) :-
```

```
          number(Expr), !,
          Dim= 1.           %   take numbers to be dimension 1
dim(Op(Expr1, Expr2), Dim) :-
          dim(Expr1, Dim1) ,
          dim(Expr2, Dim2),
          dim(Op,Dim1, Dim2, Dim).
dim(+, Dim1, Dim2, Dim1) :-
          eval(Dim1/Dim2, 1).
dim(*, Dim1, Dim2, Dim) :-
          eval(Dim1*Dim2, Dim).
dim(/, Dim1, Dim2, Dim) :-
          eval(Dim1/Dim2, Dim).
```

Notice that we use **eval** to check that we can add two dimensions together by showing that they are of the same type.

Another useful application of symbolic system analysis is for the simplification of hierarchically structured systems. Overall transfer functions can easily be obtained for subsystems and stored in the system database — perhaps as a property of the subsystem. This can then be used in further systems analysis or to reduce the complexity of a system by replacing the subsystem by its black-box equivalent. The proper use of units and other signal properties can be used to ensure consistent and correct use of sub-components thereby enabling re-use and the possible development of component libraries as advocated by Mattson [13].

5   Transformations and Automatic layout

In this section we discuss the problem of converting a block diagram into an equivalent signal flow graph both at the topological and at the graphical level [4, 7].

The transformation is carried out by scanning the block diagram and constructing the SFG by means of a set of eight rules which reflect the duality of the two representations. The predicate

```
transform(Block,Node,Rflag,Sign)
```

is invoked at each block encountered where **Block** is the block name, **Node** the node created in the SFG, **Sign** the polarity of the signal and **Rflag** is passed by the previous transformation indicating whether the node is reducible. A node is reducible if it is created from a system input or a functional block which has only outgoing connections.

The code for rule 3 is given below. This is used when a functional block with a preceding node already created is reached. A new destination node together with an edge, with the corresponding transfer function attached, are introduced in the SFG.

```
% transformation for rule 3
transform(Block,Node_s,_,_) :-
        block(Block,fun,TrFun),
        create_node(Node_d,var),    % create destination node
        create_edge(Node_s,Node_d,fun,TrFun,'+'),
                                    % form the correct edge
        scan_next(Block,Node_d),!.
% scan rest of diagram
scan_next(Block,Node) :-
        outconnection_number(Block,Num),
        Num > 0,
        node_reducible(Block,Num,Rflag),
        scan_next1(Block,Node,Rflag),!.
scan_next(_,_) :- !.
scan_next1(Block,Node,Rflag) :-
        connection(Block,Next,Sign),
        Num > 0,
        transform(Next,Node,Rflag,Sign),fail.
scan_next1(_,_) :-!.
```

Part of a transformation applying rule 3 is seen in Figure 9.

An algorithm for converting from SFG's to block diagrams is similar, but is somewhat more complex as extra information has to be introduced in the block diagram represenation.

We now turn to the problem of graphical layout of graphs from the topological represenation. We are interested in obtaining graphs which conform as much as possible to the conventional layouts adopted by control engineers.

A fully automatic algorithm has been developed in Prolog [4, 7] incorporating heuristics for aesthetic layout.

Figure 10 illustrates the main stages carried out to produce the final layout for a SFG from the Prolog representation without any graphical information. Initially a graph is produced on a simple grid (n-space) of size $n \times n$ where n is the number of nodes. A backtracking approach is then made to select an

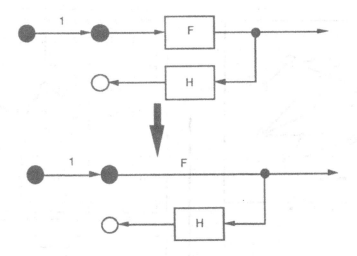

Figure 9: Transformation Using Rule 3

optimised graph in n-space based on a heuristic measure of 'goodness'. This optimised graph in n-space is then mapped into a grid based on the display size (user-space) using essentially linear interpolation. This is then improved by making use of some other heuristics. Finally curved connections can then be added in a straightforward manner taking into account some further aesthetic considerations.

6   Discrete Event systems

CES has several graphical editors for constructing DEDS (Discrete Event Dynamic Systems) catering for the three models of Petri Net, Grafcet and Ladder diagram. Simulation and manipulation tools for the three models have been written in Prolog. In this section we will concentrate only on the ladder diagram [6].

We shall briefly describe one tool for mapping ladder diagrams into code for PLCs (Programmable Logic Controllers). Figure 11 illustrates a ladder diagram where p1, p2 are system inputs and p3, p4 system outputs and the lines between them represent power rails. p5 and p6 are open contacts and p7 and p8 are closed contacts. Finally p9 and p10 are coils. All identifiers p5 to p10 lie on rung 1 of the diagram, other rungs can appear below this — hence the name.

This graphical object is represented by a set of Prolog assertions with main

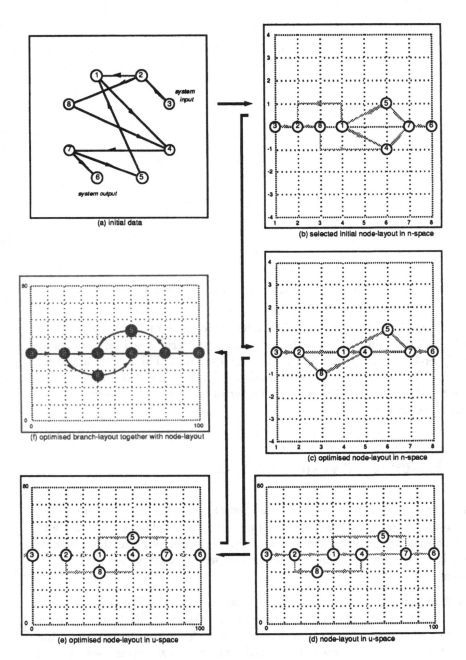

Figure 10: Main Stages in Automatic Layout

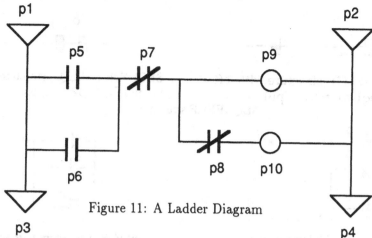

Figure 11: A Ladder Diagram

functors **state** and **state_conn**. The state assertions are of the form:

state(Identifier,PLCConn,Type,Rung,Time)

and

state_conn(Start,End)

Identifier is the name of the state (p1–p10 in Figure 11), **PLCConn** is the connection name on the PLC , **Type** is type of state, **Rung** is the rung number and **Time** is the time interval for a timer state. For a specific PLC we have the following:

> **PLCConn** begins with **x** for input, **y** for output and **t** for timer connections.
>
> **Type** can include **input**, **output**, **open** and **closed** contact and **coil**.

Without knowing too much about ladder diagrams it is fairly clear how Figure 11 is represented by the set of Prolog assertions below:

```
state(p1,T T,input,0,0).          state_conn(p1,   p3).
state(p2,T ',input,0,0).          state_conn(p2,   p4).
state(p3,T T,output,0,0).         state_conn(p5,   p7).
state(p4,T T,output,0,0).         state_conn(p7,   p9).
state(p5, x400,open,1,0).         state_conn(p8,   p10).
state(p6,y430,open,1,0).          state_conn(p6,   p7).
state(p7,t450,closed,1,0).        state_conn(p9,   p4).
```

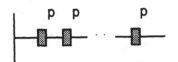 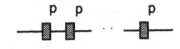

SEQUENCE (SEQ1) structure with left power rail seq1(p1, p2, ..., pn)

SEQUENCE (SEQ2) structure without pow rail **seq2**(p1, p2, ..., pn)

SEQUENCE structures

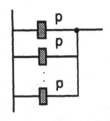 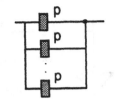

OR (OR1) structure with left power rail or1(p1, p2, ..., pn)

OR (OR2) structure without power rail or2(p1, p2, ..., pn)

OR structures

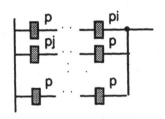 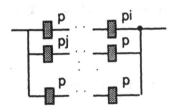

OR BRANCH (ORB1) structure with left power rail orb1(p1, p2, ..., pn)

OR BRANCH (ORB2) structure without power rail orb2(p1, p2, ..., pn)

Figure 12: Ladder Diagram Constructs

```
state(p8,x400,closed,1,0).        state_conn(p10,  p4).
state(p9,y430,coil,1,0).          state_conn(p1,   p5).
state(p10,t450,coil,1,19).        state_conn(p1,   p6).
                                  state_conn(p7,   p8).
```

Any ladder diagram can be built up recursively from structures SEQUENCE, OR or ORBRANCH as illustrated in Figure 12.

By similar techniques as described in Section 2 for reducing SFG's we can simultaneously reduce the ladder diagram by grouping components together under the classification in Figure 12 and at the same time produce the PLC code.

For example two reduction steps of Figure 11 produce the diagram in Figure 13.

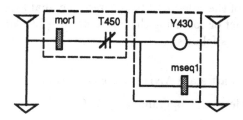

Figure 13: Two Reduction Steps

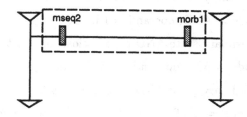

Figure 14: Next Step in Reduction

where the code for `mor1` and `mseq1` are:

```
LD  x400
OR  y430
ANI x400
OUT t450
K19
```

The next two reduction steps yields Figure 14.

where the codes for `mseq2` and `morb1` are:

```
LD  x400
OR  y430
ANI t450
OUT y430
ANI x400
OUT t450
K 19
```

The final resulting code is then the concatenation of the above.

Examples of some of the rules used to generate the final PLC codes according to the type of contact or coil using the information, PLCConn etc. associated with that state are as follows:

IF state is a start state AND type is open contact

THEN opcode = LD, operand = PLC Conn

IF state is a start state AND type is closed contact

THEN opcode = LDI, operand = PLCConn

IF state is ordinary state AND type is open contact

THEN opcode = AND, operand = PLCConn

IF state is ordinary state AND type is closed contact

THEN opcode = ANI, operand = PLCConn

IF state is ordinary state AND type is TIMER

THEN opcode1 = OUT, operand1 = PLC Conn opcode2 = K, operand2 = time

As there are many forms of PLC languages available, DCG's could be used here to translate between different manufacturers codes.

7   Conclusions

We have outlined some details of a number of applications for control engineering which have been successfully developed in Prolog for integration into CES. Features of Prolog that were particularly useful for this development:

- Pattern matching — good for symbolic processing, eliminates the need for conditionals and assignments. Gives a declarative view to programs.

- Rule-based — implementation of things solvable by repeated application of rules.

- Backtracking — good for problems with multiple solutions, especially graph analysis used in CACSD.

- Terms — Prolog terms can be used to represent mathematical expresssions in a natural manner, thus avoiding the necessity to map from expressions to some other internal representation.

In this paper we have concentrated on tools particularly developed to support the symbolic manipulation and analysis of systems described by the interconnection of subsystems.

Acknowledgements

It is a pleasure to extend our thanks to other members of the Control and Computer Aided Engineering group at Swansea including HA Barker, P Townsend, M Chen and J Song. In particular, Chen Min has discussed with us the details of his transformation and layout algorithms and Song Ji details of his Ladder diagram transformation routines.

References

[1] J. R. Abrahams. Signal flow graph methods, 1966. Control 10.

[2] H. A. Barker, M. Chen, P. W. Grant, C. P. Jobling, and P. Townsend. The development of an intelligent man-machine interface for computer aided design, simulation and implementation of control systems. In *Proceedings of the 10th IFAC Congress on Automatic Control*, volume 7, pages 255–260, 1987.

[3] H. A. Barker, M. Chen, C. P. Jobling, and P. Townsend. Interactive graphics for the computer-aided design of dynamic systems. *IEEE Control Systems Society Magazine*, 7(3):19–25, 1987.

[4] H. A. Barker, M. Chen, and P. Townsend. Algorithms for transformations between block diagrams and signal flow graphs. In Zhen-Yu [18].

[5] H. A. Barker, M. Chen, and P. Townsend. The development of a graphical environment for the computer aided design of control systems. In *Proc IEE Conference on Control '88*, pages 81–86, Oxford, 1988.

[6] H. A. Barker, J. Song, and P. Townsend. A rule-based procedure for generating programmable logic controller code from graphical input in the form of ladder diagrams. *Engineering Applications of AI*, 1990.

[7] M. Chen. *Graphical Man-machine Interface to CACSD*. PhD thesis, University College of Swansea, UK, 1991.

[8] P. W. Grant, C. P. Jobling, and C. Rezvani. The role of interactive rule based control system analysis in future cacsd environments. In IEEE [10], pages 767–772.

[9] N. Heintze, S. Michaylov, and P. Stuckey. CLP(R) and some electrical engineering problems. Technical Report CMI-CS-89-139, Carnegie Mellon Computer Science Dept., 1989.

[10] *Proc. 28th IEEE Conference on Decision and Control*, Tampa, Florida, 1989.

[11] C.P. Jobling and P.W. Grant. A rule-based program for signal flow graph reduction. *Engineering Applications of AI*, 1:22–33, 1988.

[12] S.J. Mason. Feedback theory — some properties of signal flow graphs. *Proc IRE*, pages 1144–1156, 1952.

[13] S.-E. Mattson. On model structuring concepts. In Zhen-Yu [18], pages 269–274.

[14] N. Munro. Composite system studies using the connection matrix. *International Journal of Control*, 26:831–839, 1977.

[15] N Munro and R.S. McLeod. Minimal realization of transfer function matrices using the system matrix. *Proc IEE*, 118(9):1298–1301, 1971.

[16] S.V. Salehi. Signal flow graph reduction of sampled data systems. *International Journal of Control*, 34:71–94, 1981.

[17] C-Y. Tan and J.M. Maciejowski. DB-Prolog: A database programming environment for CACSD. In IEEE [10], pages 72–77.

[18] Chen Zhen-Yu, editor. *Proc 4th IFAC Symposium on CADCS*, Beijing, PRC, 1988.

GAP: An Exercise in Model Oriented Programming

Keith Harrison

Abstract

We describe GAP, an experiment in model-oriented programming. This prototype application applied the concepts of knowledge base management, user-centred models and dialogue modelling to the domain of expense monitoring and targetting. The application area is discussed giving a motivation for the notions of ad hoc query and query-by-format. The prototype is discussed both from the point of view of the hypotheses under examination and the viability of using a logic-programming-based KBMS, namely **KBMS1**, as the sole implementation technology. We find that the use of KBMS1 enabled rapid development and resulted in an application whose performance was well within the limits of acceptability.

1 Introduction

In this paper we will discuss the results of an experiment to implement a large and sophisticated "commercial" application using a Prolog-like language.

We will describe the purpose of the experiment, the hypotheses being tested, the problem domain and the solution. Finally, we will discuss the technologies involved in implementing the solution.

2 The GAP Experiment

GAP was an exercise run by the Advanced Information Management (AIM) Department of the European centre of Hewlett-Packard Laboratories.

The AIM Department's research focus is the development of systems which provide direct access to, and maintenance of, business information by business professionals. By business information we typically mean

> Accounting data, stock levels, orders, personnel data, sales and marketing information, competitive analyses, ...

while examples of business professionals might include

> Accountants, personnel officers, marketing managers, executive officers, ...

The goals of the GAP experiment were three-fold :

- To test the Department's ideas and existing technologies within a single domain of application

- To provide an application pull for the development of our ideas and technologies by raising application issues that have not yet been addressed

- To produce a system which provides a successful solution to the information needs of the domain of financial management and which could be easily transferred to another team for further development.

The hypotheses under test within the GAP experiment were as follows:

- The knowledge base management system KBMS1 [2, 3] provides an effective and adequate rapid prototyping environment.

- Declarative representations of business models can be used by business professionals to customise and maintain their information systems.

- Declarative representations of business models can be used to facilitate dialogues between business professionals and their information systems.

- Extended dialogue supported by mixed-mode dialogue technology is feasible and facilitates the execution of ad hoc queries and 'creative rummaging'.

3   The Problem Domain

Each project manager, in our own laboratory, puts together a financial plan for the coming year. The plan consists of a number of expense categories with predicted expense items in each spread over the next twelve months. Managers then spend against this plan. They must make decisions about unexpected expenditure based on the progress of the financial plan. The progress is measured by comparing actual expenditure with **targetted**. There are, then, two basic tasks in this domain for the project manager: targetting and monitoring.

A third task which is introduced further up the hierarchy of financial accountability is consolidation. This involves combining the data from projects into departmental data and data for departments into lab data and so on. This usually takes place during targetting to arrive at a budget for the Centre. It also takes place at financial check points such as month-ends and quarter boundaries where deviations must be understood and explained. Project managers, therefore, need to monitor closely what they have spent against what they predicted they would spend.

4 The Solution

The GAP prototype provides a means by which project managers can enter expense data into a database, query the database to produce ad hoc reports and transfer data to other GAP users. In addition, information can be received from other accounting applications for reconciliation with locally-held expense data.

In a business, diverse information is stored in various data sources. Managers need to monitor and understand this information in order to perform their roles effectively. It is not sufficient to provide only a small number of inflexible routes to their data. To follow hunches, or to explore trends and anomalies, they need to access that data in a flexible and direct manner — this mode of access we have termed *ad hoc*, and we believe that this will be an essential part of future Executive Information Systems (**EIS**). GAP's user interface is designed to support ad hoc query and extended dialogues, enabling users to generate their own views of their financial data and follow up questions provoked by the data in those views. Information is entered and displayed using representations which model the existing paper system — travel request forms, equipment requisition forms — rather than the models held within the existing accounting systems. Users may augment the standard set of expense forms by defining their own. Individual expense forms may be obtained using natural language queries, or by selecting regions within a financial report, or by combining both these modes.

The GAP solution is achieved by networking a number of GAP systems: one for each project manager in the accounting hierarchy. Thus, the total GAP solution is a multi-user system that appears to its users as a collection of intercommunicating personal systems, each customised to meet the needs of its user.

5 Getting Data Out

There are four ways of getting information out of the GAP database:

- Using models of the expense domain, displayed on the screen, to create result table layouts which are subsequently populated

- Using the context of a previous answer/table to create new tables ('drill down') to more detailed information

- Using Natural Language to go straight to the expense form details or combining natural language with the context of a previous answer/report

- Turning an existing table into a spreadsheet for calculations across rows and columns.

Information about the data that is available in the GAP database is presented to the user in the form of models of the domain. These are user-centred models in that they reflect the ways that project managers view their domain. Each model represents one aspect of the domain (the company's organization, the breakdown of expense type, the process of expense tracking, and a financial calendar). The user may customise each model, or add new ones.

6 Tables

By selecting features from the displayed models, users can specify the format of the report they wish to produce. A skeleton table (**selector**) is produced during this operation. For example see Figure 1.

When the user is satisfied with the format the resulting query is evaluated against the database and the empty table filled out with the total values, giving the result in Figure 2.

In this way the user is constructing a database query by specifying the form of desired output. The query is represented by the format of the table and

		Financial Year 90			
		Planned	Committed	Accrued	Target
AIM	Neptune				
	Saturn				
	Pluto				
	Mars				

Figure 1: A skeleton selector

		Financial Year 90			
		Planned	Committed	Accrued	Target
AIM	Neptune	750.00	4622.00	528.80	5900.00
	Saturn	0.00	1107.35	4122.50	4120.00
	Pluto	115.00	140.00	10313.50	10370.00
	Mars	1426.30	1160.40	4150.00	6700.00

Figure 2: A populated selector

the answer is then displayed within this skeleton (unlike other systems, such as QBE [4], which keep the query and answer separate). This basic feature has been termed **Query By Format**.

7 Context

Within a selector, each cell represents a set of expense forms that satisfy the constraints imposed by the row and column. It is the total value associated with these expense forms that is being displayed within the cell. The union of this set with other sets from the same report may be specified by simply selecting the appropriate cells. This resulting set of expense forms may be used in a number of ways

- They may be displayed as a number of individual expense forms, thus the user may 'drill-down' through the cell to the underlying expense forms

- They may be displayed as a list giving a short description and total value of each expense form

- They may be used as a context for a natural language query

- They may be included in a package to be communicated to another GAP user.

8 Natural Language

The purpose of the natural language interface to GAP is also to access expense forms stored in the database. Thus, it would appear that the selector and natural language are performing identical roles. However, the selector performs two major roles — it produces reports giving summary information, and it provides a means of selecting sets of expense forms. Consequently we may view natural language simply as an alternative means of retrieving documents, which may suit some users better than the selector mechanism. Beyond this, there are two specific reasons for incorporating natural language into the interface:

- Direct Access.

  Natural language allows the user to retrieve expense forms directly with queries such as "List Neptune's committed expenditure". The

> same information can be accessed via the selector, but only after a table-template has been constructed and evaluated; this involves several direct manipulations.

- Added Functionality.

  In addition to providing a more direct means of access, natural language allows the expression of queries which would be either difficult or simply impossible to express in the alternative table-based mode. For example, to pose a negative query such as "Show me all documents that are not for Saturn", with the selector, would require the explicit selection of every project other than Saturn . Other sets of expense forms can not be specified at all with the selector. We can pose the query "List the expenses over $1000", but at present there is no selector mechanism for querying with restrictions on numerical values.

A natural language query can be stated in one of two ways. At any point in the interaction, the user may issue a natural language request. In this case, the context for the query is assumed to be the entire database. Alternatively, an natural language query can be made from the perspective of a particular table constructed by the selector. Here the query will be interpreted relative to the context created by the table, so that if the user asks "Which of these are for Pluto?", the expression "these" is taken to refer to the expense forms pertaining to the table. In both modes, we assume that an input sentence produces a list of documents on the screen, in the same format as those accessed via the selector.

The Natural Language subsystem was built around the Core Language Engine (**CLE**) [1]. The CLE was the result of a three-year research programme carried out at SRI's Cambridge Research Centre. The project was funded by members of the NATTIE consortium (British Aerospace, British Telecom, Hewlett-Packard, ICL, Olivetti, Philips, Shell Research, and SRI) and by a grant from the Department of Trade and Industry under the Alvey Initiative. It took six man weeks to customise the CLE to meet GAP's needs.

9 Spreadsheet

In addition to the drill-down capability provided by the selectors, users can create spreadsheets. Each spreadsheet contains a 'copy' of the results of the query represented by the originating selector.

Unlike existing spreadsheets, Lotus 1-2-3, Excel, etc, the user is only permitted to construct new rows and columns by entering a formula into a calcula-

Financial Year 90			
Planned	Committed	Accrued	Target

	Planned	Committed	Accrued	Target
AIM	2291.30	7029.75	19114.80	27090.00

Figure 3: The starting point — grand totals by accounting category for the department

		Financial Year 90			
		Planned	Committed	Accrued	Target
AIM	Neptune	750.00	4622.00	528.80	5900.00
	Saturn	0.00	1107.35	4122.50	4120.00
	Pluto	115.00	140.00	10313.50	10370.00
	Mars	1426.30	1160.40	4150.00	6700.00

Figure 4: Expanded out by project

tor. It is our belief that our spreadsheet design is more useful to the project manager because it is easy to use, and optimised to their requirements.

10   Versioning

Any selector that is on the screen may be used as the basis for a new, more complex, selector. As each selector is constructed, its parent is still available — until the user explicitly deletes it.

For example, we start with the selector in Figure 3. We then expand the AIM Department into its constituent projects to Figure 4. Both selectors are now on the screen. The first contains information that is contained in greater detail in the second. However we can go back to the first selector and

		Financial Year 90			
		Planned	Committed	Accrued	Target
AIM	Neptune	750.00	4622.00	528.80	5900.00
	Saturn	0.00	1107.35	4122.50	4120.00

Figure 5: Now expanded out to just two of the four projects

then break AIM down into only two of its projects. This gives Figure 5.

11   Recalculation

The user may have several selectors and/or spreadsheet windows on their screen. Should the user change the database by adding, deleting or amending expense forms, then these selectors/spreadsheets become out of date. Of the three options available to us

- Do not change the existing windows to reflect the changes to the database

- Mark windows as potentially out of date

- Amend all windows bringing them up to date with the current data base, otherwise called **hotlinking**

we chose to implement the second option: that is, we flag all windows as potentially out of date. By informing users which selectors are out of date, the user can decide whether more up to date information is required. Both selectors and spreadsheets store the query that they represent, rather than the expense forms that were selected. Consequently, the user may explicitly reissue the query and thus cause the entity to be redrawn. In a live application it was felt that some users would prefer this option, while others would prefer the third option.

12   KBMS1

As we have seen, GAP provides the user with a rich and sophisticated set of capabilities in the domain of expense planning and monitoring. A goal of the experiment was to test the Department's technologies, in particular the prototype Knowledge Base Management System KBMS1. KBMS1 was chosen as the sole programming language for GAP, to test its maturity and its suitability for implementing business-oriented applications.

The GAP prototype took a total of five and a half man months, an elapsed time of two and a half months. Of this, four man months were taken in 'coding' the application in KBMS1, one and a half man months were spent implementing the natural language subsystem, in Quintus Prolog.

A major part of the research activity was to explore our evolving ideas about dialogue modelling and, as a result, the development of the GAP system comprised a number of computational experiments. The turnround was frequently of the order of hours rather than the more traditional turnround period measured in days, if not weeks.

KBMS1 can be loosely regarded as a Prolog in which operations on the global database have been replaced by non-side-effecting operations on theories, coupled with a number of facilities related to persistence.

A theory is a partition of the knowledge base; it is an unordered set of procedures, where a procedure is an ordered set of clauses which possess the same primary functor and arity. The customary global database of standard Prolog is eliminated since theories represent an exhaustive partitioning of the knowledge base. Theories are first-class objects whose updating is treated in a wholly declarative manner (theories $T1$ and $T2$ differ by update U, or equivalently $T2$ is the result of applying U to $T1$). As a result many of the commonly criticised features of standard Prolog disappear, for example a program is no longer able to make side-effecting updates to itself. The powerful versioning facility that naturally arises from declarative updating enables many useful techniques to become easily accessible, such as hypothetical reasoning and mutually inconsistent theories. From an implementation point of view, sharing of substructure is used heavily to make the theory versioning mechanism space efficient.

System theories provide a logical organization of theories, theory names and the names of metatheories. A set of triples of named metatheories is associated with each theory, each triple naming an interpreter theory, an assimilator theory and an attribute theory. In general the set contains just one triple.

Interpreters are the querying interface to named theories — all queries to that theory are handled by its interpreter. In a similar fashion, assimilators are the updating interface to named theories. Attribute theories hold metadata about the named theory. This metadata is generally used by interpreters and assimilators when performing specialised inference and assimilation control. The metadata could be folded into the relevant interpreters and assimilators but that would specialise those metatheories to that particular object theory. So an attribute theory is a way of abstracting out object-theory-specific metadata which allows interpreters and assimilators to be re-used with many different object theories. Examples of metadata useful in inference and assimilation control include: functional dependencies between arguments, number of clauses in a procedure, integrity constraints to be observed when updating a procedure, the 'cost' of evaluating a goal in that theory given a certain instantiation pattern.

Since metatheories are themselves theories, they in turn have three sets of metatheories associated with them. This apparent infinite regress is quickly terminated by three built-in metatheories: **prologInt** which is the system interpreter that performs Prolog-like inference; **prologAss** which updates theories exactly as told (adds clauses when instructed to add, deletes clauses when instructed to delete); and an attribute theory which is empty.

KBMS1 is now a mature system. It comprises a novel interpreter (written in C), which has built-in support for theories and their associated operations, closely coupled to a storage manager based on DBCore, the record manager of Hewlett-Packard's relational database product.

In practice GAP treats theories in one of two ways :

- Code Modules.

  These theories are loaded at start-up time and are never changed.

- Data Theories.

  These theories contain facts which are "looked up" whenever they are needed. The models, selectors, spreadsheets, expense forms, etc are implemented as a set of named data theories. When changes are made to a named theory, a new system theory is generated which associates that name with the updated theory.

GAP, as implemented, did not require the development of specialised interpreters and assimilators, the defaults proving adequate. However future enhancements will require update control through the use of assimilators, and inference control through specialised interpreters.

The versioning of theories is also realised in the persistent store which results in the support of versioned knowledge bases. Systems may be stored on disc and then recovered at a later stage. This facility was used naturally to provide a save-state capability within GAP.

GAP makes extensive use of the X-Widget integration provided by KBMS1 for its user interface. This interface technology was adequate for GAP because

- it was able to provide the style of interface we were investigating

- it is a *de facto* standard

- it performed all of the low-level tasks, such as repainting, automatically, thereby allowing the developers to concentrate on the appearance and functionality of the interface.

Because KBMS1 is an interpreted language, it was felt that the response time of a large application would prove unacceptable. However, this was not the case, performance was well within the limits of acceptability. Indeed, analysis revealed that only 25time went into the interpretation, the rest going to the handling of X-Widgets.

The KBMS1 application specific code resulted in 11500 lines of Prolog in 1860 clauses, organised as 1100 procedures. These procedures were spread amongst more than 50 theories. Estimates provided by our own MIS Department suggest that COBOL or C would have required in the region of 50,000 lines of code to implement an equivalent application.

13   Where Next ...

GAP is a demonstrator of technologies, it is not intended to be an application. However it is complete enough, as an application, to permit its use internally within the Centre for evaluation purposes.

GAP is also being used as a testbench for future research within the Department. For example, two areas of research currently being pursued are

- the impact of size on KBMS1. What changes are needed to KBMS1 to support large numbers of expense forms.

- the incorporation of other modes of interaction in the user interface.

It is our belief that KBMS1 should be regarded as an assembly language and that programmers should develop applications in higher-level "Model-Oriented Languages". Research is proceeding into the design of such languages and the associated notion of Model-oriented Programming.

GAP revealed a number of shortcomings in KBMS1 as a development environment, particularly in the area of debugging support. These are being addressed.

14 Conclusion

All of the original stated goals of the project were met.

- KBMS1 proved to be not only a suitable environment for prototyping this application but also proved adequate for its delivery. Evaluation of the user interface demonstrated that the support of an extended dialogue through mixed-media interaction is feasible and natural. The use of user-centred models is a powerful method of presenting and maintaining such a dialogue.

- Many avenues for future research have been opened.

- GAP is now in active use within the Centre.

From the point of view of Logic Programming we feel that this exercise has proved the viability of persistent Prolog-like languages, such as KBMS1, for major commercial applications, and, by extension, other related application domains.

Acknowledgements

The author wishes to express his appreciation for all those whose effort made GAP successful. This includes Alasdair Cox, Nick Haddock, John Manley, Chris Mitchell, Andrew Nelson, Ian Page, Phil Stenton and Steve Whittaker.

References

[1] H. Alshawi et al. Research programme in natual language processing. final report, Alvey project no. ALV/PRJ/IKBS/105. Technical report, SRI Cambridge Research Centre, 1989.

[2] D. S. Black and J. C. Manley. A logic-based architecture for knowledge management. In *Proc of the Tenth International Joint Conference on Artificial Intelligence*, pages 87–90, Milano, 1987.

[3] J.C. Manley. kbProlog: A language for knowledge management. In *Proc SERC/IED Workshop on Handling Large Knowledge Bases Declaratively*, University of Essex, September 1989.

[4] M. M. Zloof. Query-by-example: a data base language. *IBM Systems Journal*, 16(4):324–343, 1977.

Using Prolog to Animate Mathematics

Ron Knott

1 Introduction

A library of Prolog rules has been developed which makes much of mathematics directly executable on a computer. We describe why Prolog was chosen as opposed to a functional programming language, the benefits of the Prolog notation and portability.

Although originally employed for the animation of Z in the context of specifying software systems, the Library of rules seems to have potential on its own, not only for the working mathematician, but for the software developer who is interested in mathematically based notations which are nevertheless executable on a computer, and not just the Z notation.

The work was originally applied to the animation of Z (a set theoretic notation from PRG, Oxford, which is proposed as a notation for specifying software) in two Alvey projects: SuZan (SE/090) which was later subsumed into FORSITE (SE/090).

A description of this method of animating mathematics which is directed towards mathematicians rather than those familiar with Prolog, will be found in [6]. The application, and initial development of the animation library and its application to animating Z is reported in [7, 8, 9].

2 The Animation of Mathematics

Much, but by no means all, of mathematics is constructive in that it describes processes for building objects and materialising them, especially Discrete mathematics. The areas of Discrete mathematics that we have investigated to date include set theory and logic, combinatorics, number theory, graph theory and group theory.

We describe here an experiment which uses a subset of Prolog to provide the vehicle for animating those parts of mathematics described above. We will compare Prolog as the representative of logic programming languages, with functional programming and show how the relationship between the two is subtle and how each can provide challenges and insights into the use of the other.

Since we are interested in exploiting the precision of mathematics in an executable notation, we wish to adopt a style of programming that relates closely to that of mathematics itself. We want to be able to prove properties of our programs, writing first in a clear style, and, if necessary, later transforming them into more efficient forms in the same notation, using correctness-preserving transformations. These are the premises on which our animation is founded.

Given these aims, a declarative language seems the obvious first choice. The functional programming and logic programming languages are becoming increasingly more available and well known. We will describe our findings that indicate that functional languages like Miranda and Hope have certain advantages over Prolog, but Prolog can be made to mimic the effects we want, and that Prolog has other advantages that functional languages do not have.

3   The advantages of Prolog for Animating Mathematics

3.1   Relations versus functions

Functional programming uses functions, Prolog uses relations. This is one difference which characterises the two styles of programming. Relations are more flexible since a function is a relation which, for a given x, produces a unique y that x is related to. Removing this restriction gives a relation where a given x may be related to many y's, or to just one.

However, functional programming allows arguments to its functions to be left unevaluated, if not needed. A function may be 'curried' (after Haskel B Curry) in that only some of the initial parameters need be provided and the result is another function of the remaining ones, with the supplied arguments bound in. Results of functions may be tuples (lists) so that several objects may be returned.

Not only may functions be called with only some of their parameters supplied, but lists may be materialised partially. This is a consequence of 'lazy evaluation' — that is, not evaluating expressions until they are needed. Lazy evaluation provides a very flexible approach to programming and gives the programmer freedom to program with unbounded lists in a manner which still terminates when executed. (For a fuller description of currying and lazy evaluation, see most Functional programming books — e.g. [1]).

On the other hand, Prolog provides backtracking to materialize alternative solutions to a rule. The results of a query are reported one at a time, so we can materialize as many as we want.

3.2 Rules with any flowmode

Prolog therefore lets us describe certain functions (for example, the appending of two lists to give a third list) by a rule that can not only be driven forwards mimicking a mathematical function ('What is the join of two given lists?') but also backwards producing the parameters that would give rise to a given result of the 'function' ('What two lists could be joined to give a specified list?').

This 'any flowmode' feature of Prolog, although it does not apply to every rule, is very elegant and worthwhile. It turned out to be of fundamental importance for some of the basic rules of the animation library, and, in particular, in the four basic selection rules of combinatorics. To select objects from a given collection, we may want to choose a set or a sequence of them, i.e. does the order in which they are chosen matter? Independently, we may want to remove or allow a repeat of an object in our collection, that is, once chosen, does the object go back into the pool as a possible choice in the remainder of our selection or is it removed? This is detailed in [6] and reproduced in Table 1.

Using these definitions, it is easy to prove by list induction that, given a list C,

$$
\begin{aligned}
setrem(P,C) &\rightarrow bagrep(P,C) \\
seqrem(P,C) &\rightarrow setrem(P,C) \\
seqrem(P,C) &\rightarrow seqrep(P,C) \\
seqrep(P,C) &\rightarrow bagrep(P,C).
\end{aligned}
$$

The essential symmetry of these operations is captured for the first time in a single notation which is open to proof.

There are further benefits from using Prolog in a declarative style. Many of the common operations of mathematics can be expressed using these four rules.

	samples with removal	samples with replacement

```
s  seqrem([],_).                    seqrep([],_).
e  seqrem([H|T],Objs) :-            seqrep([H—T],Objs) :-+
q     append(Before,[H|After],Objs) append(Before,[H|After],Objs)
s  &  append(Before,After,Others)   & append(Before,[H|After],Others)
   &  seqrem(T,Others).             & seqrep(T,Others).


s  setrem([],_).                    bagrep([],_).
e  setrem([H|T],Objs) :-            bagrep([H|T],Objs) :-
t     append(Before,[H|After],Objs) append(Before,[H|After],Objs)
s  &  setrem(T,After).              & bagrep(T,[H|After]).
```

Table 1: The symmetry in the Four Combinatorial Sampling Methods
(Rewritten to show that samples with removal are included in samples with
repetition and that sets are included among the sequences).

3.2.1 Permutations, subsets and powersets for free

If the list we are selecting is as long as the list of objects from which we
are choosing, and, if we are choosing sequences with removal (i.e. seqrem),
we have a permutation of the collection (where the rule $samelength(A, B)$
states that A and B are lists of the same length):

```
permutation(Perm,Seq):- samelength(Seq,Perm)
                 & seqrem(Perm,Seq).
```

If we consider choices of arbitrary size, we can find all the subsets of a given
set of objects:

```
hassubset(Subset,Set):-setrem(Subset,Set).
```

and the collection of all subsets is the powerset:

```
powerset(Set,Powerset):-
         set_of(S, hassubset(S,Set), Powerset).
```

We can further extend these rules to give compositions of a number and the
use of sets, sequences or cycles of sets or sequences to partition a collection
(introducing the *Stirling numbers* [4] of both kinds). Also *functions* (implemented as a relation — that is, as a list of pairs $\langle x, y \rangle$ where $f(x) = y$),
one-to-one or *partial, one-to-one* , *onto*, *composition* of functions, etc.

This was an unexpected benefit of using Prolog to describe these basic operations of combinatorics.

3.3   Higher Order Functions

Another feature of functional languages is that they allow functions to be supplied as arguments to 'higher order' functions. Often, a single higher-order function can capture the pattern of several 'smaller' functions. Two useful higher order functions are **map** and **reduce**. Map applies a function to every element of a list (for example, to add 1 to each element, or to apply a predicate to each element), and reduce applies an operator across a list so that we can combine all the elements together (for example, to sum them). They can usefully be applied together. To see if there exists an element in a given list with a certain property p, we map p across the list and reduce the result by 'or'-ing the list of booleans.

In Prolog, we can employ the 'call' rule (or $= ..$) to evaluate a term given as an argument to a rule. Such fundamental higher-order rules in Prolog include *bag_of* (collect all the solutions of a rule into a list), *set_of* (as *bag_of*, but remove duplicates and order the collection in some standard order), *exists_* (succeed once if a clause succeeds at all), *for_all* (succeed once if all successes of a generating clause also succeed with a predicating clause), *if* (choose one of two depending on whether a given clause succeeds at all), and *nthsoln* (return the number of the solution when a clause succeeds). In terms of these, we can define others such as map, reduce, while (while a generating clause succeeds together with a predicating clause, then succeed, but as soon as a generating case fails the predicate, terminate with failure), and sigma (the sigma sign of mathematics to sum the elements of a series).

3.4   Types

Most functional languages have a type mechanism that checks for consistency in a program before the program is executed. On the other hand, Prolog implementations are usually type-free; or rather, perform run-time type checking.

We have found that although types certainly do help track down errors in programs, they can be unnecessarily restrictive. Some functional languages distinguish between tuples that are of a fixed size but whose objects may have different types, and lists, which can be arbitrarily long, but only contain objects of the same type.

For instance, when writing rules which format the result of a Prolog query, we wish them to apply to objects of many types, but we may wish to return the solutions as a list.

A type-checker for Prolog would certainly be useful, but it is not clear that it should be a strict as some functional programming type checkers.

3.5   Unbounded Lists

Functional programming's lazy evaluation allows objects to be specified which have an unbounded number of components. Above, we mentioned that we can write rules in Prolog which return an unbounded number of results. For instance, the natural numbers are definable as:

```
nat(0).
nat(Next):-nat(N) & Next is  N+1 .
```

This is a useful rule when we need to generate the natural numbers since we can generate as many as we like, but is not efficient if we want to check that a given value is a non-negative integer (e.g. "?nat(13255)."}.

However, to use lists instead can mean excessive amounts of memory are needed since elements are kept that are no longer needed. In cases where we need elements of an unbounded collection but only once, such items are swept up by the garbage-collector in functional languages when they are not needed, but Prolog may hang onto them (since the rules generating them have not exited).

An example is the definition of the cartesian product of two sets(lists). If the sets are finite, a *list* of pairs is a valid representation. If the sets are unbounded (e.g. pairs of natural numbers), a *rule* generating pairs is useful. The cartesian product rule then materialises as many elements as we need.

Experimentation with such definitions has shown us that we need few primitive rules in order to successfully handle rules which produce an unbounded number of solutions.

Functionally, it is easy to produce the first few elements of an unbounded list. In Prolog, difference lists can provide an efficient way to deal with partially instantiated lists (for example, see [10]).

When writing Prolog programs which need to process rules producing an unspecified number of solutions, a few higher-order functions are useful, which avoid the need for cut.

One of these is 'while'. Given a clause which generates instantiations of a variable, and a predicate clause which applies to the instantiated variables, we can avoid non-termination when searching through an ordered unbounded collection for items with a given property. The query which finds all natural numbers in the range *Lo* to *Hi* for which a given property *p* holds, is written:-

```
? while( (nat(N), N>=Lo),     (p(N),N=<Hi) ).
```

The one other rule is 'nthsoln' which returns solutions to a clause together with the number of solutions found so far. Such a rule is very useful when formatting results from queries. For example, to write out all solutions to a rule called 'solve', three to a line:-

```
?- nthsoln(N, solve(X)),  write(X), mod_(N,3,0), nl,fail.
```

3.6   Memoization

The lazy list in functional languages provides us with a mechanism for remembering previous results. By writing a recursive definition of a function of natural numbers in terms of a list of values, we can compute items as we progress down the list. The advantage is that, unlike the recursive definitions which need to recompute the earlier values, we need only look them up when they are needed again, once they have been noted after initial computation. This is called memo-ization since we make a memo that this value has been computed already.

One method of memoizing a rule in Prolog is to use assert to note the computed values. We have avoided using assert in every other circumstance (apart from the definitions of certain of the underware rules, where it cannot be avoided), but, if the following prescription is followed, it is both safe and very efficient. Sterling and Shapiro give an alternative form, but use cut. Our version avoids cut. The recursive definition of the fibonacci numbers is given as an example, followed by its memoized form.

```
/*Recursive form*/
fib(0,0).
fib(1,1).
fib(N,FN):-N>1,N1 is N-1,fib(N1,F1),N2 is N-2,fib(N2,F2),
          FN is F1+F2.

/*Memoized form*/
```

```
fibmemo(0,0).
fibmemo(1,1).
fib(N,FN):-fibmemo(N,FN).
fib(N,FN):-not fibmemo(F,_),
           N>1,N1 is N-1,fib(N1,F1),N2 is N-2,fib(N2,F2),
           FN is F1+F2
           assert(fibmemo(N,FN)).
```

3.7   Avoiding Extra-Logical features

All the Prolog books that the author has seen introduce cut. Some distinguish
between green and red cuts (such as Sterling and Shapiro). We wish to avoid
them since they inhibit the multi-flowmode use of rules and destroy any
possibility of program transformation. Indeed, all the animation libraries
(apart from the underware rules) have been written without cut.

Cut can be avoided by guarding rules. Thus, the first term in a definition of
a rule is often the conditions on the parameters that apply for this case to
hold. Where applicable, the rules need to be defined with mutually exclusive
guards. This deals with many of the cases where cut is used in current
textbooks. True, Prolog may backtrack to try the following cases, which is
avoided if cut is used, but the advantage of not using cut is a logical purity
which means that we can transform our programs. However, there is another
case where guards may be inefficient.

If a guard is computationally expensive, we need to recompute it in each
guard clause. In this case, we can use the → and ; operators that are provided
for describing an if-then-else clause. To avoid the lack of this facility in some
implementations of Prolog, we explicitly provide an 'if' rule in the basic
library. This not only allows the user to write efficient forms of rules but also
gives us semantic information when transforming a Prolog rule using 'if'.

It is advantageous to avoid using 'if' since then more general flowmodes and
a wider class of program transformations apply. If the condition of the 'if' is
not computationally expensive, we can unfold the 'if' and replace its call as
if it had the following definition which uses guards:-

```
if(Cond,Then,Else) :-      exists_(Cond), call(Then);
                       not exists_(Cond), call(Else).
```

Occasionally, where a rule provides for the generation of several objects, we
may wish to know merely if any exist rather than generating all of them.
For example, a rule to check if two given networks (graphs) are the same

(isomorphic) uses the rule (isomorphism) which generates all the mappings of a graph onto itself preserving an operation. For this case, the rule 'exists_' is supplied in the basic library. This is essentially a hidden cut, but it has the advantage that the cut IS hidden, so that transformations can still be applied, and also shows the extent of the clauses controlled by the cut.

4   The Library of Fundamental Rules

One application of animating mathematics was to animate Z specifications. The software specifiers could animate the abstractions of a specification partly so that they could experiment with descriptions and partly to help the customer buying the software. If the customer (who need know nothing of Z or formal methods) could see the specification in action, then feedback could be given to the specifier to ensure the specification has correctly captured the client's ideas for the software. Since the client may well want to change his mind once he sees the working form of his project, such rapidly produced prototypes give very early feedback, with little effort at producing an implementation. Also, misconceptions about the meanings of terms used by the client can be tested by the specifier to help the transfer of the knowledge in the client's mind to a notation on the specifier's page.

Thus our animation was to be based on a library of a small set of basic rules taking the basic definitions of Z as our starting point. See, for example, the glossary of Z notation in [5].

4.1   Standardisation

Since Prolog has no commonly accepted Standard yet, apart from the informal standard of [2] as the library developed, we filtered out those rules that varied across different implementations of Prolog. The library was then written in terms of our own standard names and semantics (e.g. append, member and length should be usable with any flowmodes). Since some Prologs do not allow the user to redefine system rules such as length or member, we decided on names for the basic rules which could be defined in all the systems we encountered. Thus we could supply a version of each of our standard rules for every Prolog.

Such rules, once defined, are treated as if they were built-in to Prolog. The only way to implement such rules as set_of where, for instance, $set\_of(X, P(X), S)$ is to succeed always and to be semantically equivalent to the mathematical expression $S = \{x : p(x)\}$, is to resort to the 'assembly language'

Higher-order rules:	Arithmetic rules
bag_of/3,	(after [4])
set_of/3,	fix/2, round/2, floor/2, ceiling/2,
exists_/1,	div/3,mod_/3,ln_/2,topow/3,topowmod/3,
for_all/2,	gcd/3
if/3,	**Random numbers** random/1, randint/3
sorted/2, setsorted/2, seqsorted/2	
nthsoln/2	**Input/Output**
List rules	writespaces/1, atom_to_string/2
max_/2, min_/2,length_/2,	
member/2, append/3,reverse/2	**Timing** cpu_time_mow/1,cpu_time_clause/3

Table 2: The Underware Rules

features of Prolog and use 'assert', 'retract' and cut. For this reason, these rules are NOT to be viewed by the general public and we termed them the 'underware'.

Once defined, these rule-names are used in the Library built above them. To port the library to another Prolog, we need only redefine the underware rules and the whole of the library is then available.

Currently, the Library runs under Salford PrologIX (on Primes), NIP (on UNIX systems) and LPA MacProlog 2.5 and 3.0 (on the Apple Macintosh range). As our experience of other Prolog systems widens, we may need to incorporate a few other rules from the basic rule library into the underware.

Currently, the underware consists of a small set of about 30 rules given in Table 2.

4.2   The Library of Fundamental rules

On top of the underware we build the library of fundamental rules. These are given in Table 3. They provide definitions of common operations on sets and other common arithmetic rules.

On top of this, the next layer of Library rules is built, consisting of rules for some specific areas of mathematics. They were originally developed to test the extent of the underware and basic library, but gave useful experience on the practicality of the style of Prolog advocated above.

functions: (in the style of Z, i.e. finite lists of pairs) onto, 1-1, total and combinations of these, functional composition, inverse, identity, domain, range.
sets and sequences: isapermutationof, equalbags, equalsets, hassubset, haspropersubset, subsetofsize, subsetofsize, powerset, partitions, compositions, cartesian products, disjoint, intersection, union, setdifference, randelt (of a sequence).
numeric: count, sigma, odd, even, factorial, bincoeff, lcm, add, sub, mul, (for use with reduce/map) intsfromto,intsfrom.
output formatting: askyou, readint, writelist, writeprolog (write a Prolog term that makes sensible splits across line boundaries), writeintfw(write an integer in a field of a given width).

Table 3: Fundamental Mathematical Objects

4.3   The other Mathematics Libraries

Large libraries of rules have been developed during the course of testing the proposed style of use of Prolog advocated above. The rules are simple transliterations of the mathematical descriptions into Prolog. Some of them have been transformed into more optimal forms and, once written, provide a pool of rules available for later use.

The current extent of the libraries may be judged from the tables of their contents (see Tables 4 and 5).

The Graph theory rules have been detailed in [6] where their use to generate the 206 abstract graphs with from 1 to 6 nodes takes a few minute using these techniques. The generation of up to 70 properties per graph takes about 10 minutes. The author then expressed well known theorems of graph theory in the Prolog form and verified that they held across the example collection. This uncovered some ambiguities and errors in the Graph Theory text book being used. The rules also allow us to produce conjectures that hold across the collection of examples — that is relationships amongst the properties of the graphs. It produced about one conjecture every three seconds for about an hour. Some of these were trivially true, others may be true merely for the example collection and not true in general. The mathematician is then free to classify a conjecture and to seek a proof if it was thought to be true in general. The library has thus become a resource for the computer to act as a super-fast research assistant.

Basic rules: nbedges, nbvertices, degree, degrees, hasloop, hasmultipleedge, issimple, isolatednode, adjacent, isregular, bipartite, cliquenb, omega, perfectgraph

isomorphism: isomorphic, automorphism

operations: deleteedge, contractedge, indentifyvertices, removevs, subgraph, linegraph, unite, complement, crossproduct

colourings: chromatic polynomials,chromatic nb,chi,kchromatic, colouring, edgecolouring, colouredges, chromaticindex

connectivity: isconnected,component,disconnectingset,cutset,bridge, isthmus,edgeconnectivity, lambda, separatingset, cutvertex, kappa, cyclomaticnb, gamma, circuitrank

defining graphs: null, pathgraph, circuitgraph, wheel, platonic(tetrahedron, cube, octahedron, dodecahedron, icosahedron), star, kcube, petersen, grotzsch, complete, completepartitioned

generating graphs on a given number of vertices including generating functions for the number of graphs of v vertices and e edges,Polya enumeration theorem coded directly, paths and trails unique vertex and edge

walks/tours/paths: circuits, girth, euleriantype, hamiltoniantype

trees: istrees, isforest, rootedtrees, free, binary, ordered, labelled, labelledrooted, both counting and generating them. hrightr, weight, cutsetrank, componentrank, spanningtrees, prufersequences, planarity checking using Hopcroft-Tarjan algorithm (in Prolog)

(133 rules)

Table 4: Graph Theory Rules

isprime (a predicate), prime (a generator), primesto, primefactors, factor table producer, hasdivisor, totient, numberofdivisors, sumofdivisors, moebiusmu, areamicable, mersenne, lucastest, egcd (extended gcd solving $a * x + b * y = gcd(x,y)$), egcdlist (extended gcd but of a list of numbers) , solve(Diophantine equations) legendresymbol,quadraticresidues, sumofsquares, polygonal numbers, continued fractions (conversion to/from rationals), egyptian fractions, perfect and psuedo-perfect numbers, farey sequences

(¿40 rules)

Table 5: Number Theory Rules

5 Prolog program transformation

Although we have not developed an overall strategy of improving Prolog which uses the library, we have identified certain results that bear on the process of transformation.

5.1 The optimising measure

It is not enough to have a collection of rules which optimise programs. What is being optimised? In some cases it is the minimising of calls to a rule which has a large collection of cases. In other cases, it is cutting down on the search space of instantiations. Also, a rule used in one flowmode may be optimal, but non-optimal if used in another flowmode. Transformations then need to be applied with an actual query in mind.

5.2 Non-implicit facts

Often, the optimisation relies on *external facts* that are in no way implicit in the rules. If we were writing rules about family trees, transformations which speed up the execution times of queries can be performed since we know that everyone has only two parents, one of each sex, and that a person from a list of sons of a given couple will not appear as a daughter or mother.

5.3 Boolean algebra rules

Given our more pure style of using Prolog, which uses fixed names for rules in the basic library that have precise semantics, the main process of transformation is to apply the rules of boolean algebra. Obvious candidates which do not rely on an optimising measure nor external facts are the distributive laws. It is usually true that $(a, b; a, c)$ is better written as $(a, (b; c))$ and that (a, b) is better written as b if we can prove that a is always true. However, during the course of folding and unfolding rules, we may need to apply these transformations in the non-obvious direction.

5.4 Theorems = Speed

By the introduction of true clauses (that is, clauses which represent theorems proved true) we can introduce extra information into the rules which can help speed up the execution speed. If we want to specify that a solution of the cryptarithm $SIX + SIX = NINE$ where each letter stands for a different non-zero number, we can state the problem declaratively as:

```
puzzle([S,I,X]+[S,I,X]=[N,I,N,E]):-
    seqrem([S,I,X,N,E],[1,2,3,4,5,6,7,8,9]),
    2*(100*S+10*I+X) =:= (1010*N+100*I+E).
```

which tests 15120 combinations of the 5 variables chosen from 9 possibilities, generating them and testing which have the given property of the puzzle. However, we know the biggest three-digit number is 999 so that $NINE$ must be less than $999+999 = 1998$. Thus we have shown that "$N = 1$" is a theorem true for this puzzle. By introducing the theorem into the specification, we reduce the number of possibilities to try and have speeded up the execution time.

```
puzzle([S,I,X]+[S,I,X]=[N,I,N,E]):-
        N=1,
        seqrem([S,I,X,N,E],[1,2,3,4,5,6,7,8,9]),
        2*(100*S+10*I+X) =:= (1010*N+100*I+E).
```

Only one-ninth of the original cases need be tried now. This is an example of the boolean algebra law "$(True, a) = a$" applied in the 'wrong' direction.

5.5   Common patterns

It was found that when Prolog is used for expressing rules, the patterns common to the rules become clear. This was the case for the four combinatorics laws above, where it was noticed that they could be written in a common style which gave new insight into their construction. This is not the only case where we found the benefits of using Prolog.

5.6   Tail recursion and iteration

When we have transformed recursive rules into tail recursive form, some Prologs will apply an internal optimisation which saves stack space. Essentially, tail recursive rules are implementable by iterative methods. We found that using the equivalent of foldl and foldr rules of functional programming (see [1]) we were able to transform the definition of powerset into a tail recursive form. This could then be implemented in an imperative language and provides a fast and efficient algorithm for the generation of subsets of a given set. It also had the advantage that only one element at a time changed from subset to subset, so that the method was related to the generation of Gray Codes.

6 The animation library and the executable specifications

The application of the animation library to the direct execution of Z specifications has been referred to above. Since no tools existed for the automatic manipulation of Z at the inception of the project, we decided to take the approach of translating Z into calls of Prolog rules by hand. This meant that the rules in the Prolog library must closely match the fundamental Z constructs. Also, the Z animation library only deals with finite sets. Above we have described how the library has been extended to other constructs of mathematics, not just those of Z.

Since no software existed which allowed the user to check Z specifications for consistency, let alone prove theorems about such specifications, we also decided that our efficiency improving transformations would be carried out on the Prolog code, until such times as Z theorem provers became available. However, the work has wider applications than to Prolog transliterated from Z, but with the proviso that the Prolog has been produced in the 'pure' style argued for above.

Such a naive approach to animating Z often produced acceptably fast animations of Z specifications. One case where this lamentably failed was the animation of a Telephone Network, as specified by Carroll Morgan in [5] (see [9]). Krause found that one simple transformation (involving moving delta schemas from near the start of the schema rule to the end) produced a speed-up of several orders of magnitude (from several hours to 70 seconds). Other transformations applied by Knott were applications of the laws of boolean algebra on the terms of the clauses in the rules, made possible by the purely logical style employed in their production. They produced a further reduction in execution time to less than one second. A. J. J. Dick has experimented on a prototype system to help the user fold and unfold Prolog clauses in order to aid in the production of efficient Prolog code ([3]).

Such advantages of transformation more than justify the strictures of a pure logic programming style.

References

[1] R. Bird and P. Wadler. *Introduction to Functional Programming.* Prentice Hall, 1988.

[2] W. F. Clocksin and C. S. Mellish. *Programming in Prolog.* Springer International, 1984.

[3] A. J. J. Dick. Computer aided transformation of Prolog specifications. Technical report, Racal Research Limited, Worton Drive, Reading, UK, 1989.

[4] R. L. Graham, D. E. Knuth, and O. Patashnik. *Concrete Mathematics.* Addison Wesley, 1989.

[5] I. Hayes, editor. *Specification Case Studies.* Prentice Hall, 1987.

[6] R. D. Knott. Making discrete mathemtics executable on a computer. In *Proceedings of the IMA Conference on 'The Mathematical Revolution Inspired by Computing'*, April 1989.

[7] R. D. Knott and P. J. Krause. An approach to animating Z using Prolog. Technical Report Alvey Project SE/090 and SE/065 Report A1.1, Maths Dept, Surrey University, 1988.

[8] R. D. Knott and P. J. Krause. Library system — an example of the rapid prototyping of a Z specification in Prolog. Technical Report Alvey Project SE/090 and SE/065 Report A1.2, Maths Dept, Surrey University, 1988.

[9] R. D. Knott and P. J. Krause. On the derivation of an effective animation: Telephone network case study. Technical Report Alvey Project SE/090 and SE/065 Report A1.3, Maths Dept, Surrey University, 1988.

[10] Leon Sterling and Ehud Shapiro. *The Art of Prolog.* MIT Press, 1986.

Term-Encodable Description Spaces

Chris Mellish

Abstract

Spaces of descriptions arise in many branches of Computer Science, being known, for instance, as *types* [13, 7, 1], *concepts* [14, 19], *categories* [10] as well as *descriptions* [5]. In all these cases, it makes sense to talk about there being a space of possible descriptions that can be applied to objects and a subsumption ordering on these descriptions. Moreover, in all these cases it is useful to compute both the conjunction of two descriptions (the most general description subsumed by both) and to determine whether this conjunction is $\perp$ (the description that does not apply to anything).

A number of logic programmers have noticed that a convenient way to implement the conjunction operation on descriptions is often to encode the descriptions as terms of logic in such a way that standard unification produces the term encoding of the conjunction and fails if the result is $\perp$. When a space of descriptions is amenable to such treatment we will call it *term encodable*. The purpose of this paper is to begin to investigate what the limits of term encodability are.

1 Description Spaces

Given a set of ways of describing something, it is usually appropriate to consider the relation of *subsumption* that may hold between a pair of descriptions. Description d_1 is subsumed by description d_2, $d_1 \leq d_2$ when it is an equally or more specific description and hence covers a subset of the possible objects covered by d_2. We will assume here that two descriptions, each subsuming the other, are considered to be "the same" description. Given this, $\leq$ is a partial ordering on descriptions, and often any two given descriptions α and β will have a (unique) least upper bound $\alpha \vee \beta$ and greatest lower bound $\alpha \& \beta$ in the space and so the space will be a lattice. In this paper, we will only require that greatest lower bounds exist and we will concentrate on the greatest lower bound operation, which usually computes the conjunction of the two descriptions involved (although in some impoverished

description spaces it may compute a more specific description than this).
Thus the following will be our starting point:

Definition 1 *A* description space *is a countable meet-semilattice with zero
and unit elements,[1] ordered by a relationship of subsumption. The elements
of a description space are called* descriptions.

Figures 1 and 2 show two examples of portions of description spaces displayed
graphically. Figure 1 shows an example of a finite description space (from
[3]). Figure 2 shows part of an infinite description space that might be used
to represent a patient's record as regards contact with a particular disease.
A patient's record indicates his/her sex, possibly an indication that (s)he is
known to carry or suffer from the disease (the latter is assumed to imply
the former), as well as possibly a similar partial record for the (combined)
parents. We have used a subset of the formalism of the FL language of [5] for
this. These diagrams use a standard convention for displaying lattices, where
elements early in the partial order (specific descriptions) are shown below
elements later in the partial order (more general descriptions). From such a
diagram, it is possible to locate the greatest lower bound of two descriptions
(usually the conjunction) as the highest element that is below both. We will
not use any information about least upper bounds that is available from the
diagrams.

Notice that in this paper we will consider two description spaces to be "equivalent" if they have the same "shape" as semilattices. We will thus be viewing
description spaces in a way that does not depend on the particular formalisms
used to create them. In particular, if we are discussing a particular description space and two different expressions in some notation are equivalent with
respect to subsumption, then we will simply regard those expressions as "the
same" description (i.e. we essentially consider equivalence classes of descriptions with respect to logical equivalence).

2   Term Spaces

The set of terms used in logic is partially ordered by the relation "at least as
instantiated as". We can form a lattice from logical terms, collapsing together

---

[1]Although we shall require that greatest lower bounds exist and be unique, [2] provide a
way of extending any partially ordered set into a semilattice, and so our assumption is not
very restrictive. Note that we require that a description space is augmented if necessary
to contain a zero element $\perp$ — a description that is subsumed by everything and a unit
element $\top$ — a description that subsumes everything.

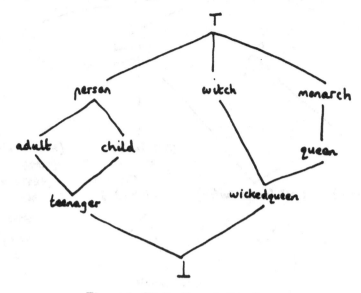

Figure 1: Finite Description Space

terms which are "variants" (i.e. pairs of terms, each of which is at least as instantiated as the other) and adding extra ⊤ and ⊥ elements. This lattice is the lattice of Generalised Atomic Formulae ("GAF lattice") discussed by [15]. In this lattice, the greatest lower bound operation is term unification [16] (which produces ⊥ on failure), although for various sublattices the actual operation may be simpler.

Any meet-subsemilattice of the GAF lattice would satisfy our definition of a description space, although one might reasonably expect a description space also to come equipped with a way of obtaining semantic interpretations of descriptions. This fact means that it makes sense to consider whether there are useful mappings from term spaces to other description spaces and *vice versa*.

3 A Logic Programming Trick

A number of logic programmers have noticed that operations on descriptions can sometimes be performed by encoding those descriptions as terms and performing the corresponding operations in the appropriate term space. In particular, given the right kind of encoding, computing the conjunction of two descriptions can be achieved by unifying their encodings and decoding the result (Figure 3). Some logic programmers [9, 12, 6] have even explicitly introduced encoding functions to deal with spaces of descriptions that are originally defined using some quite different notation.

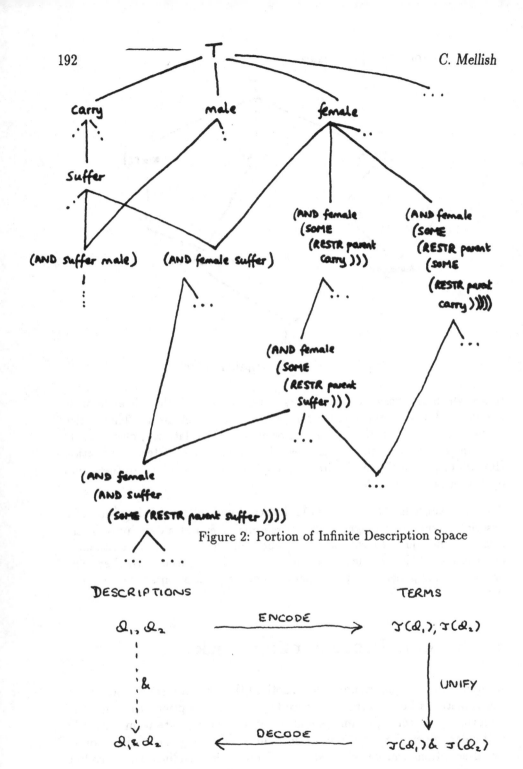

Figure 2: Portion of Infinite Description Space

Figure 3: Using a Term Encoding

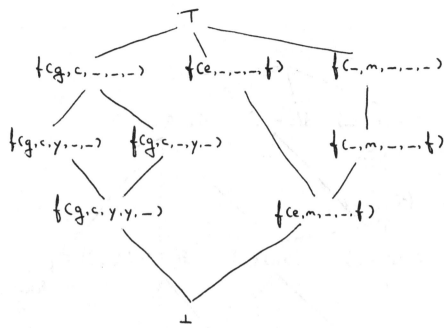

Figure 4: Reconstructed version of Figure 1

Figure 4 shows an example of a term description space that is exactly the same "shape" as the description space shown in Figure 1. Here the original description space has been recreated, using just part of the term space obtainable using the function symbols f, g, c, e, m and y (singly occurring variables are indicated by _). Thus a space that was not originally thought of in terms of logic terms can be reconstructed as a space of this form. Operations in the original space can be carried out in the term space without any loss of precision.

Figure 5 shows another example of the same idea, this time reconstructing the portion of the description space given in Figure 2 (though the reconstruction will extend to an infinite description space). Let us formalise what is going on in these two examples.

Definition 2 *A description space D is term encodable iff for some term description space G there is a mapping $\tau : D \to G$ satisfying the following:*

If $\tau(d_1) = \tau(d_2)$ then $d_1 = d_2$

$\tau(\perp) = \perp$[2]

---

[2]For simplicity, we use $\perp$ to refer to the bottom element, $\leq$ to refer to the partial ordering and & to refer to the greatest lower bound (unification) operation in all description spaces, even though, of course, each description space has its own version of these things.

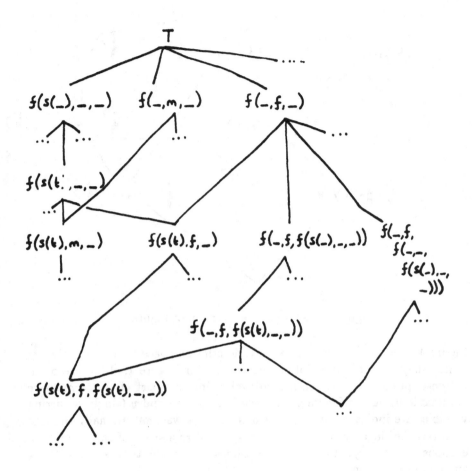

Figure 5: Reconstructed version of Figure 2

$$\tau(d_1 \& d_2) = \tau(d_1) \& \tau(d_2)$$

This amounts to τ having to be a 1-1, 0-preserving meet-homomorphism. Since we are only requiring description spaces to be meet semilattices, this criterion suffices for the relevant structure of the encoded description space to be modelled in the encoding description space. If we were interested in more of the structure of description spaces, then it would be easy to augment this criterion to ensure that, for instance, information about least upper bounds and the covering relation was also preserved, but a discussion of this would be beyond the scope of this paper.

The aim of this paper is to characterise the description spaces that can be encoded as terms in this way. Unfortunately, many properties that apply to complete term spaces generated by sets of function symbols do not hold in all subspaces which are closed under &, and it is these (i.e. the images of 1-1 meet-homomorpshisms) that we have to study. For instance, in a complete term space with at least two different function symbols, every description d is uniquely determined by its set of ground instances. This property does not hold in all subsets of a term description space closed under & (even if there are at least two different function symbols). Similarly, for any complete term space with a finite number of function symbols each element only covers a finite number of other elements; once again this is not true in every subspace of such a space that is closed under &. It follows that existing results characterising complete term lattices generated by sets of function symbols cannot be used directly to characterise term encodability.

It is convenient to subdivide the question of term encodability according to the kinds of terms used in the encoding (Figure 6). At the simplest level, we can consider limiting ourselves to terms that are essentially trees. An alternative is to allow what we call "flat terms" essentially directed acyclic graphs where every node is reachable from a root note by a path of length at most 1. Generalising this, we obtain the whole set of terms. It might even be possible to go further and consider the use of rational trees [8], although we only speculate about that in this paper.

4   Spanning Sets

In order to express a description as a structure of function symbols and arguments we need to have a way of determining the description's "components" in some sense. In its most abstract form, a "component" can be thought of as a set of descriptions, the descriptions which have that piece of substructure. Since if a particular description has a "component" we would expect every

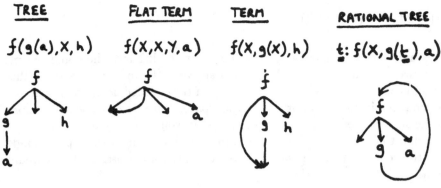

Figure 6: Types of terms

more specific description to have that "component", such a set will satisfy
the following requirement:

Definition 3 *A set of elements I in a description space is an* ideal[3] *iff whenever* $d_1 \in I$ *and* $d_2 \leq d_1$ *then* $d_2 \in I$.

Thus the task of finding a way of splitting descriptions into components is
equivalent to finding a set of sets of descriptions that behaves as follows:

Definition 4 *A set of ideals S is a* spanning set *for the description space D
iff the function* $\lambda x.\{s : x \in s \text{ and } s \in S\}$ *is a 1-1 mapping from D into* 2^S.

In accordance with our motivation, we will call an element of a spanning set
a component and the function $\lambda x.\{s : x \in s \text{ and } s \in S\}$ the *component mapping* of the spanning set. This definition simply says that every description
can be mapped into the set of components it has (the elements of the spanning set that it belongs to) and that each element is uniquely determined by
its components.

The concept of a spanning set will be vital for our study of term encodability,
and we will use the following terminology in talking about sets of descriptions.
We will say that a description *has* a component iff it is an element of that

---

[3]The traditional definition of an ideal (see [11], p17) for a lattice requires that in
addition the set be closed under & and ∨. The former is a consequence of the condition we
give. The latter does not arise directly because we are dealing with meet semilattices. We
could introduce an extra criterion which would reduce to closure under ∨ if the description
space happened to be a lattice, but with such a strict definition of an ideal most of our
results (e.g. Lemma 1, Theorem 1) would not be valid.

set and that two components are *incompatible* iff each element of the first is incompatible with each element of the second.[4]

One particular kind of spanning set will be of particular interest to us:

Definition 5 *A spanning set S for the description space D is* locally finite *iff, for every non-$\perp$ $d \in D$, $\{s : d \in s \text{ and } s \in S\}$ is a finite set.*

In a description space with a locally finite spanning set, every element only has a finite number of components.

5 Prime Ideals

In Artificial Intelligence there is ample precedent (e.g. [17]) to talk about a description as being composed in some way of a set of *primitives*. We will now present one possible formalisation of this idea, which turns out to be very appropriate for describing the limits of term encodability. Intuitively, an ideal P is *prime* if it has the monopoly of some special "ingredient", and any way of manufacturing a description with this ingredient must use some description already in P:

Definition 6 *An ideal P of descriptions is* prime *iff whenever $p \in P$, $\alpha \& \beta = p$ and $\alpha \& \beta \neq \perp$, then either $\alpha \in P$ or $\beta \in P$.*

The notion of a prime ideal is standard in lattice theory.

Lemma 1 *Every description space has a countable spanning set of prime ideals.*

This shows that much of the structure of a description space is captured by the properties of a spanning set of prime ideals and that we do not need to worry about such spanning sets being uncountable.

6 A Characterisation of Tree Encodability

Theorem 1 *A description space D is tree encodable iff it has a locally finite spanning set of prime ideals S such that, if d_1 and d_2 are elements of D,*

---

[4]Two elements α and β are incompatible iff $\alpha \& \beta = \perp$.

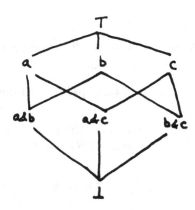

Figure 7: Non Tree Encodable Decsription Space

$d_1 \& d_2 = \perp$ *iff there are two incompatible sets* P_1 *and* P_2 *in* S *such that* $d_1 \in P_1$ *and* $d_2 \in P_2$.

Corollary 1 *In a tree encodable description space a conjunction of elements is* $\perp$ *iff two of the conjuncts are incompatible.*

Corollary 2 *In a tree encodable description space, the set of elements incompatible with a given element is a prime ideal.*

Corollary 3 *It is impossible to have a tree encodable description space in which there are elements subsumed by* $\alpha \vee \beta$, $\neg\alpha$ *and* $\neg\beta$, *for some independent descriptions* α *and* β.

It follows from this that not all finite description spaces are tree encodable. Since [9, 12, 6] all only use tree-shaped terms in their encoding schemes, these results indicate to some extent the limitations of their methods. For instance, Figure 7 shows a simple finite description space that is not tree encodable (for instance, it does not have the property of Corollary 1).

That infinite description spaces can be tree encodable is demonstrated, for instance, by the infinite flat lattice (Figure 8) of natural numbers. For this description space, the sets $\{i, \perp\}$ ($i \in N$) form a locally finite spanning set of prime ideals. In this lattice every two non-$\top$ elements are incompatible.

Description spaces built using the frame languages FL^-[5] and the *Tbox* of Krypton [4] are always tree encodable (we assume that no terminological axioms are allowed). Indeed, the same is true of of spaces constructed using the augmented version of FL^- mentioned at the end of [5], which includes all the features available in FL^- and the Krypton *Tbox*. The elements in

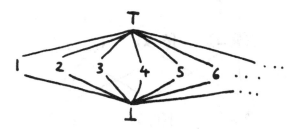

Figure 8: The flat lattice of natural numbers

a description space created with this framework are expressions of the type
$\langle Concept \rangle$ (plus an extra $\perp$ element), defined by the following rules:

$\langle Concept \rangle ::=$
 $\langle Atomic\ concept \rangle |$
 $(AND \langle Concept_1 \rangle \cdots \langle Concept_n \rangle)|(n \geq 0)$
 $(ALL \langle Role \rangle \langle Concept \rangle)|$
 $(ATLEAST \langle Role \rangle \langle Number \rangle)$
$\langle Role \rangle ::=$
 $\langle Atomic\ role \rangle |$
 $(ROLE - CHAIN \langle Role_1 \rangle \cdots \langle Role_n \rangle)(n \geq 1)$

For the augmented FL^-, subsumption is defined in terms of the semantics
of the constructs. Informally, AND indicates conjunction, ALL describes
an object all of whose fillers for a given role satisfy a given description and
$ATLEAST$ describes an object which has at least some given number of
different fillers for a specified role. Roles may be atomic, or may be chains
of role names. Thus, for instance, the description

$$(AND\ person(ATLEAST\ child3)(ALL\ child\ male))$$

could be used to indicate a person with at least 3 children, all of whom were
male.

The full language FL includes the construct $(RESTR \langle Role \rangle \langle Concept \rangle)$ as
a kind of $\langle Role \rangle$ but does not include $ROLE - CHAIN$. It includes a
construct $SOME$ which is the same as $ATLEAST$ with argument 1. It can
be shown that there are FL description spaces that have no locally finite
spanning sets of prime ideals (and hence are not tree encodable). It is very
interesting that, as well as representing a step from tree encodability to non
tree encodability, the transition from FL^- to FL corresponds to a significant
step in the complexity of computing subsumption [5].

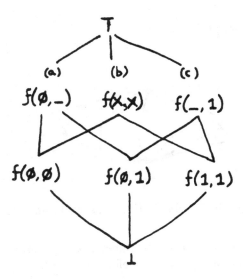

Figure 9: Term Space

7 Flat Pseudo-prime Spanning Sets

The criterion of Corollary 1 does not hold for general terms. For instance, in Figure 9 the conjunction of terms (a), (b) and (c) is $\perp$ but no pair of them is incompatible. One is therefore tempted to hypothesise that, if one is allowed to use general terms, rather than just trees, then the necessary and sufficient condition for term encodability will simply be the existence of a locally finite spanning set of prime ideals. Indeed this condition is sufficient for encodability, but in fact there is a wider range of description spaces that can be encoded.

Recall that if P is a prime ideal then for every conjunction that belongs to the set one of the conjuncts must belong. We can generalise this by allowing there to be some other set, P', of elements that can appear as conjuncts in an element of P when no conjunct is actually in P:

$$\alpha \& \beta \in P \text{ iff } \alpha \in P \cup P' \text{ or } \beta \in P \cup P'.$$

Generalising further, we can let the set P' depend on the elements involved:

$$\alpha \& \beta \in P \text{ iff}$$
$$\alpha \in P \text{ or } \beta \in P$$
$$\text{or } (\alpha \in Q_i \text{ and } \beta \in C_i)$$
$$\text{or } (\beta \in Q_i \text{ and } \alpha \in C_i)$$

where $\{Q_i : i \in N\}$ is a countable set of sets. Each C_i then corresponds to a set of elements that "convert" elements of Q_i into elements of P. We then have to choose the sets Q_i (it makes sense for them to be sets like P) and determine how the sets C_i behave. Here is one possible way that this could be done:

Definition 7 *A flat pseudo-prime spanning set is a spanning set consisting of the following components:*

$$S_\sigma^k \qquad\qquad \sigma, k \in N$$
$$C_{\sigma_1 \sigma_2} \qquad\qquad \sigma_1, \sigma_2 \in N$$

such that for every non-$\perp$ α and β:

1. *$\alpha \& \beta \in S_\sigma^k$ iff $\langle \sigma, k \rangle \in S(\alpha, \beta)$*

2. *$\alpha \& \beta \in C_{\sigma_1 \sigma_2}$ iff $\langle \sigma_1, \sigma_2 \rangle \in C(\alpha, \beta)$*

3. *$\alpha \& \beta = \perp$ iff for some $k, l, \sigma, \langle \sigma, k \rangle \in S(\alpha, \beta), \langle \sigma, l \rangle \in S(\alpha, \beta)$ and $k \neq l$*

where $C(\alpha, \beta)$ and $S(\alpha, \beta)$ are the least sets C, S satisfying:

$$
\begin{aligned}
C \ = \ & \{\langle \sigma_1, \sigma_2 \rangle : \alpha \in C_{\sigma_1 \sigma_2} \text{ or } \beta \in C_{\sigma_1 \sigma_2}\} \cup \\
& \{\langle \sigma_1, \sigma_2 \rangle : \text{for some } k, \langle \sigma_1, k \rangle \in S \text{ and } \langle \sigma_2, k \rangle \in S\} \cup \\
& \{\langle \sigma_1, \sigma_2 \rangle : \langle \sigma_2, \sigma_1 \rangle \in C\} \cup \\
& \{\langle \sigma_1, \sigma_3 \rangle : \text{for some } \sigma_2, \langle \sigma_1, \sigma_2 \rangle \in C \text{ and } \langle \sigma_2, \sigma_3 \rangle \in C\} \\
S \ = \ & \{\langle \sigma, k \rangle : \alpha \in S_\sigma^k \text{ or } \beta \in S_\sigma^k\} \cup \\
& \{\langle \sigma_1, k \rangle : \text{for some } \sigma, \langle \sigma, k \rangle \in S \text{ and } \langle \sigma_1, \sigma \rangle \in C\}
\end{aligned}
$$

Intuitively one can think of each σ as naming a position in a term and each k as a possible function symbol that may appear there. A set S_σ^k then corresponds to the set of descriptions that have value k in position σ. The elements of a set $C_{\sigma_1 \sigma_2}$ enable one to convert a description with a value in position σ_1 to one which (also) has a value in the position σ_2. A set of the form $C_{\sigma\sigma}$, which contains all the sets $C_{\sigma\sigma_1}$ and S_σ^k, then represents the set of descriptions which have position σ. It follows from the above that such a set is a prime ideal.

Given an encoding for a flat term encodable description space we can divide up the descriptions according to the principal function symbol of their encoding; descriptions allocated different principal function symbols must be incompatible. Since there are only finitely many flat terms constructable using a given function symbol, the elements of the description space must therefore divide up into a number of finite, pairwise incompatible, sets. The

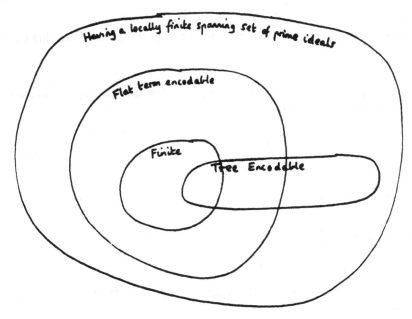

Figure 10: Classes of description space

condition of having a locally finite flat pseudo-prime spanning set does not in itself guarantee that this structure will be present. In order to state this extra condition, we need to define the function *compats*, which is essentially the transitive closure of the relation "is compatible with". If d is an element of a description space D then

$$compats(d) = \bigcup_{d_1 \in D} \left\{ \begin{array}{ll} \emptyset & \text{if } d_1 = \top \text{ or } d \& d_1 = \bot \\ \{d_1\} \cup compats(d_1) & \text{otherwise} \end{array} \right.$$

We can now state the conditions for flat term encodability.

Theorem 2 *A description space D is flat term encodable iff it has a locally finite flat pseudo-prime spanning set and for each element $d \neq \top$, $compats(d)$ is a finite set.*

In fact, it turns out that the class of flat term encodable description spaces is a proper subclass of the class of description spaces with locally finite spanning sets of prime ideals (Figure 10) and so there is still room to consider more general classes of description space.

8 Hierarchical Pseudo-prime Spanning Sets

It is easy to construct examples of description spaces that are tree encodable but not flat term encodable, because flat term encodable spaces cannot contain infinite descending chains (whereas tree encodable ones can). So, for instance, in an FL^- space with d_i being the description $(ATLEAST\ R\ i)$, for some fixed role R, the set of all $d_i, i = 1, 2, \ldots$ is an infinite descending chain. Hence in general FL^- description spaces are not flat term encodable.

Clearly full term encodability encompasses both tree encodability and flat term encodability, and we now introduce a characterisation of full term encodability, which in fact covers both those description spaces that are flat term encodable and also those which have locally finite spanning sets of prime ideals (and possibly more).

In a lattice of non-flat terms, the unification of two terms can have a value in a position that does not exist in either of the terms individually. For instance, the unification of $f(X, X)$ and $f(g(a), Y)$ has the value a in the position "the first argument of the second argument of the term", even though this description makes no sense for either of the terms on its own. Such a position depends for its existence on the existence of less specific positions (here, "the second argument of the term"), and we can capture this idea through the notion of hierarchically organised components.

To introduce the idea of hierarchically organised components in an abstract way, we will consider sequences of numbers, rather than simple numbers, as the possible values for the σ elements in a pseudo-prime spanning set. The more general definition now runs as follows:

Definition 8 *A* hierarchical pseudo-prime spanning set *is a spanning set consisting of the following components:*

$$S_\sigma^k \qquad\qquad k \in N, \sigma \in N^*$$
$$C_{\sigma_1\sigma_2} \qquad\qquad \sigma_1, \sigma_2 \in N^*$$

such that for every non-$\bot$ α and β:

1. *$\alpha \& \beta \in S_\sigma^k$ iff $\langle \sigma, k \rangle \in S(\alpha, \beta)$*

2. *$\alpha \& \beta \in C_{\sigma_1\sigma_2}$ iff $\langle \sigma_1, \sigma_2 \rangle \in C(\alpha, \beta)$*

3. *$\alpha \& \beta = \bot$ iff for some $k, l, \sigma, \langle \sigma, k \rangle \in S(\alpha, \beta), \langle \sigma, l \rangle \in S(\alpha, \beta)$ and $k \neq l$*

where $C(\alpha, \beta)$ and $S(\alpha, \beta)$ are the least sets C, S satisfying:

$$
\begin{aligned}
C \;=\; & \{\langle \sigma_1, \sigma_2 \rangle : \alpha \in C_{\sigma_1 \sigma_2} \ or \ \beta \in C_{\sigma_1 \sigma_2} \} \cup \\
& \{\langle \sigma_1, \sigma_2 \rangle : for \ some \ k, \langle \sigma_1, k \rangle \in S \ and \ \langle \sigma_2, k \rangle \in S \} \cup \\
& \{\langle \sigma_1, \sigma_2 \rangle : \langle \sigma_2, \sigma_1 \rangle \in C \} \cup \\
& \{\langle \sigma_1, \sigma_3 \rangle : for \ some \ \sigma_2, \langle \sigma_1, \sigma_2 \rangle \in C \ and \ \langle \sigma_2, \sigma_3 \rangle \in C \} \cup \\
& \{\langle \sigma_1.\sigma, \sigma_2.\sigma \rangle : \langle \sigma_1, \sigma_2 \rangle \in C \ and \ either \ \langle \sigma_1.\sigma, \sigma_1.\sigma \rangle \in C \\
& or \ \langle \sigma_2.\sigma, \sigma_2.\sigma \rangle \in C \} \\
S \;=\; & \{\langle \sigma, k \rangle : \alpha \in S_\sigma^k \ or \ \beta \in S_\sigma^k \} \cup \\
& \{\langle \sigma_1, k \rangle : for \ some \ \sigma, \langle \sigma, k \rangle \in S \ and \ \langle \sigma_1, \sigma \rangle \in C \}
\end{aligned}
$$

It is the last clause for C which legitimates the possibility of values in a position in a conjunction when neither conjunct has that position. Clearly a hierarchical pseudoprime spanning set reduces to a flat one if $C_{\sigma\sigma}$ is empty whenever σ is of length greater than 1.

For term encodability, we are concerned with locally finite spanning sets. A locally finite hierarchical pseudoprime spanning set is simply one where each element of the description space only belongs to a finite number of S_σ^k and $C_{\sigma_1 \sigma_2}$. An element d will fail to do this iff it is $\perp$ or at least one of $C(d, d)$ and $S(d, d)$ is infinite. It follows that in a description space with a locally finite hierarchical pseudo-prime spanning set the only element d with infinite $C(d, d)$ or $S(d, d)$ can be $\perp$.

It might seem that the rather esoteric definitions of pseudo-prime spanning sets mean that these will not arise often in practice, but the following results show that they represent a real generalisation of countable prime ideal spanning sets.

Lemma 2 *If a description space D has a countable spanning set S of prime ideals, then it also has a hierarchical pseudo-prime spanning set S_1 where S_1 is locally finite iff S is.*

Corollary 4 *Every description space has a hierarchical pseudo-prime spanning set.*

9   Term Encodable Description Spaces

Theorem 3 *A description space D is term encodable iff it has a locally finite hierarchical pseudo-prime spanning set.*

Figure 11: Non term encodable description spaces

There are certainly description spaces that are not even term encodable, and Figure 11 shows examples of how this can happen. In fact, these examples are description spaces for which no locally finite spanning set can be found at all, let alone a hierarchical pseudo-prime one. In the first case, there is an infinitely ascending chain of descriptions d_i. This could arise in a language similar to FL^- but with an $ATMOST$ construction similar to the existing $ATLEAST$. In such a language, letting d_i be the description $(ATMOST\ R\ i)$, for some fixed role R, would create such a chain. The second case involves an infinite descending chain of elements d_i, together with a non-$\perp$ lower bound d for that chain. This could arise with a version of FL^- that allowed the special number ∞. In this case, letting d_i be $(ATLEAST\ R\ i)$ and d be $(ATLEAST\ R\ \infty)$, for some fixed role R, would create the desired configuration.

It is interesting to speculate what extra description spaces would be encodable if we allowed rational trees (and the appropriately modified notion of unification). We speculate that rational tree encodability can be characterised exactly as term encodability, except that the local finiteness condition is further relaxed. Certainly lattices of rational trees can contain infinite descending chains with non-$\perp$ lower bounds. The ψ-terms of [3] are almost certainly rational tree encodable, even though in general they are not term encodable.

Acknowledgements

This work would not have been possible without the assistence of research grant GRE 57376 and an Advanced Fellowship provided by the Science and Engineering Research Council.

References

[1] H. Ait-Kaci. *A Lattice-Theoretic Approach to Computation Based on a Calculus of Partially-Ordered Type Structures.* PhD thesis, Dept of Computer and Information Science, University of Pennsylvania, Philadelphia, 1984.

[2] H. Ait-Kaci, R. Boyer, P. Lincoln, and R. Nasr. Efficient implementation of lattice operations. *TOPLAS*, 11(1), 1989.

[3] H. Ait-Kaci and R. Nasr. Login: A logic programming language with built-in inheritance. *Journal of Logic Programming*, 3(3), October 1986.

[4] R. J. Brachman, V. P. Gilbert, and H. J. Levesque. An essential hybrid reasoning system: Knowledge and symbol level accounts of Krypton. In *Proceedings of IJCAI 1985*, 1985.

[5] R. J. Brachman and H. J. Levesque. The tractability of subsumption in frame-based description languages. *Procs of AAAI*, 1984.

[6] A. Bundy, L. Byrd, and C. Mellish. Special purpose, but domain independent, inference mechanisms. In *Procs.of the European Conference on Artificial Intelligence*, Orsay, France, 1982. Also appears in [18].

[7] L. Cardelli. A semantics of multiple inheritance. In G. Kahn, D. MacQueen, and G. Plotkin, editors, *Semantics of Data Types*. Springer Verlag, 1984.

[8] A. Colmerauer. Prolog and infinite trees. In K. Clark and S-A Tärnlund, editors, *Logic Programming*. Academic Press, 1982.

[9] V. Dahl. Un système deductif d'interrogation de banques de donnes en espagnol. Research report, Groupe d'Intelligence Artificielle, University of Marseille-Luminy, 1977.

[10] G. Gazdar, G. Pullum, R. Carpenter, E. Klein, T. Hukari, and R. Levine. Category structures. *Computational Linguistics*, 14(1), 1988.

[11] G. Graetzer. *General Lattice Theory*. Birkhauser Verlag, 1978.

[12] M. C. McCord. Design of a Prolog-based machine translation system. In E. Y. Shapiro, editor, *Proc. of 3rd International Logic Programming Conference*, July 1986.

[13] R. Milner. A theory of type polymorphism in programming. *Journal of Computer and System Science*, 17, 1978.

[14] T. M. Mitchell. Generalisation as search. *Artificial Intelligence*, 18:203–226, 1982.

[15] J. C. Reynolds. Transformational systems and the algebraic structure of atomic formulas. In B. Meltzer and D. Michie, editors, *Machine Intelligence 5*. Edinburgh University Press, 1970.

[16] J. A. Robinson. A machine-oriented logic based on the resolution principle. *JACM*, 12:23–41, 1965.

[17] R. C. Schank. Conceptual dependency: A theory of natural language understanding. *Cognitive Psychology*, 3, 1972.

[18] L. Steels and J. Campbell, editors. *Progress in Artificial Intelligence*. Ellis Horwood, 1985.

[19] P. H. Winston. Learning structural descriptions from examples. In P. H. Winston, editor, *The Psychology of Computer Vision*. McGraw-Hill, 1975.

Logic, Language and the Quest for Intelligence

Chris Moss

Abstract

There has been a widespread confusion of cause and effect in the relationship between intelligence and symbolic systems. Although historically it has been intelligent beings that have created symbolic systems there has been a continuing belief, fostered by many researchers in their promotional writing, which suggests that symbolic programming offers a serious prospect of creating systems equalling or surpassing human intelligence. This has been fostered by inaccurate interpretations of the significance both of Turing's thesis about the computational equivalence of machines and his test for recognizing intelligence.

The role of symbolic reasoning in human intelligence is still far from clear despite much recent activity in the area of cognition. It is linked with the use of language by human beings, but the differences between natural language and formal systems mean that one must be very careful in choosing the correct problems to tackle using computer systems. An understanding of the limits of symbolic methods can encourage better design of the human computer interface in logic programming systems and avoid some of the expectations aroused by terms like artificial intelligence.

1 Introduction

The Analytic Engine does not occupy common ground with mere "calculating machines". It holds a position wholly its own ... In enabling mechanism to combine together general symbols in successions of unlimited variety and extent, a uniting link is established between the operation of matter and the abstract mental processes of the most abstract branch of mathematics. A new, a vast, and a powerful language is developed for the future use of analysis, in which to wield its

208

truths so that these may become of more speedy and accurate practical applications for the purposes of mankind than the means hitherto in our possession have rendered possible.

Since Ada Augusta, only child of Lord Byron, grasped, in the quotation above which was written around 1842 [1], the import of Babbage's invention, the potential of the computer has risen so far in the view of many people that it has become difficult to place any bounds on it. It is now commonplace for people to regard the human mind as simply an advanced form of computer, and a valid exercise to try to emulate the subtleties of intelligence by writing computer programs.

By the time technology had caught up with ideas, and the notion of artificial intelligence was born — in 1956 at a conference in Dartmouth, in the United States — the notions of logic and the computable had become immensely refined. Not only had an attempt been made to capture the laws of mathematics logically (by Russell and Whitehead) using a new notation (by Frege) and been proved incomplete (by Gödel), but the equivalence of abstract mathematical and mechanically computable functions had been shown (by Church and Turing).

Thus it is not surprising that the nature of reasoning and the human mind should be a matter of intense speculation: how far could the processes of human reason be clarified by models of computations orders of magnitude more efficient than those previously imagined?

Three generations of research in Artificial Intelligence are now commonly observed. The first was the pre-paradigmatic era, with the research of Newell and Simon on problem solving, McCarthy on LISP and Rosenblatt on the Perceptron. It ended with Minsky and Papert's [21] critique of the shortcomings of the neural network programme. The second was the symbolic era which peaked not long afterwards with the publication of Winograd's [30] thesis on SHRLDU and gave rise to the notion of expert systems. The third was ushered in the early 1980's with developments such as Hopfield's networks [14] and christened as connectionism by the publication of Rumelhart and McClelland [26].

Logic Programming was in many ways an offshoot of that second era, relating back the idea of search as a general problem solving mechanism to the earlier notions of the completeness of first-order predicate logic and combining this with an efficient computational mechanism, using unification and Horn clause resolution [17]. It succeeded in the 1980's, by virtue of its expressiveness and efficient implementations, in becoming a basis for many projects outside the traditional goals of AI, as well as for others (such as the Japanese ICOT project) which were closer to those traditional goals.

As the ad hoc nature of AI's methods is questioned, the association of logic programming with the goals of AI is in danger of limiting the progress of logic proogramming and needs to be reviewed. However it is important not to its destroy the internal dynamic. We need therefore to review the relationship between three related topics: formal systems, intelligence and natural language. The last of these three is important not only because it is one of the foremost applications of logic programming systems but because it represents the meeting point of the first two topics which have served as the twin foci of logic programming.

The plan of this paper is as follows: In the first section we discuss various uses of thje word intelligence and distinguish several levels at which it can apply. Then we discuss the evolution of intelligence, language and invention of formal systems. Finally we discuss the implications of this for logic as a computational formalism, in relation to AI, cognitive science and linguistics.

2 Intelligence

One of the curious aspects of many modern treatments of Artificial Intelligence is they scarcely bother to define intelligence. For example [11]:

> How shall we define intelligence? Doesn't everything turn on this? Surprisingly, perhaps, very little seems to turn on it. For practical purposes a criterion proposed by Alan Turing [29] satisfies nearly everyone.

The assumption is that we all know what intelligence is. Of course it is a word that like many others has changed in meaning subtly with the years. Johnson's dictionary [16] has as its primary definition:

> Commerce of information; notice; mutual communication; account of things distant or secret.

and not until the 4th and last definition do we come across the more recognizable "understanding; skill". If we compare this with a typical modern dictionary [4], we find as its first definition

> the capacity for understanding; ability to perceive and comprehend meaning.

and if we consult the word "meaning" we find

> the sense or significance of a word.

Thus the understanding of symbols, or words, has become the accepted measure, and even the aspect of "skill" has been downgraded.

Of course the definition of Artificial Intelligence has also changed. The Handbook of AI gives what may still be considered a mainstream definition:

> the part of computer science concerned with designing intelligent computer systems, that is, systems that exhibit the characteristics we associate with intelligence in human behaviour — understanding language, learning, reasoning, solving problems and so on.

We may see here a conscious adoption of Turing's [29] formulation, which is essentially a behaviourist definition: intelligence is something that yields intelligent characteristics. It is only explained by reference to human examples and is an unashamedly circular definition.

Rather than attempting a definition of the word intelligence which generations of psychologists have been unable to agree about, we may usefully distinguish three distinct levels at which intelligence may be defined:

1. reason

2. language

3. animal behaviour

"Reason", said Hobbes in 1651 [13], "is nothing but Reckoning (that is, adding and subtracting) of the consequences of general names agreed upon for the marking and signifying of our thoughts". This is the level of logical thinking, first examined systematically in an AI setting by Newell and Simon, starting with the General Problem Solver. It is the characteristic of the adult educated human mind and is the aspect in which most success has been achieved by symbolic methods.

Language is seen more and more clearly as the distinctive characteristic of human beings since the recent attempts to teach chimpanzees sign language are often perceived to have failed (see [27]). Every human has this ability and even those without hearing or sight usually develop it in some form.

Animal behaviour refers to the capabilities of our brains which we share with the rest of the animal world. Other names for it are survival ability and common sense (but it should not be identified with *behaviourism*). It is the most baffling and hard-to-program aspect of intelligence and includes the ability to learn, to plan, the emotions and the senses. The word "intelligence" has only recently been applied to animals. As Hoage and Goldman [12] point out,

> In the years since Charles Darwin, people have come to accept the fact that the human body is the product of millions of years of evolution, and is quite analogous to the body structure of many other animals... Brains have also evolved, as has the behaviour they control, but the evolution of mental capabilities as an analogue to the evolution of physical characteristics is not so easily accepted.

Yet many of the hardest problems of AI arise precisely from this continuity. As Dreyfus & Dreyfus [6] point out,

> the commonsense knowledge problem has blocked all progress in theoretical AI for the past decade. Winograd was one of the first to see the limitations of SHRDLU and all script and frame attempts to extend the microworlds approach. Having "lost faith" in AI, he now teaches Heidegger in his computer science course in Stanford and points out "the difficulty of formalizing the commonsense background that determines which scripts, goals and strategies are relevant and how they interact".

These characteristics are not uniquely human; most of them can be observed in the higher animals. It is tempting to ignore these "lower" levels of intelligence when considering artificial intelligence, and indeed it is common practice. But Reeke and Edelman [25] point out that one is then in danger of overlooking the real problems of intelligence:

> In the standard AI paradigm, as presented by Winston [33], the key to finding powerful procedures that can solve these problems is to discover appropriate representations of the relevant information. Once a representation is given that "makes the right things explicit and expose[s] the natural constraints," it is a much simpler matter to devise purely computational procedures to manipulate the information, still in its encoded representation, so as to obtain the desired solutions. Winston is right. Once an appropriate representation is available, many problems do become amenable to automatic solution. In our view, however, the problem requiring intelligence is the original one of finding a representation. To place this problem in the domain of the system designer rather than in that of the designed system is to beg the question and reduce intelligence to symbol manipulation.

It was perhaps then fortunate for Turing [29] that he chose the middle level aspect of the trio we have identified, language, as the key test of intelligence. It is not clear that there is any clear focus on language *per se* in his thinking. It was simply the obvious communication channel through which to query the human mind, and it avoided what to him were tediously irrelevant aspects, such as motor skills and the senses. But the experience of AI is that language encapsulates its problems. For instance, Winograd now says [32]:

> There may be practical applications for computer processing of natural language formalisms and for limited processing of natural language, but computers will remain incapable of using language in the way human beings do, both in interpretation and in the generation of commitment[1] that is central to language.

Yet it was being seriously argued as long ago as 1972 by no less a person than Christopher Longuet-Higgins [19] that:

> The only trouble with Turing's test is that a computer programme [*sic*] has already passed it. Here's a dialogue which actually developed between Weizenbaum's programme, Eliza, and a salesman who called it up by mistake, thinking he was connected to one of the professors at M.I.T.

There follows a dialogue whose style would be familiar to anyone who has played with the program. Although Longuet-Higgins subsequently averred that "Eliza has only passed the Turing test by cheating", the damage was done. Any program which can hold its own among humans for however short a time can be said to "pass the Turing test".

In terms of the original criteria laid down by Turing :

> I believe that in about fifty years' time it will be possible to program computers, with a storage capacity of about 10^9 to make them play the imitation game so well that an average interrogator will not have more than 70 percent chance of making the right identification after five minutes of questioning.

one may well still argue about its possible achievement until one remembers the basic intention of the game which is so regularly forgotten: the interrogator is consciously trying to "spot the computer" and devises the

---

[1]The notion of commitment is not dissimilar to the notion of intention used by Searle and others.

interrogation with this in mind. For this purpose, use of language is a devastatingly sharp weapon. Despite claims about the use of language for carefully regulated uses, no serious researcher will claim that ten years is a sensible time frame for achieving competence in free and wide-ranging conversation with humans.[2] HAL will not be delivered by 2001!

A corollary of this is that most areas in which human reason operates (the law, philosophy and the arts) remain so far immune to treatment by formal means, though progress is made and will continue to be made. Thus our original definition must be refined to distinguish what can be formally treated from that which cannot. This is doubtless a moving distinction, just as our understanding of the linguistic traits of animals will change.

Much of the work in AI has been concerned with the lower level capabilities which we share with the animals: vision, planning, learning, concept formation, and so on. None of these *require* the use of symbols in animals as far as we can tell and many are well advanced in relatively primitive animals. If there is one overriding characteristic of biological systems it is that they are programmed for survival. (Conversely, computer programs are notoriously brittle.) The reason for this central emphasis is that living creatures are continually in contact with their surroundings, finding sustenance and avoiding hazards. In contrast, a symbolic system may be entirely isolated, without even a semantic correspondence to the world.

Attempts have been made to bridge this gap by building up symbolic stores of commonsense knowledge about the world (see [18]). Apart from the inevitably incomplete nature of this project (even in the indefinite future), one is still dealing with the effect not the cause of intelligence. If used by an intelligent being (whether animal or computer!), commonsense is a useful mine of information. But otherwise it can be simply banal.

There is therefore also a crucial interface between pre-symbolic intelligence and symbols which must be understood if we are to understand the true nature of language and symbolic communication. The last thirty years of artificial intelligence have been an experiment which has taught people many things and led to profitable exploitation. But in terms of creating true intelligence, the chief lesson should be that we cannot ignore the biological basis of intelligence any longer.

---

[2]On the other hand, his projections of memory sizes available on an average machine in the year 2000 has already been achieved.

3   The evolution of Symbolic Systems

A key question that has to be answered is whether intelligence is *essentially* symbolic. Initially one may be surprised that the suggestion has been made: since we share so many capabilities with animals who do not have the same capacity for language, why should we take symbolic systems, whether formal or linguistic, as the defining paradigm? Yet this thesis is strongly argued from two different camps: from the school of AI, and from the linguistic camp. Thus Newell and Simon [24]:

> A physical symbol system has the necessary and sufficient means for generating intelligent action. By 'necessary' we mean that any system that exhibits general intelligence will prove upon analysis to be a physical symbol system. By 'sufficient' we mean that any physical system of sufficient size can be organized further to exhibit general intelligence.

The strongest statement from linguistics is the influential though heterodox view of Richard Montague [22]:

> I reject the contention that an important theoretical difference exists between formal and natural languages.

An entirely different but equally comprehensive approach is Chomsky's quest for a Universal Grammar (UG), as outlined by Cook [5]:

> UG theory holds that a speaker knows a set of principles that apply to all languages, and parameters that vary within clearly defined limits from one language to another. Acquiring language means learning how these principles apply to a particular language and which value is appropriate for each parameter.

In making the distinction between three stages in the evolution of intelligent systems: animal intelligence, language and formal systems, it may help by trying to put tentative dates on their appearance in evolutionary history.

Many of the underlying characteristics which we call intelligence are seen in animals, even quite primitive ones. The following example, quoted by Gould & Gould [8] would be recognizable to any programmer:

> When the nineteenth century French naturalist Jean Henri Fabre interfered with the prey-capture ritual of a cricket-hunting wasp by

moving its paralysed victim, he stumbled across some of the wiring
that runs the wasp's routine. The wasp, whose behavior appears ec-
centric but intelligent, invariably leaves the cricket she has caught ly-
ing on its back, its antennae just touching the tunnel entrance, while
she inspects her burrow. Each time Fabre moved it even slightly away
from the entrance, the reemerging wasp insisted on precisely reposi-
tioning the cricket and inspecting the tunnel again. Fabre continued
this trivial alteration 40 times and the wasp, locked in a behavioral
"do-loop" never thought to skip an obviously pointless step in her program. Clearly the wasp is a machine in this context, entirely inflexible
in her behavior.

Capabilities vary widely across species, and the most advanced behaviour
does not always occur in the most advanced species. For example, the well-
known message system of bees in which they indicate by dancing the direction
and distance of food sources has many of the characteristics of a language
system but is an isolated and almost entirely instinctual behaviour. Yet it
discloses some remarkable underlying abilities, such as the ability to form a
mental map and then formulate appropriate behaviour. This is recounted in
the same article by Gould and Gould:

> The first hint of such an ability in bees came years ago when von
> Frisch discovered that bees that had flown an indirect route to a food
> source were nevertheless able to indicate by their famous communica-
> tion dances the straightline direction to the food. By itself, it is easy
> to interpret this ability as some sort of mindless, automatic exercise
> in trigonometry. Three years ago we trained foragers along a lake and
> tricked them into dancing to indicate to potential recruit bees in the
> hive that the food was in the middle of the lake. Recruits refused to
> search for these food sources, even when we put a food source in a
> boat in the lake at the indicated spot. At first we thought that the re-
> cruits might simply be suffering from some sort of apian hydrophobia,
> but when we increased the distance of the station so that the dances
> indicated the far side of the lake, recruits turned up on the opposite
> shore in great numbers. Apparently they "knew" how wide the lake
> was and so were able to distinguish between sources allegedly in the
> lake and sources on the shore. We see no way to account for this
> behavior on the basis of either associative or trial-and-error learning.
> This ability is accounted for most simply if we assume that the re-
> cruits have mental maps of the surroundings on which they somehow
> place the spots indicated by the dances.

The ability to recognize classes of objects, discriminate conceptually, to communicate in limited but effective ways, to learn new behaviour, to form plans,

to show affections and dislikes and so on can be shown in most vertebrates and can be ranked in very approximate hierarchies of learning skills [28]:

1. Habituation (ignoring a stimulus that has no consequences)

2. Signal learning (Pavlovian conditioning)

3. Stimulus-response learning (operant conditioning)

4. Chaining (several actions required to gain a reward)

5. Concurrent discriminations (how many it can remember at the same time; only mammals show more than 6 or 7)

6. Affirmative concepts (generalizations e.g. pigeons)

7. Conditional/conjunctive/disjunctive concepts (e.g. chimpanzees)

8. Biconditional concepts (unknown)

Although the last of these can only be demonstrated in primates, many of the earlier techniques are found in animals which evolved many hundreds of millions of years ago but are not yet incorporated with any generality into present programmed systems.

Language appears to be a uniquely human attribute, at least in the sense of complex sentences. Most of the studies teaching chimpanzee to speak have concluded that there are definite limitations on the complexity of speech that chimpanzees can be taught, even using various techniques to circumvent their lack of adaption to complex sound production. For example, Terrace [27] points out:

> The initial results of the various ape-language projects produced exciting evidence of an ape's ability to form sentences. For example, in an early diary report, the Gardners noted that their chimpanzee Washoe, who had been taught in American Sign language for the deaf (ASL) used her signs 'in strings of two or more...in 29 different two-sign combinations and four different combinations of three signs'. ...By 1980, it became apparent that the evidence purporting to show that apes can create sentences could be explained without any reference to grammatical competence. ...in each case, what is learned is a *rote sequence*. It would be just as erroneous to interpret a rote sequence of pecks [by a trained pigeon] to the colours red, green, yellow and blue in that order, as a sentence, as a sentence meaning PLEASE MACHINE GIVE GRAIN as it would be to interpret the sequence that a person produces while operating a bank cash machine as a sentence meaning PLEASE MACHINE GIVE CASH.

It is conventional to assume that the need for speech as we understand it began with the development of hominids after their transition into hunters on the plains around two million years ago, when the increased need for communication is obvious — cooperative signals, plans of attack, recounting the layout of the land, and even the hunter's tale all have their part (e.g. [2]). (The failure of experiments with chimpanzees may simply be due to the lack of this type of motivation.) Clearly the age at which speech developed can only be inferred indirectly and approximately, but it is likely to be of the order of a million years.

When we come to formal systems we are on rather different ground. Here we are positing an explicit set of rules which can be recognized as a formula that is adequate for achieving some specified ends. Thus the calculation of areas in the Nile flood plain formed such a system. The architypes of these are Aristotle's logic and Euclid's geometry. One may exclude counting but include a proper understanding of arithmetic operations (addition etc.). Thus the development of formal systems are already mature with the Greeks in the first millenium b.c., but they would not appear to be too much older. Perhaps the only way to gauge their age is to extrapolate backwards from the known history counting the number of different formal systems developed. Though this exercise would need to be carried out scientifically, one might hypothesize a co-occurrence with writing systems, which developed from 3,000 b.c. to 1,500 b.c. A link between the "objectifying" of an idea by writing it down, and the recognition of a formal set of rules would appear plausible.

Thus we have three very widely different dates: 500 million years for intelligent behaviour, 1 million years for language, 5,000 years for formal systems.

The primary reason for recalling this progression is to point out that, historically at least, language arose in creatures that were intelligent and formal systems arose in creatures that had language. Of the three, intelligence is undoubtedly the most complex, since it produces the other two in any human individual, and may well be the most complex of all artifacts.

We may also point out two very obvious points about language which are often overlooked by computer scientists: first, there is no reason to expect that human language could be elegantly formalized in a general fashion. This is easy to demonstrate in the area of lexical semantics, because the meanings of words are essentially fuzzy and vary from one person to another. But syntax is equally variable and it may be only the influence of writing that has made it as standard as it is now. Second, language depends intrinsically on many of the abilities which we share with the animals: the ability to recognize items within categories (pigeons are adept at this), form plans (as one can observe in any dog) etc. If we aver that these are essentially symbolic, then we have to widen substantially the class of animals that can perform such actions (there is no intrinsic objection to this though we might need to redefine what we mean by symbols).

But the most important point of all has not to do with science or philosophy but with engineering. Animals are self-sustaining and propagating entities. The will to survive is the most basic of instincts. In this they differ totally from current computers, which are artifacts which derive all their abilities second-hand from their manufacturers and programmers. Any attempt to replicate brain features which ignores this basic motivating force must be suspect if as seems evident, brain function as we know it is essentially a control function for a body. The disappointing results of the first forty years of research into AI would seem to confirm this. For the first time biologists are pursuing distinctively biological models of intelligence. For instance, Reeke and Edelman [25]:

> It is very curious that AI, even in its new connectionist guise, has for the most part neglected the fundamental biology of the nervous system, from which the very definition of intelligence is derived. We suggest that in order to make progress in overcoming the obstacles we have discussed, AI must recognize these origins and incorporate what can be learned from a study of nervous systems....This change will require AI to abandon the notion of intelligence as a purely abstract information-processing device.

What the analysis above does *not* prove of course is that it is impossible to represent the totality of intelligent behaviour as a mathematical function. While it can be realized, in theory, in a totally non-illuminating simulation, as discussed in Moss [23], the Church-Turing thesis has always been one of the strongest motivations behind the quest for AI, though its proponents are usually cautious about the way in which they use the argument. Two of the less cautious are Churchland and Churchland [3]:

> These two results [Church's & Turing's] entail something remarkable, namely that a ...suitably programmed symbol manipulating machine should be able to pass the Turing test for conscious intelligence.

Yet even they do not accept either the Turing test or any recognizable definition of computer:

> When brains are said to be computers, it should not be implied that they are serial digital computers, that they are programmed,

that they exhibit the distinction between hardware and software or that they must be symbol manipulators or rule followers. Brains are computers in a radically different style.

It seems that there is an increasing agreement that whatever the Church-Turing thesis proves, it does *not* justify the belief that intelligence can be achieved by programming.

4 Logic or Cognition

Logic as classically understood is simply a manipulation of symbols, which, as Hobbes recognized, are names of things. These symbols are empty of meaning, except when considered as a relation between a symbol and an object in the world. How the symbols behave logically simply accords with the rules of logic. It is a game. To relate the symbols to the world one uses the concept of a *model*. This is an explication of the correspondence between true statements of the logic system and what is believed to be true in the world.

An attempt to change this definition was made by Newell and Simon [24] in their definition of a "physical symbol system". This is an entirely materialistic interpretation of mind, expressing the fact that the computers behave in accordance with physical laws. They introduce new definitions of the notions of *designation* and *interpretation*:

> *Designation.* An expression designates an object if, given the expression, the system can either affect the object itself or behave in ways dependent on the object.

This presupposes a direct interaction between the "system", which is a symbol manipulating machine, and the objects of the world, which encompass both symbols and everything else. Their definition of interpretation mirrors the normal computer use of this word rather than the logical use:

> *Interpretation.* The system can interpret an expression if the expression designates a process and if, given the expression, the system can carry out the process.

So physical symbols have some direct connection with the world, unlike human symbols, whose connection with the world is mysterious, and logical symbols, which have no connection except that agreed by their users.

But what is the nature of this connection? Here Newell and Simon are evasive. Indeed many of the types of designation they talk about are not covered by the definition above.

A symbol may be used to designate any expression whatsoever

This appears to correspond to the notion of a variable in a computer process; i.e. a symbol which has as its value another symbol, which association can be changed arbitrarily. It is not clear how the symbol "affects" its value. Indeed all that has happened is a canonization of existing practice:

> The type of system we have just defined is not unfamiliar to computer scientists. It bears a a strong family resemblance to all general purpose computers. If a symbol manipulation language, such as LISP, is taken as defining a machine, then the kinship becomes truly brotherly.

It is not necessary to recount the dissatisfaction that has subsequently been expressed with this type of system as a way of explaining how things are. AI has tried and failed in its attempt (and this is only one of several) to replace more traditional understandings of meaning, such as logic, by a new "procedural" understanding.

But given the nature of the problem that AI has set itself, problems will recur over the nature of symbolic systems. An example is the frame problem [20]: what stays constant and what changes in a changing world? The combinatorial problem that results derives from the fact that one is essentially trying to perform a simulation of an extremely complex situation. Is this how an animal copes with, for instance, a planning situation? Almost certainly not. By a combination of remembering similar situations and real-time feedback from the current situation it avoids nearly all of the difficult task of simulation. Its strategy copes at the same time with the closely allied problem of a simulation which omits some vital detail and is thereby "fragile".

The frame problem is thus a symptom of a deeper malaise which Harnad [10] has christened the "symbol grounding problem": how it is that a symbol acquires its "grounding" in the world. This is *not* a problem of logic but one of *cognition*. To attempt to tackle this problem within a logical framework is inappropriate. To quote again from Reeke and Edelman [25]

> The essential requirement for learning, logic and the other mental functions of AI research is the prior ability to categorize objects and events based on sensory signals reaching the brain. ...The categories themselves are not present in the environment but must be

constructed by each individual according to what is adaptive for its species and its particular circumstances. ... Our first task, then, is to build a satisfactory theory that goes beyond the formal processing of information to a consideration of how that information comes to exist in an unlabeled world, what relationship exists between signals in the brain and the categories it has constructed, and how the interactions of those signals yield behaviour without the benefit of prearranged algorithms to process them.

We can illustrate this problem with a simple example. Most adults can tell the difference between "left" and "right" reliably although children have a great deal of difficulty. Yet the author has observed the following phenomenon several times when navigating for other car drivers on the road. Take a driver who normally drives on the left hand side of the road to a country where one drives on the right hand side (or vice versa). If you say "turn right" to the driver, they are quite likely to turn left; if you say "turn left" they are quite likely to turn right.

What is happening? I would suggest that there is an unconscious association of "right" with the concept "across the traffic" and "left" with "away from the traffic" (and the converse for someone who normally drives on the right). Moving from one country to another changes this association and causes the error. If this is brought to the person's conscious attention they will correct themselves and indeed slowly "undo" the association.

Thus the brain is operating in a way that is unobserved by the individual and even working against the "proper" definition of the words. This "labelling" is an example of what is occurring all the time whether we are aware of it or not.

If we want to construct intelligent artifacts and Reeke and Edelman's analysis is correct, then we need to establish an interface between the approaches to cognition and the inference systems that can control what is done with the information so created. The sensible goal is a partnership, not a competition.

Indeed the major shift that occurred during the late 1970's and 80's was the emergence of the discipline of cognitive science (see for instance [7]) as a meeting point between psychologists, linguists and computer scientists. Its aim was not to create intelligence but to understand it. The computer was seen as a tool for testing hypotheses about the functioning of the brain and for clarifying the nature of mind. In this endeavour logic can play a double role both as formalism and computer representation.

The more radical outworkings of the ideas of cognition can lead to some significant differences in the interpretation of semantics. For instance, Jackendoff [15] points out the centrality of the perceived world to an individual making a statement (which may be as much about a dream or a pain, as about a event in the outside world) and thereby challenges the traditional notion of truth:

> We have conscious access only to the projected world — the world as unconsciously organized by the mind; and we can talk about things only insofar as they have achieved mental representation through these processes of organization. ...we must question the centrality to natural language semantics of the notions of truth and reference as traditionally conceived. Truth is generally regarded as a relationship between a certain subset of sentences (the true ones) and the real world; reference is regarded as a relationship between expressions in a language and things in the real world that these expressions refer to. Having rejected the direct connection of the real world to language, we should not take these notions as starting points for a theory of meaning[p. 29].

This difference in perspective leads Jackendoff to some valuable insights in, for instance, the analysis of word meanings and spatial expressions, that would be difficult otherwise.

It can also affect the way in which computer systems are designed. We suggested in an earlier section that the emergence of formal systems was approximately contemporaneous with the emergence of writing systems. Writing has played a highly significant role in the development of human culture: for instance most of the world religions were established soon after writing became widespread and used the new medium to record and spread their ideas. Computers have the potential for revolutionizing the way in which knowledge is recorded and disseminated and logical inference is an essential part of this process. But we need to recognize what is hard or even impossible for computers to recognize unaided.

An example suggested by Winograd [31] is called a "coordinator system". This recognizes the function of language referred to as "speech acts" — whether a sentence is used to make a request, answer one, give a command etc. But because it is very often an extremely subtle matter to deduce these functions from natural language, the system expects these functions to be indicated explicitly. In this way we utilize our understanding of the ways in which language works without requiring the computer system to be totally intelligent.

5   Conclusions

We have tried to show that much confusion has been caused within computing by the failure to distinguish various manifestations of intelligence. By
distinguishing the levels of formalized reasoning, natural language and animal behaviour one can clarify the contribution of each. Whereas formalized
reasoning is essentially symbolic, it is unlikely that abilities shared by most
animals will themselves be symbolic in nature in our brains. Natural language is a borderline case: it is intended for intelligent recipients and so its
interpretation in general depends on intelligence.

Systems based on logic do not necessarily encounter the problems faced by
AI, but only by being aware of these problems and staying abreast of developments in cognitive science. It is often better from an engineering point of
view to avoid the problem rather than try to solve it.

References

[1] A. Augusta. Notes on the memoir sketch of the analytic machine in-
    vented by Charles Babbage, by L.F. Menabrea. In P.Morrison and
    E.Morrison, editors, *Charles Babbage and his Calculating Engines*.
    Dover Publications, 1842.

[2] B. B. Beck. Tools and intelligence. In Hoage and Goldman [12].

[3] P. M. Churchland and P. M. Churchland. Could a machine think? *Sci-
    entific American*, 262(1):26–31, 1990.

[4] *Dictionary of the English Language*. Collins, 1976.

[5] V. J. Cook. *Chomsky's Universal Grammar*. Basil Blackwell Ltd, Ox-
    ford, 1988.

[6] H. L. Dreyfus and S. E. Dreyfus. Making a mind versus modelling a
    brain. In Graubard [9].

[7] H. Gardner. *The Mind's new Science. A history of the Cognitive Revo-
    lution*. Basic Books, New York, 1985.

[8] J. L. Gould and Carol Grant Gould. Invertebrate intelligence. In Hoage
    and Goldman [12].

[9] S.R. Graubard, editor. *The Artificial Intelligence Debate*. MIT Press,
    1988.

[10] S. Harnad. Category induction and representation. In S. Harnad, editor, *Categorical Perception: the Groundwork of Cognition.* Cambridge University Press, New York, 1987.

[11] J. Haugeland. *Artificial Intelligence: The Very Idea.* MIT Press, Cambridge, 1985.

[12] R. J. Hoage and L. Goldman, editors. *Animal Intelligence.* Smithsonian Institution Press, 1986.

[13] T. Hobbes. *Leviathan.* Everyman's Library. J.M.Dent & Sons, London, 1914. Originally published in 1651.

[14] J.J. Hopfield. Neural networks and physical systems with emergent collective computational abilities. *Proc. Nat. Acad. of Sciences*, 79:2254, 1982.

[15] R. Jackendoff. *Semantics and Cognition.* MIT Press, Cambridge, London, 1983.

[16] S. Johnson. *A Dictionary of the English Language.* Henry G. Bone, London, 1752.

[17] R. A. Kowalski. Predicate logic as programming language. In *Proc IFIP 74*, pages 569–574. North-Holland, 1974.

[18] D. Lenat, M. Prakash, and M. Shepherd. CYC: Using commonsense knowledge to overcome brittleness and knowledge acquisition bottlenecks. *AI Magazine*, 6(2), 1988.

[19] C. Longuet-Higgins. To the mind via semantics. In A. Kenny, H. Longuet-Higgins, J. Lucas, and C. Waddington, editors, *The Nature of Mind.* Edinburgh University Press, 1972.

[20] J. McCarthy and P.J. Hayes. Some philosophical problems for the standpoint of artificial intelligence. In D. Michie and B. Meltzer, editors, *Machine Intelligence 4*, pages 463–502. Edinburgh University Press, 1969.

[21] M. Minsky and S. Papert. *Perceptrons: An Introduction to Computational Geometry.* MIT Press, 1969.

[22] R. Montague. English as a formal language. In R.H.Thomason, editor, *Formal Philosophy: Selected Papers of Richard Montague.* Yale University Press, New Haven, 1970.

[23] C. D. S. Moss. Artificial intelligence and symbols. *Artificial Intelligence and Society*, 3(4), 1989.

[24] A. Newell and H. Simon. Computer science as empirical inquiry: Symbols and search. Turing award lecture. *CACM*, 1976.

[25] G. N. Reeke, Jr. and G.M. Edelman. Real brains and artificial intelligence. In Graubard [9].

[26] D.E. Rumelhart and J.L. McClelland, editors. *Parallel Distributed Processing: Explorations in the Microstructure of Cognition*. MIT Press, Cambridge, 1986.

[27] H.S. Terrace. In C. Blakemore, editor, *Mindwaves*. Oxford University Press, 1987.

[28] R.K. Thomas. Vertebrate intelligence: A review of the laboratory research. In Hoage and Goldman [12].

[29] A. Turing. Computing machinery and intelligence. *Mind*, 59:434–60, 1950.

[30] T. Winograd. *Understanding Natural Language*. Academic Press, New York, 1972.

[31] T. Winograd. Computer software for working with language. *Scientific American*, 1987.

[32] T. Winograd and F. Flores. *Understanding Computers and Cognition*. Ablex, New Jersey, 1986.

[33] P. H. Winston. *Artificial Intelligence*. Addison-Wesley, Reading, Mass, 2nd edition edition, 1984.

A Model for OR-Parallel Prolog Execution using Graph Reduction

S. M. S. Syed-Mustaffa

Abstract

The concept of graph reduction has been used, in recent times, as a model for functional language implementation. The aim here is to show how graph reduction and its associated techniques can be extended and applied to an implementation of OR-parallel Prolog. In applying the technique to OR-parallel Prolog, the first concept that will be presented is a visual representation of OR-parallel graphs. These graphs are different from the usual AND-OR trees in that they are used only for exhibiting OR-parallel execution via a series of graph rewritings. These rewrites are determined by the computation rule which, in this case, incorporates OR-parallelism in the usual SLD-resolution mechanism of Prolog. In moving towards a more concrete representation, for the purpose of implementation, each node of a graph is transformed into a packet. An attractive feature of graph reduction is that it lends itself naturally to parallel execution. If a parallel machine were used to execute graph reduction each of the packets can be thought of as a process. The parallel architecture that is used in this case, i.e. the Flagship machine, is a non-shared memory multiprocessor. In order to efficiently exploit the parallelism of the machine the execution model must ensure as much locality as possible. The method that has been employed in this case is the closed environments method. The application of the method using the packet based model is explained.

1 Introduction

In the last few years the concept of graph reduction has been used extensively in the exploitation of parallelism in functional programming languages. Its use ranges from the abstract representation of parallel execution of such programs to the construction of parallel (graph-reduction) machines [7, 5]. The

227

Flagship machine [9, 8] is a particular example of a graph-reduction machine which can efficiently execute functional programs in parallel. Whereas most of the work done on the Flagship project has concentrated on functional programming, the work described here is an implementation of OR-parallel Prolog based on the Flagship architecture. Since the Flagship machine is a non-shared memory multiprocessor, to reduce the overheads of communication requires as little inter-processor communication as possible. Thus any program which is able to spawn independent processes, which may subsequently be executed on different processors, serves as a good starting point in the exploitation of parallelism on the Flagship machine. As far as logic programming is concerned, OR-parallel programs satisfy this initial criterion. A particular implementation of OR-parallel Prolog based on the Flagship architecture is described here. An outline of the Flagship machine architecture and the method of graph reduction applied to functional programs is presented first. These will introduce the basic concepts from which extensions will be introduced in the implementation of OR-parallel Prolog on the Flagship machine.

2   Functional Program Execution on the Flagship Machine

The starting point in the construction of the Flagship machine is that it is intended to be a very efficient machine in the execution of functional programs. One of the ways of viewing functional program execution is via graph reduction. This methodology views programs as graphs and the execution of a program is done by a sequence of modifications on the graph. The modifications are determined by the rewrite rules which constitute the program. The computation starts from a graph representing the initial expression to be reduced and terminates in a graph representing its normal form.

As an example consider the program for defining the Fibonnaci sequence written in Hope [1].

$$fib(0) \Leftarrow 1;   \qquad \text{% rule 1}$$
$$fib(1) \Leftarrow 1;   \qquad \text{% rule 2}$$
$$fib(n) \Leftarrow fib(n-1) + fib(n-2);   \qquad \text{% rule 3}$$

To illustrate diagrammatically the way in which graph reduction is performed the reduction of the initial redex fib(2) is shown in Figure 1.

One of the characteristic features of graph reduction is that it exhibits the possibility of parallel execution. This is explicit in the second graph above

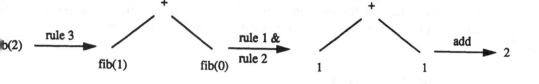

Figure 1: Reduction of `fib(2)`

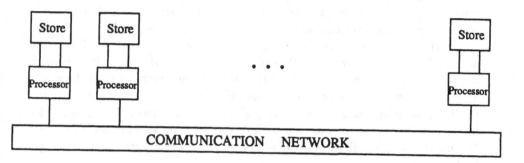

Figure 2: The Flagship machine architecture

whereby both the subgraphs $fib(1)$ and $fib(0)$ can be evaluated independently, and therefore, in parallel. A machine that would best suit the requirements for such computations would necessarily treat its programs as graphs and reduce them by graph reduction. In order to exploit the parallelism inherent in the program it would also need to be a parallel machine.

The Flagship machine is based on these principles and it is, physically, a non-shared memory multiprocessor. Within this framework the machine consists of closely-coupled processor-store pairs which are connected together via a communication network (see Figure 2).

It is to be expected, therefore, that the execution of parallel programs on the Flagship machine allows the possibility of computations performed on different processing elements. In addition to this a particular graph (especially if it is a very large one) may have its subgraphs distributed over different processing elements. Any computation involving inter-procesor communication would necessarily reduce the speed of that computation. Thus the locality of computations is an important factor in determining the speed of computations.

This is one of the main factors that will be addressed in the execution of

OR-parallel Prolog on the Flagship machine. Before getting to the implementation details of the method employed a visual representation of graph reduction applied to logic programming execution is presented below.

3   OR-Parallel Graphs

In applying graph reduction to OR-parallel Prolog a computation views the initial goal to be solved as a graph and the program clauses constitute the rewrite (or reduction) rules. These graphs are represented in a similar way to the ones in the previous section in the sense that the graphs reflect the transformations that the initial graph undergoes as subsequent rewrite rules are applied. This concept is different from the AND-OR trees [3] whereby the paths of a tree constitute a derivation of the results starting from the goal at the root node. However since the model of computation is an extension of SLD-resolution the graphs are very similar to SLD-trees [4]. Instead of having one SLD-tree to trace the path of the program execution a series of OR-parallel graphs will show the different phases of the program as it is being reduced.

As an example consider the familiar Prolog program which defines a grand-parent-grandchild relationship :

```
p(a, b).
p(b, c).
p(b, d).
g(X, Y) :-
    p(X, Z),
    p(Z, Y).
?- g(A, B).
```

The object of this program is to find pairs, A and B, such that the relationship $g(A, B)$ is satisfied, i.e. some A is the grandparent of B. OR-parallelism is possible if a goal predicate matches more than one head predicate of a clause.

In the following diagrams OR-parallelism is indicated whenever a goal spawns two branches of matching head clauses. The variable bindings are represented by the θi's. The variable bindings in this case is the usual one employed by Prolog; i.e. given a chain of variable bindings, in the case of variable-to-variable bindings, variables lower down the tree diagram dereference to variables higher up.

?- g(A, B).

Figure 3: The initial graph

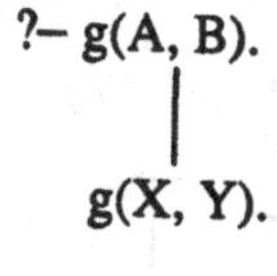

?- g(A, B).
|
g(X, Y).

Figure 4: Matching

Using the grand-parent program, the initial graph is simply the representation of the initial goal (Figure 3).

The goal matches with only one program clause (Figure 4).

On unifying, the substitution, $\theta 1$ is indicated along the arc of the tree and the head of the program clause can now be replaced by (the goals that make up) its body (Figure 5).

The goal that is to be executed next, i.e. the "active" goal, is ?- p(X, Z). This goal can match with the three clauses that define the parent-of relationships (Figure 6).

This goal unifies successfully with each of the three facts producing substitutions $\theta 2$, $\theta 3$, $\theta 4$ as indicated in Figure 7. Additionally the successful unifications result in the rewriting of the unit clauses to null clauses which are denoted by □. This is to be expected since unit clauses such as p(a, b). can be thought of as the program clause p(a, b) :- □.

So far the OR-parallel graph has progressively expanded as the computation proceeded. The effect of the, successful, null clauses is to collapse the graph by one level and activate the next goal. The goal ?- p(A, Z) has succeeded

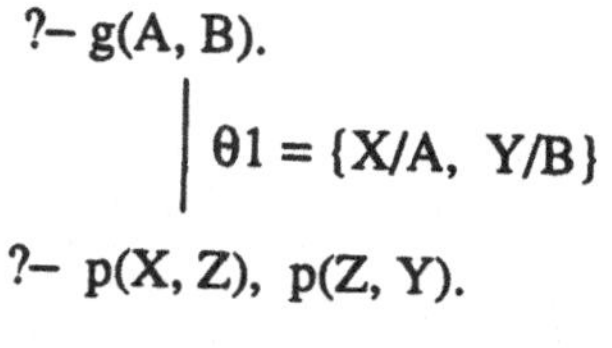

?- g(A, B).

$\theta 1 = \{X/A, \ Y/B\}$

?- p(X, Z), p(Z, Y).

Figure 5: Unifying

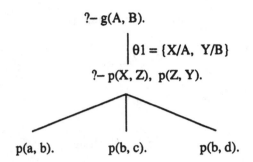

Figure 6: Matching

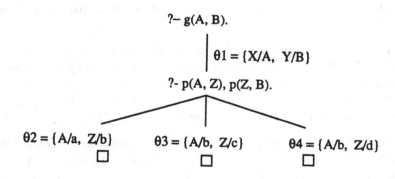

Figure 7: Unifying

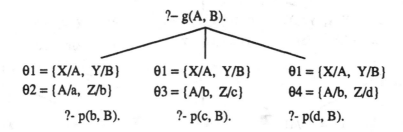

Figure 8: Applying substitutions

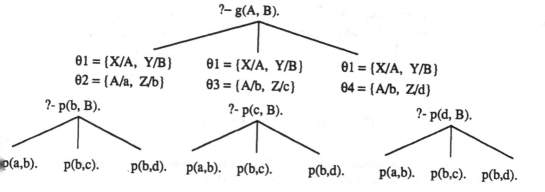

Figure 9: Matching

and the next goal to be executed is ?- p(Z, B). The previous unifications, performed in OR-parallel, also resulted in the substitutions $\theta 2$, $\theta 3$, and $\theta 4$. Applying these substitutions, appropriately, to the goal ?- p(Z, B) results in Figure 8.

Each of these active goals can now match with the fact clauses (Figure 9).

Unification results in only two successful cases, denoted by the null clauses together with the associated substitutions, and each of the remaining failure cases are denoted by the failure clause (Figure 10). A failure clause is denoted by ■.

All the leaves of the graph are either successful (i.e. null) or failure clauses. The graph can be further collapsed because of each of these. At this point it is wise to ignore the failure cases and the graph can be pruned and reduced as in Figure 11.

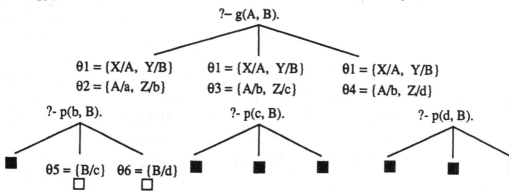

Figure 10: Unifying

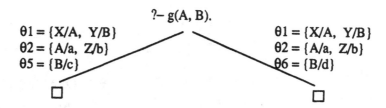

Figure 11: Pruning out the failure cases

Finally the substitutions can be applied to the variables in the original goal to yield the results: $\{A/a, B/c\}$ and $\{A/a, B/d\}$.

These diagrams also illustrate, very cursorily, a number of potential problems in the implementation of OR-parallel Prolog. The first of these is that, wherever there is an OR-branch, every child goal needs to have its own copy of the parent goal's variables to avoid a clash in the instantiation of these variables. This can be seen, for example, in Figure 7 where the variables A and Z are bound differently in the substitutions $\theta2$, $\theta3$ and $\theta4$. However this problem, the multiple bindings problem, is common to all implementations of OR-parallel Prolog and is not unique to any particular type of parallel architecture.

A problem that is specific to the Flagship machine, however, is the way in which the bindings environment is implemented. In most Prolog implementations, the binding environment is a single large data structure. If such a schema were adopted on a non-shared memory implementation then the need arises for maintaining some sort of single memory address space for the environment. This results in the problem of non-local accesses.

In the normal (Warren Abstract Machine [6]) implementation of the bindings environment, the result of a variable-to-variable binding is that "younger" variables lower down the tree dereference to "older" variables further up the tree, e.g. in Figure 5 the bindings in the substitution $\theta 1$ are X/A and Y/B. In a nonshared memory implementation this may reduce performance if the tree is arbitrarily deep; for example, in the worst possible case, if a variable at the leaf dereferences to a variable at the root such that the leaf and the root are held in different stores (due to the distribution of the bindings environment) then the dereferencing requires an inter-processor communication. If there are a lot of such cases then the overheads in interprocessor communication will hamper any possible speed-ups.

In brief, therefore, a conventional approach to OR-parallel implementation on a Flagship-type machine results in the problems of non-locality. To overcome the problem above a method has been devised, known as the "closed environments method" [2], which is described below.

4   The Closed Environments Method

Before describing the closed environments method it is necessary to describe the framework within which the method will be applied. This includes a description of the representation of terms, and definitions of stack frames and environments. These are defined below.

Definition 1 (representation of terms) *Terms are represented as* tagged cells *whereby non-structure terms, i.e. constants and variables, and pointers to other terms occupy one cell. Structured terms, of the form $f(T_1, \ldots, T_n)$ are stored using consecutive cells with the first cell for the functor and the remaining cells for the arguments.*

Definition 2 (frame) *A* stack frame, *or* frame *for short, consists of an array of cells. The number of cells in a frame correspond to the number of different variables in the frame.*

Definition 3 (environment) *An* environment *consists of a set of frames.*

In carrying out a unification a frame corresponding to the goal is set up containing all the variables of the goal. This frame is referred to as the *top frame*. If there is a matching clause then a new frame is constructed for the clause containing all the variables of the clause. This frame is known as the *bottom frame*. All the variables in the initial top frame and all variables in the bottom frame are initially set to unbound. When two unbound variables are unified a relative pointer, known as a *link*, is used to indicate the binding of one to the other.

The first problem of locality that has to be solved is the locality of variable bindings. In this case the closed environments method reverses the direction of the bindings of variables in the bottom frame to terms in the top frame. This is performed as follows.

Consider unifying a term T in the top frame (i.e. from the goal) and an unbound variable V in the bottom frame (i.e. from the matching clause). Unification results in V dereferencing to T, i.e. there is a link from V to T. The closure procedure can be subdivided into two sub-procedures depending on the nature of T.

If T is a non-structural term, i.e. it is either a constant or a variable, then :

1. if T is a constant then bind V to T;

2. if T is an unbound variable then dereference T to V, i.e. the link from V to T is reversed and T now points to V; and

3. if T is a variable which dereferences to a variable X (and $X \neq V$), where X belongs to the same frame as V does, i.e. the bottom frame, then dereference V to X.

If T is a structural term, of the form $f(T_1, \ldots, T_n)$, then for each argument T_i that dereferences to a link in the top frame :

4. if T_i is a non-variable term, U, then replace T_i by U and repeat this procedure on the terms of U;

5. if T_i dereferences to an unbound variable in the bottom frame then replace T_i with a link to that variable; and

6. if T_i dereferences to an unbound variable V_t in the top frame then create a new unbound variable V_b in the bottom frame, replace T_i with a link to V_b and bind V_t to V_b.

When the closure procedure has been applied to the two frames all the variables in the bottom frame no longer dereference to any term in the top frame. The bottom frame is now said to be *closed*, i.e.

Definition 4 (closed frame) *A closed frame is a frame in which all the references, of the cells in the frame, are within that frame only. It does* not however preclude the possibility of pointers originating from other frames pointing to it.

Hence a *closed environment* can be defined as follows.

Definition 5 (closed environment) *Given a set of frames that constitute an environment, E say, a* closed environment *is one in which there are no cells, in any of the frames in E, that dereference to cells that are not in E.*

The closure procedure solves the problem of locality of variable dereferencing. In doing so the closure procedure updates the state of the variables in the top frame after unification. In order to secure the locality of the binding environment the following control flow must be complied with.

So far the computation involves only unification and closure which can be summarised as follows.

1. Before unification is performed two frames are set up corresponding to the goal and the matching clause i.e. the top and bottom frames respectively.

2. The cells of the bottom frame, which represent all the variables of the matching clause are initially set to unbound.

3. When the top frame and the bottom frame have been unified, the bottom frame is closed with respect to the top frame by application of the closure procedure.

On completion of the application of the closure procedure the bottom frame is closed with respect to the top frame. These steps ensure that :

• the frame corresponding to the first goal is always closed;

• the corresponding bottom frame for the matching clause is always initially closed since it only contains unbound variables;

• the two frames together constitute a closed environment; and

• after unification and closure the bottom frame is always closed and is ready to initiate the next unification.

The closed bottom frame corresponds to the first goal of the resolvent of the previous unification and therefore represents the subsequent goal to be solved. In order to satisfy the second locality condition, i.e. the locality of binding environments three further measures have to be observed. These are as follows.

4. If the matching clause is a unit clause then the top frame is closed with respect to the bottom frame and the bottom frame can then be discarded. Unlike the steps above, which expand the execution tree, this step reduces it. The closed top frame can then be used to solve any subsequent sibling subgoal.

5. If the matching clause is a program clause then the closed bottom frame, which corresponds to the first subgoal in the body of the clause, now becomes the top frame and a new bottom frame is created corresponding to the clause matching the subgoal. The unification and closure operations are repeated, as above, until there are no more subgoals to be solved.

6. If there are no more subgoals to be solved then the top frame of the last subgoal is closed with respect to the bottom frame. The closed top frame can now be used to solve sibling goals.

The application of this technique to OR-parallel Prolog is presented below.

5   The OR-Parallel Packet-Based Model

The ideas that have been presented in the last two sections are now combined to produce a model that can easily be implemented on the Flagship machine. The first step involves a move from the abstract graph representation, in Section 3, to a more concrete representation. For a Flagship model, quite naturally, this means that nodes of the graph are now represented as packets. The packet structure that will be adopted is summarised as follows :

$$
\begin{aligned}
\langle packet\rangle &::= \langle packet\_state\rangle\langle packet\_fields\rangle \\
\langle packet\_state\rangle &::= \langle ground\rangle|\langle active\rangle|\langle dormant\rangle|\langle suspended\rangle \\
\langle packet\_fields\rangle &::= \langle continuation\rangle\langle parent\rangle\langle bindings\_list\rangle \\
\langle continuation\rangle &::= \langle ans\rangle|\langle c\_end\rangle|\langle user-defined\ function\rangle \\
\langle parent\rangle &::= \langle root\rangle|\uparrow\langle packet\rangle \\
\langle bindings\_list\rangle &::= []|\langle binding\rangle\langle bindings\_list\rangle \\
\langle binding\rangle &::= \langle variable\_identifier\rangle : \langle variable\_state\rangle \\
\langle variable\_state\rangle &::= \langle Ubv\rangle|\langle identifier\rangle|@\langle identifier\rangle
\end{aligned}
$$

The nodes of a graph are represented by packets and the pointers from child packets to their parents form the arcs of a graph. Each packet can have one of four states, as defined above. These are the usual packet states used in Flagship. The usual packet annotations apply, i.e.

! denotes an active packet,

˜ denotes a dormant packet, and

# denotes a suspended packet.

A ground packet does not have any annotation.

An active packet is one in which the function contained in its "continuation" field is ready to be applied by the rewrite rules. A dormant packet is a packet that has been created and will be used later in the computation. An active packet is set to dormant if on application of the function in its "continuation" field results in the packet requiring a number of its bindings to be updated before the reduction of the packet can proceed further.

In applying the concepts of the closed environments method each packet may be viewed as a frame. Each packet has at least two fields, i.e. the "continuation" and a pointer to a parent packet with the exception of the initial, or root, packet which does not have a parent. A packet may also have a (variable length) list for storing the variable bindings associated with the packet.

The function defined in the "continuation" field dictates the control flow of the program. The "ans" function can only appear in the root packet. If the state of the root packet is active and the value of its "continuation" field is "ans" then this signifies that the program has terminated and that the results as represented by the bindings list may be output. The "c_end" is used in two situations. Firstly "c_end" is the function that is placed in the "continuation" field of packets corresponding to unit clauses. This corresponds to step 4 of the closed environments method as outlined in the preceding section. The other case in which "c_end" is placed in the "continuation" field corresponds to step 5, i.e. when the last subgoal from the list of goals in a matching clause has been executed then the top frame is closed with respect to the bottom frame. All the atomic formulae of the program constitute the remaining "user defined functions".

The variable bindings are contained in a bindings list. Each binding denotes whether a variable is unbound (Ubv), bound to a term, or dereferenced to another variable.

The basic execution step involves the unification and closing of two packets. One packet corresponds to a goal and the others correspond to the matching clauses. A general program is of the form :

$$q_1(\ldots) \quad :- \quad \ldots$$

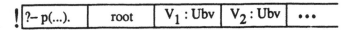

Figure 12: An active goal packet

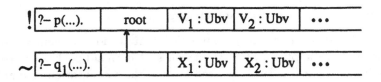

Figure 13: Matching packets

$$\vdots$$

$$q_m(\ldots) \quad :- \quad r_1(\ldots),\ldots,rk(\ldots).$$

$$\vdots$$

$$q_n(\ldots) \quad :- \quad \ldots$$

$$\vdots$$

$$p(\ldots) \quad :- \quad q_1(\ldots),\ldots,q_m(\ldots),\ldots,q_n(\ldots).$$
$$?- \quad p(\ldots).$$

The execution mechanism using the packet-based model, incorporating the closed environments method, can be summarised as follows. Firstly a packet corresponding to the goal is constructed. The goal that is to be executed, i.e. $?- p(\ldots)$, is placed in the "continuation" field and since this is the initial packet it has no parents therefore "root" is placed in its parent field. The variables of p, if any, occupy one slot each in the bindings field and each is set to unbound. The state of this packet is active and this is diagrammatically represented as in Figure 12.

There is a clause whose head matches the goal, and a packet is set up for the clause. If unification of the goal with the clause is successful then the resolvent is $?- q_1(\ldots),\ldots,q_m(\ldots),\ldots,q_n(\ldots)$. This means that the first subgoal that has to be executed next is $?- q_1(\ldots)$. This is then placed in the "continuation" field of the child packet and its parent field naturally has a pointer to the root packet. All the variables of the clause, at this stage, are all unbound. So the current state of the packets is as in Figure 13.

If unification is successful then the variable bindings would have to be modified accordingly. In this case, for simplicity, X_1 is bound to V_1 and X_2

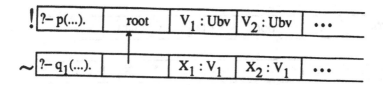

Figure 14: Successful unification of packets

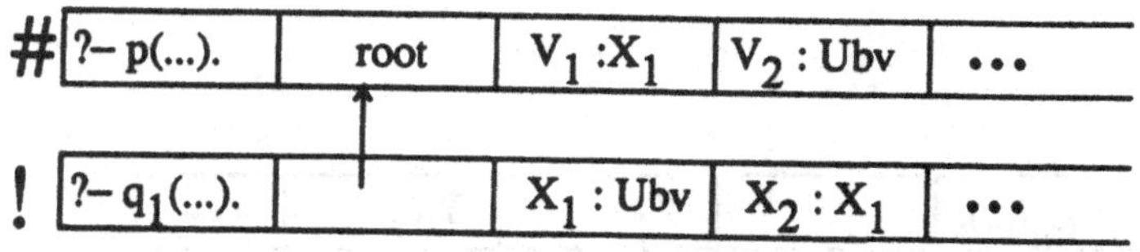

Figure 15: Closing (down)

is also bound to V_1. The "continuation" field of the parent (root) packet now becomes "ans". On completion of unification the graph, so far, is as in Figure 14.

The closing operation is applied, reversing the direction of the variable bindings, and the states of the packets are amended accordingly. The parent (root) packet is set to suspended, awaiting the results, while the child packet is set to active and is ready to perform the next unify and closing operations. This is represented in Figure 15.

Since there is a clause that matches the goal $?- q_1(\ldots)$ a packet is set up corresponding to the clause and the graph now becomes as in Figure 16.

The program proceeds with the unification and closing operations as these expand the graph as described above.

Let us consider a general position in the execution of the program, i.e. at the point when the subgoal $?- q_m(\ldots)$ is about to be executed. At this point the area of interest, of the graph, is shown in Figure 17.

Assume that there is a clause that matches this goal and that the two can be unified. If the matching clause is a program i.e.

$$q_m(\ldots) :- r_1(\ldots), \ldots, r_k(\ldots).$$

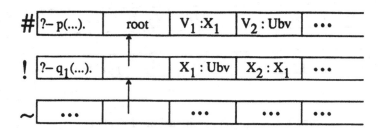

Figure 16: Matching the current active packet

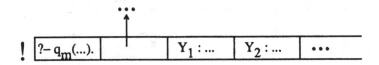

Figure 17: The part of the graph that is currently active

then the graph expansion continues in the fashion described so far. However if the matching clause is a unit clause, i.e. $k = 0$, then the packet corresponding to the unit clause has "c_end" as its "continuation" field. On completion of unification and closure the child packet is active. This part of the graph is represented in Figure 18.

On applying the "c_end" function, the top packet is closed with respect to the bottom packet and the top packet is now closed. This corresponds to step 4 of the closed environments method. The bottom packet can be garbage collected and the graph is reduced to that in Figure 19.

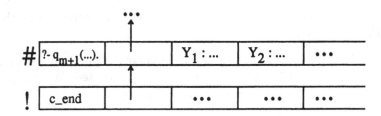

Figure 18: Matching results in a child packet that is a "c_end".

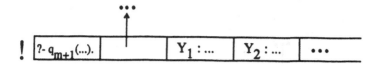

Figure 19: On closing (up) a "s_end" packet.

The computation can then proceed with the goal $?- q_{m+1}(\ldots)$.

The other case in which the "continuation" field of a packet is a "c_end" is at the point where the goal that is about to be executed is the last subgoal from a goal list. This is exemplified by the two cases $?- r_k$ and $?- q_n$. This corresponds to step 6 of the closed environments method. In each of these cases when the "c_end" function is applied to the packet the graph is reduced by one level.

So far the compound actions of unification and environment closing have only been considered for the case of a goal and one matching clause. If there is more than one clause that matches a goal, thereby resulting in OR-parallelism, the multiplicity of packets (corresponding to the OR-parallel choices) in forming the graph is an extension of the case considered so far. This extension comprises of two separate cases : graph expansion and graph reduction.

In the case of a goal having more than one matching clause each of its child packets would have the goal packet itself as its parent. For example, in the program :

$$p(X,Y) \quad :- \quad q_1(\ldots), q_2(\ldots), \ldots$$
$$p(X,Y) \quad :- \quad r_1(\ldots), r_2(\ldots), \ldots$$
$$?- \quad p(A,B).$$

the graph expansion after unification of the goal with the clauses and closing results in Figure 20.

Conversely if sibling packets are each in an active state and each has "c_end" as its "continuation" function then the graph can be reduced. In doing so copies of the parent packet are made to handle the different bindings imposed by each child packet.

As an example of this, consider the program fragment :

$$p(a).$$
$$p(b).$$
$$?- \quad \ldots, p(X), q(X), \ldots$$

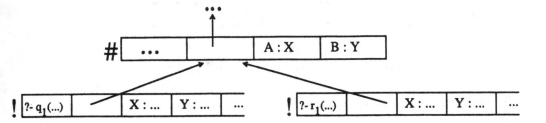

Figure 20: Multiple matching of packets

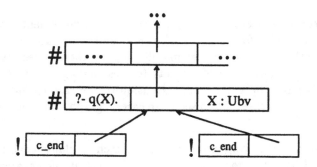

Figure 21: A graph with multiple "c_end" packets.

At the point where unification has succeeded in matching the goal $?- p(X)$ with the unit clauses the graph has the form in Figure 21.

On applying the "c_end" functions the parent packet is closed with respect to the children packets. The situation that now arises, as a result of the OR-parallel cases, is that different parent packets are needed to correspond to the different variable bindings. This means that another parent packet is needed to represent the two different bindings. On applying the "c_end" function to each of the child packets the graph reduces to Figure 22.

The grandparent example (Section 2) can be executed in OR-parallel since the goals $?- p(X, Z)$ and $?- p(Z, Y)$ can each match with the three unit clauses. The execution of this program, using packets and a computation rule that incorporates the closed environments method, is illustrated below.

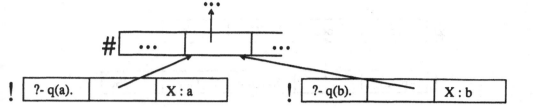

Figure 22: Result of reducing multiple "c_end" packets.

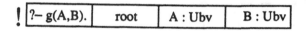

Figure 23: The initial packet.

6   Example : the grandparent program using packets

The execution is initiated by the goal $?- g(A, B)$. A packet is set up corresponding to the goal; this being the root packet means that it has "root" placed in its parent field. The computation proceeds by executing the goal itself so the goal is placed in the "continuation" field. The goal has two variables, A and B, and these form the elements of the bindings list. All variables are initially unbound, so the states of these two are set to "Ubv". This initial packet constitutes a closed environment.

The goal matches with the clause defining g and so a packet is set up for the matching clause. The parent of this packet is the root packet and a pointer is placed in the parent field of the child packet linking it to the root. The matching clause has three variables, namely X, Y and Z, and these are placed in the bindings list and each of them initially set to unbound. If unification is successful then the computation proceeds with the reduction of the resolvent of $?- g(A, B)$ with $g(X, Y) :- p(X, Z), p(Z, Y)$, i.e. $?- p(X, Z), p(Y, Z)$.' This means that the next goal to be solved is $?- p(X, Z)$ and it is placed in the "continuation" field. This child packet is also closed and these two packets together form a closed environment. Unification succeeds with X being bound to A and Y to B. The child packet is no longer closed since two of its variable bindings now dereference to terms belonging to a different packet. The closing operation is applied to the child packet with respect to

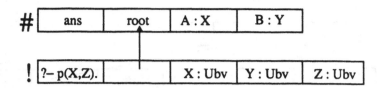

Figure 24: After matching, unifying and closing.

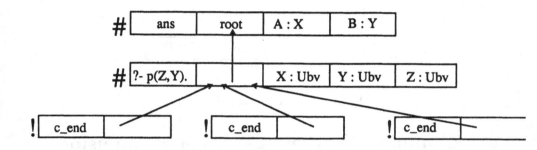

Figure 25: Three successful cases after closing (down).

the root packet and the net result is shown in Figure 24.

The child packet is now closed and it can therefore proceed with executing the goal $?- p(X, Z)$. There are now three matching unit clauses. A packet is set up corresponding to each and, being unit clauses, each has "c_end" in its "continuation" field and no bindings list.

The active child packet now becomes the parent packet in the next unification step and has three packets, corresponding to the unit clauses, as its children. Unification is successful and the parent packet's "continuation" field is set to $?- p(Z, Y)$ to activate the next goal when this packet is reactivated. On completion of closing the children packets are active and the "c_end" function is ready to be applied (Figure 25).

Applying the "c_end" function, i.e. the parent packet is closed with respect to the children packet, requires three copies of the parent packet : each corresponding to the different bindings imposed by the children packets. Each of these are then ready to be executed (Figure 26).

The three active sibling packets represent the goals $?- p(b, Y)$, $?- p(c, Y)$ and $?- p(d, Y)$. Each of these can match with the three unit clauses. The

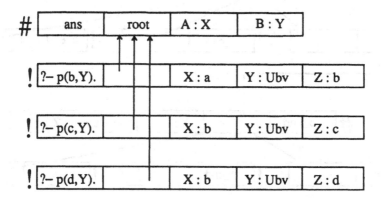

Figure 26: Copying as a result of closing (up).

result is a graph with nine active leaf packets (Figure 27).

Unification is successful in only two of these cases. This is reflected by the graph after the "c_end" function is applied to the nine active sibling packets (Figure 28).

The "c_end" functions can now be applied to the two successful cases and this results in two root packets representing the two results (Figure 29).

The "ans" function can then extract the results from the active root packets to yield the expected results.

7   Implementation Issues

Although this example has illustrated how a logic program may be executed by the use of graph reduction it has not considered any potential problems when such an activity is carried out during an actual program execution. A hint of one of the drawbacks of the method can be seen by having multiple copies of the parent packet during the closing up operation of OR-parallel sibling packets. Copying is even more problematical if the terms involved are structured terms. Furthermore structures can lead to even more problems related to unification, the backbone of the rewriting rule that has so far been kept in the background. These issues are examined below.

The first problem related to copying is that of copying structures when pack-

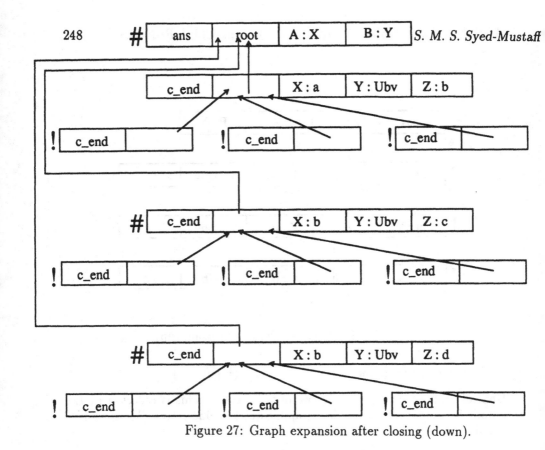

Figure 27: Graph expansion after closing (down).

Figure 28: Reduction of graph to successful packets only.

Figure 29: Final state of packets.

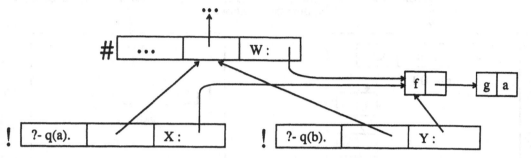

Figure 30: Structure sharing.

ets are exported to other processors. As an illustration of this, consider the program fragment :

$$p(X) \;\; :- \;\; \ldots$$
$$p(Y) \;\; :- \;\; \ldots$$
$$?- \;\; \ldots, p(W), \ldots$$

at the point where the variable W has already been instantiated to the term $f(g(a))$ and the unification and closure operations have been performed. The graph at this stage of the program is shown in Figure 30.

The term $f(g(a))$ is built in the heap using consecutive packets (see Definition 1). Ideally the structured term should be shared by the three packets. The diagrammatic representation of the graph does not convey any information regarding the spread of the graph over multiple processors and copying will be necessary should either, or both, of the two active child packets be exported to another processor. In such circumstances the structure can no longer be shared but must be copied and exported to the appropriate processor.

In this respect the implementation of the copying mechanism of the Flagship machine is not really helpful in the implementation of the type of copying that is required here. This is to be expected since the machine was primarily designed to handle functional languages and the kind of structure copying that occurs there is not as complicated as those encountered in logic programming. The copying mechanism on the Flagship machine does not allow the copying of whole graphs but, rather, a level of the graph at a time. Since structured terms are built up by the linking together of packets into a graph, in order to copy a term then requires a sequence of copying steps for every level that constitutes the term. Thus the copying of nested structures, that occur in logic programs, would decrease execution time.

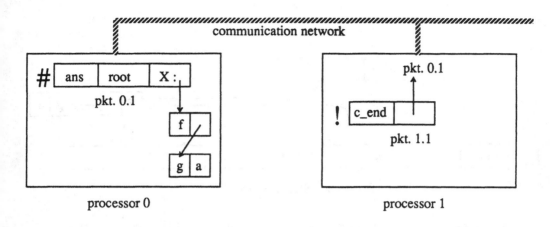

Figure 31: A graph distributed over two processors.

The other problem related to copying is the application of the "c_end" function, i.e. when a parent packet is closed (up) with respect to a child packet. A simple, but potentially problematical, case is the program :

$$p(f(g(a))).$$
$$?-\ p(X).$$

at the point when the "c_end" function is about to be applied to the active child packet. If the two packets involved are in two physically separate processors the distributed graph may be visually represented as in Figure 31.

Before the "c_end" function can be applied to the child packet (whose packet address is 1.1) it needs to have a local copy of its parent packet. This example illustrates the worst possible scenario in that the parent packet has a reference to a structured term which, in turn, needs to be copied as well.

In addition to the copying overheads, as shown above, structured terms can also add further overheads at run-time if the general unification procedure has to be used when unifying two terms. Although a compiletime analysis may usually reduce the complexity of unifying these terms there is one case which still needs to resort to the use of the full unification algorithm. As an illustration of this consider the program for appending lists

```
append([], L, L).
append([A|B], C, [A|D]) :-
    append(B, C, D).
?- append([1], [2], [1,X]).
```

The point of interest is at the second unification step, i.e. when the goal
?- append(B, C, D) is about to be unified with the unit clause. A compile
time analysis would breakdown the unification to the three specialised steps:

```
unify_variable_constant(B, []),
unify_variable_variable(C, L),
unify_variable_variable(D, L).
```

However the first unification step would have bound the variables A, B, C,
and D, i.e. A/1, B/[], C/[2], D/[X]. Thus by the time the second unification
is performed the unification steps that need to be performed are actually :

```
unify_constant_constant([], []),
unify_structure_variable([2], L),
unify_structure_structure([X], [2]).
```

The last of these specialised cases is radically different from the expected
step as predicted at the compiler stage. The problem with having to perform
general unification at run-time is that the rewrite rule needs to be more
complex to handle such a general case. However this is a general unification
problem rather than one that is specific to either the closed environments
method or the implementation that has been adopted.

8   Conclusions

The main conclusion that can be drawn from this work is that it is possible to execute logic programs using graph reduction performed on a graph
reduction machine. The implementation, based on the closed environments
method, was easily mapped onto the existing packet structure of the Flagship
machine without any significant alterations. The most important addition
is the introduction of the concept of a variable-to-variable binding. The
closed environments method has proved to be useful in the determination
of locality. However the copying mechanism, which is tailored to functional
programming execution, may result in inefficiencies when performing copying
of structures in logic programs. The work is still progressing and, therefore,
definite conclusions on the performance of the implementation cannot be
drawn.

Acknowledgements

The author would like to express his thanks to Paul Watson and Suresh Patel both of whom contributed significantly in the undertaking of this research project. Thanks also to John Keane and Fernando da Silva for the useful comments regarding the writing of this paper.

References

[1] R. M. Burstall, D. MacQueen, and D. T. Sannella. Hope : An experimental applicative language. Internal report, University of Edinburgh, 1980.

[2] J. Conery. Binding environments for parallel logic programs in non-shared memory multiprocessors. In *Proc. of the 4th. Symp. on Logic Programming*, pages 457–467, San Francisco, 1987.

[3] R. A. Kowalski. *Logic for Problem Solving.* North-Holland, 1979.

[4] J. W. Lloyd. *Foundations of Logic Programming.* Symbolic Computation Series. Springer Verlag, 2nd, extended edition edition, 1984.

[5] S. L. Peyton-Jones. *The Implementation of Functional Programming Languages.* Prentice-Hall, 1987.

[6] D. H. D. Warren. An abstract PROLOG instruction set. Technical Note 308, SRI, 1983.

[7] I. Watson, P. Watson, and V. Woods. Parallel data driven graph reduction. In *Proc. of the IFIP TC 10 Working Conf. on Fifth Generation Computer Architectures*, pages 203–220, Manchester, UK, 1986.

[8] I. Watson, V. Woods, P. Watson, R. Banach, M. Greenberg, and J. Sargeant. Flagship : A parallel architecture for declarative programming. In *15th. Annual Int. Symp. on Computer Architecture*, pages 124–129, Honolulu, Hawaii, 1988.

[9] P. Watson and I. Watson. Evaluating functional programs on the Flagship machine. In *Proc. of Functional Programming Languages and Computer Architecture*, volume 274 of *LNCS*, pages 80–97, Portland, Oregon, 1987. Springer Verlag.

Reconciling Systems and Deductive Capabilities in Knowledge Based Systems Using Logic Programming

Hamish Taylor

Abstract

A comprehensive approach to programming concurrent knowledge based systems in logic must cater for both knowledge processing and systems handling capabilities. This paper reviews requirements for supporting both capabilities in a resolution based framework, and considers logic programming schemes which sustain each kind of capability. It then considers attempts to reconcile these schemes to support both capabilities efficiently together. It argues that no approach so far advocated is ultimately satisfactory, although a hybrid approach of coupling resolution engines supporting each kind of capability is a workable compromise.

1 Introduction

This paper considers how the requirements for programming knowledge base querying and systems handling capabilities in logic interact with each other. It is argued that resolution which is open to interpretation as the execution of concurrent communicating processes and which can exhibit don't know non-determinism [20] is able to support the systems and knowledge base querying aspects of concurrent knowledge based systems. Being able to interpret resolution as the execution of concurrent communicating processes enables multiple interacting knowledge processing tasks to be executed, and resolution exhibiting don't know non-determinism enables query evaluation procedures to perform complete searches of knowledge bases top down. However, it has proved hard to combine the ability to support both kinds of resolution together in an efficient and expressive way. A number of different ways of reconciling their requirements are reviewed and their limitations discussed.

253

2   Programming Proof by Deduction in Logic

A knowledge base querying capability requires the combination of the following elements:

- knowledge representation scheme

- query evaluation procedure

Mainstream logic programming uses Horn clause logic as its knowledge representation scheme and forms of resolution as its query evaluation procedures [20]. Query evaluation procedures can be realised directly by using the resolution strategy of the logic program evaluator or indirectly by meta-programming in the logic programming language. The trade-off is between efficiency and flexibility. Meta-programming is more useful, because it enables the query evaluation procedure to be programmed explicitly to have the required characteristics [31]. However, meta-interpretation runs an order of magnitude slower than direction execution. Techniques like partial evaluation [33], which specialise meta-interpreters over a knowledge base, can close the performance gap significantly. However, the impure primitives of canonical logic programming languages create significant difficulties in doing this fully automatically, and some problems with partial evaluation, like its global control, remain unsolved [32].

Ideally a resolution based query evaluation procedure needs to be efficiently implemented and to be

- complete

- sound

- terminating

Soundness creates less difficulties than completeness and termination. Although SLD resolution is complete in the sense that each solution belongs to a finite branch of the SLD resolution tree [23], its implementation by a canonical Prolog engine is neither complete nor guaranteed to terminate. The engine can be trapped into exploring infinite paths in the SLD resolution tree, and miss finding finite solution paths on unexplored branches. A breadth first query evaluation procedure can make evaluation complete at the price of much less efficient use of memory. However, it is not guaranteed to terminate when searching for every one of a finite number of solutions, because it does not know when it has found all solutions and should stop.

SLD resolution trees can also have an infinite number of solution branches. A basic limitation is that first order logic is only semi-decidable. This means that a query evaluation procedure can only guarantee termination for all provable queries and not for all queries.

The chance of a complete search over its knowledge base by a canonical SLD resolution engine depends crucially on whether it supports don't know non-determinism in resolution or not. Since every solution is on some finite branch of the SLD resolution tree, don't know non-deterministic traversal of the tree top down offers the prospect of finding each solution eventually. By contrast the don't care non-determinism of committed choice resolution would make the query evaluation procedure incomplete in general.

Another cause of non-termination is the function symbol. The goal $man(A)$ over the Prolog program

```
man(X)   :-  man( father_of(X) ).
man(adam).
```

has a solution which is never found. One solution to such non-termination introduces two restrictions

- function-free literal arguments

- stratification of clauses

The first restriction rules out Horn clauses like the first clause for $man/1$ above, and is observed by tuples in a relational database. Hence it fits in well with a strategy of coupling Prolog to a relational database [4]. Stratification or layering addresses the other cause of non-termination by precluding SLD resolution trees from having infinitely long branches or infinitely many finite branches. Stratification requires the knowledge base be built up in a series of layers and precludes the use of recursive clauses which cause non-termination. The base layer of level 0 is the set of clause facts (bodiless clauses), and the nth layer is the set of clauses, among whose body literals at least one is defined by a level $n - 1$ clause, and none of whose literals are defined by clauses of level greater than $n - 1$ [7]. There are complete top down query evaluation procedures for recursive Horn clause databases without function symbols like OLD resolution with tabulation [34] and SLD-AL resolution [36] which terminate for all provable queries. Prolog can realise them by meta-programming although the efficiency is poor. An alternative is to compile away recursive query processing using bottom up methods which compute least fixed points [24]. Such methods preserve completeness but are less efficient than top down methods which restrict the search space better. Complete methods that combine top down and bottom up procedures also exist [2].

A resolution based query evaluation procedure should be able to use knowledge base relation arguments in a multi-moded way. A query should be able to match on some arguments' values to access related arguments' values, or be able to have their values supplied when matching on related arguments' values. Ideally any argument should be open to use in either way. Prolog's use of the bi-directional unification operation sustains this capability directly. By contrast the synchronisation constraints of concurrent logic programming or CLP languages like Parlog [15] and GHC [35] interfere with multi-moded use of clause head arguments. Each head argument can only be used for matching on or for supplying values.

3 Programming Systems in Logic

Concurrent knowledge based systems need a number of concurrency and control capabilities including

- multiple threads of control

- dynamic synchronisation of interacting tasks on dataflow among them

- asynchronous input/output

- fair multi-tasking with fine granularity concurrency

- interactive task control

Concurrent knowledge based systems need multiple threads of control to handle multiple users and work streams at the same time. Furthermore knowledge processing tasks need to be able to synchronise their execution dynamically on data flow among them and to handle input/output asynchronously to utilise available concurrency effectively. Each user's knowledge processing tasks should also receive (relatively) fair allocations of execution opportunities even over small time scales to ensure an even distribution of responsiveness. This requires fine granularity concurrency. Lastly, adequate task management requires the ability to suspend, resume and abort tasks interactively and to react locally to task execution outcomes. The attempt to realise these capabilities lead to the development of a conception of resolution as the execution of a network of concurrent processes interacting via shared variables [9, 28].

A goal is viewed as a process, while it is being resolved away. It begins to exist on being created and ceases to exist on being completely resolved away. Multiple processes can coexist if conjoined goals are executed concurrently. A process can create one or more other processes dynamically by being reduced to them. A process is conceived of as persistent, if it is recursively defined so that it reduces to itself. This may involve argument changes and the spawning of siblings. The resolution tree forms processes into a hierarchy of process dependencies, where parent goals depend for their satisfaction on the satisfaction of one or all of their children goals. Goals conceived of as processes can communicate by passing messages via shared variables. Although goals can execute concurrently in or-parallel as well as in and-parallel, and-parallelism is needed for dynamic message passing. These messages can be passed one way by one goal instantiating the shared variable to some value and the other goal receiving it. In the query

```
| ?- sender(Message), recipient(Message).
```

the *sender*/1 goal can bind *Message* to a value, and this event can be recognised and acted upon by the *recipient*/1 goal. Communication in this way via progressive instantiation of lists is called *stream and-parallelism*. However, this technique depends for its usefulness upon the *recipient*/1 goal being able to delay being executed until the shared variable is relevantly instantiated.

This interpretation of resolution as the execution of concurrent communicating processes embodies a fine grain of concurrency, communicates via shared variables, and uses means of synchronisation which delay reduction of goals over clauses until message passing variables have been bound by producer goals. It can support multiple threads of control by executing goal conjunctions concurrently.

```
| ?- task(one), task(two), task(three).
```

Dynamic synchronisation of multi-tasking can be achieved by introducing dataflow constraints. They make further execution of some goals wait upon data being supplied by bindings made to variables shared with other goals which are being executed. A CLP language, like GHC [35], enables this by introducing a synchronisation rule which makes unification between a goal and a clause head suspend until it is possible without binding or sharing goal variables. Although CLP languages, like Oc and Fleng [26], mostly use just this suspension rule, it is not very expressive to synchronise program execution primarily by this means. A more general method introduces suspending primitives and a computation restriction which delays execution of some goals until such a primitive is satisfied. One way of doing this is to introduce guards. Only when goals in the guard section of a clause body are satisfied (including any suspending primitives), are goals in the rest of the clause executed. Guards provide a general way of framing test conditions which can be evaluated in parallel to decide which way a goal is reduced. Suspending primitive goals can also serve as a simple means for handling input/output asynchronously. A goal $read(A,'/dev/ttyp1')$ can suspend execution while siblings goals continue executing. When input arrives on $/dev/ttyp1$, A is unified with the first term of that input. The binding of A in turn can awaken further goals suspended waiting on that dataflow.

However, concurrent execution of conjoined goals does not by itself guarantee any fairness in determining what gets executed when. That requires a scheduling policy. At least three factors are involved

- resolution tree traversal strategy

- multi-processor load balancing policy

- newly awakened goal scheduling

The SLD resolution tree can be traversed breadth or depth first or in some mixed manner. Breadth first traversal is fair to siblings but overly intensive in its use of memory, whereas depth first traversal is totally unfair but much more compact in its use of memory. Compromises between them like bounded depth first scheduling can combine the merits and avoid much of the disadvantages of each approach at a relatively constant extra overhead. Load balancing policy determines how multiple processors share the processing burden among themselves. It usually aims at minimising inter-processor communication overheads and processor idle time, but it should also ensure that multi-tasking remains fair. Newly awakened goals can be scheduled early or late. Most implementations favour early scheduling of newly awoken goals to preserve immediacy in input/output goal handling and because such activity biased scheduling is good at reducing goal suspension frequencies [19]. However, any such policy must be careful not to allow unrestricted preempting of goals near the top of scheduling queues which would undermine overall fairness in distributing execution opportunities. Clearly an implementation's design affects scheduling fairness more directly than a logic programming language's operational semantics. However, as language design is largely shaped by an intention to exploit a particular execution model, it already contains a bias in favour of a particular strategy of implementation. It will be seen in what follows that different logic programming schemes favour implementations which differ radically in their ability to support fairness in scheduling.

Interactive task control is programmed using resolution by meta-calls [17] as follows:

```
call(Goals, Result, Control)
```

Control is an input stream which takes control instructions like *suspend*, *resume* and *stop*, and implements that instruction over the meta-called sub-computation *Goals*. *Result* reports results by being bound to *success*, *failure* or *stopped*. *call/3*'s behaviour can be realised by flavoured meta-interpreters or directly by control call primitives [16]. The overhead of flavoured meta-interpreters can be reduced by partial evaluation or the same effect can be had by directly transforming the original code to code with extra arguments for *Result* and *Control*. Control meta-calls are more flexible and probably more efficient [13] chapter 5, but program transformation is still effective.

The systems programming interpretation of logic programs depends on the idea that the binding of a variable can be used to signal the happening of an event or the passing of a message. However, logic programming implementations, which exhibit don't know non-determinism, may generate alternative bindings for a variable when executed in parallel or may withdraw previously made bindings during the course of execution. This means that if a binding is taken as a signal, then it is not finally settled whether the signal is to be taken as sent until the don't know non-determinism in execution ends. This is inconvenient for systems programming purposes. It interferes with a modular event-based approach to managing concurrent tasks, which requires the ability to control and interact with tasks in definite states — to put them into further states by suspending, resuming or aborting them, and to respond to the results of task execution like success, failure, or exceptional outcomes. If a task's state depends on dynamic interplay with the states of other tasks mediated by variable bindings and relationships across the resolution tree, no task can be assumed to be in any definite state until the dynamic interplay has ceased. Modular and scrutable programming of the systems and querying aspects of knowledge based systems suggests a clean separation should be kept between a systems programming approach using committed bindings to signal messages, and a don't know non-deterministic search approach using trial or alternative bindings.

4 Knowledge Based Systems in Prolog

Prolog's ability to support don't know non-determinism in SLD resolution enables its query evaluation procedure to be complete, sound and terminating for function-free stratified databases, which establishes its ability to support a knowledge base capability. Canonical Prologs use backtracking to find alternative solutions and this unbuilds a canonical Prolog system's three run-time stacks, enabling the computation space used to find the previous solution to be reclaimed. Also because Prolog uses depth first search, it makes reasonably compact use of memory. With effective memory recycling, compact use of computation space, a complete search for function-free stratified databases and a reasonable execution speed, Prolog is clearly suitable for programming single tasking and single user knowledge based systems. However, Prolog's sequential execution strategy mars its ability to program systems by being unable to model multiple threads of control and dynamic synchronisation among multiple tasks being processed at the same time. Parallel execution of Prolog does not help because or-parallel Prologs do not support communication between parallel processes via a shared logical variable, and and-parallel Prologs avoid executing goals with shared variables concurrently to avoid the inefficiencies of coping with binding conflicts to variables shared between and-parallel goals while engaging in don't know non-deterministic search [11]. Furthermore execution of Prolog in parallel does not by itself provide a mechanism for synchronising execution of goals upon dataflow, for fair multi-tasking, nor for interactive task control.

5 Knowledge Based Systems in CLP Languages

The and-parallelism of the CLP languages like GHC [35], FCP [29], and Parlog [15] allows them to support concurrent execution of goals with shared variables even on a single processor implementation. They can synchronise goal execution via dataflow constraints and by the combination of suspending primitives and sequencing constructs like guards. Most CLP implementations support asynchronous input/output and single processor implementations of CLP languages use bounded depth first scheduling as a good compromise between efficient use of memory and the need to ensure a relatively fair distribution of opportunities for execution across runnable goals [16, 19]. Multiprocessor CLP implementations tend to use pure depth first scheduling on the local processor [12, 27] to improve data access locality and to avoid the overheads of operating more complex scheduling mechanisms. On-demand load sharing (with a pragma annotated goal bias) to idle processors of lower priority goals on local processor scheduling queues is used to mitigate the partiality of their purely depth first policy. Recently awoken goals are scheduled early which helps to make implementations responsive to input and output. Without some such means for distributing around execution opportunities for concurrently executable goals, implementations of CLP languages cannot hope to meet the requirements of concurrent knowledge based systems for multiple users. Interactive task control is achieved by flavoured meta-interpreters in the FCP Logix system, and by control meta-calls in Parlog implementations [16], and in GHC (i.e. KL1-B) implementations [6]. All three CLP languages only bind variables committedly, which ensures that signalling by bindings is free from retroactive interference by search which undoes bindings. Hence each of these CLP languages has the right sorts of capabilities to support the interpretation of resolution as the execution of concurrent communicating processes and suffices for programming systems [13, 15, 28].

Execution models [15, 27] for the sort of fine grained concurrency employed by CLP languages allow a memory management policy for implementations which enables effective and complete recycling of the space used by processes and their arguments, except where complex terms and some shared variables are concerned. That space needs to be recovered by garbage collection. Although computation space recovery in CLP implementations cannot match a Prolog implementation's ability to unbuild stacks during depth first search and backtracking, it remains manageable and economical.

CLP languages execute efficiently by pruning exploration of alternative solutions early using committed choice resolution and by only making committed bindings to variables. This means they cannot support resolution exhibiting don't know non-determinism. Thus in making themselves apt at handling the systems programming requirements of concurrent knowledge based systems, they sacrifice the capability to be sure of finding a solution to a query, if it exists. Furthermore, as has been seen already, the synchronisation constraints of CLP languages, like GHC and Parlog, preclude multi-moded use of knowledge base clauses. For this reason, and despite all their ability to support the model of systems programming developed earlier, they cannot support the querying requirements of knowledge based systems directly.

6   Combined Resolution Policies

It has been seen that support for an interpretation of resolution as the execution of concurrent communicating processes enables concurrent systems to be programmed in logic, while resolution exhibiting don't know non-determinism enables logic programs to support knowledge base querying in knowledge based applications. Both enable concurrent knowledge based systems to be programmed in logic. The problem is how to square their different requirements efficiently. Proposals for combining the complete search offered by don't know non-determinism with a systems programming capability are

- interpret complete search in CLP language

- compile away complete search in CLP language

- program systems with delayed goal extensions to Prolog

- devise integrated language capable of supporting both

- couple resolution engines with systems and search capabilities

6.1 Exhaustive Search Interpreter

A complete or exhaustive search interpreter can be written in a reasonably expressive CLP language so long as it can copy goals and perform full test unification. FCP [30] is able to do this, but other CLP languages, like GHC and Parlog, only support committed unification and cannot restore variables bound during unification if the unification as a whole fails. GHC cannot define goal copying or full unification in itself, but Parlog is able to copy the terms to be unified and then to unify the originals committedly only if the copies unify committedly. Although such unification is not atomic, the order independence of full unification enables Parlog to support or-parallel Prolog execution by meta-programming [8].

Fujita [14] has proposed supporting full unification in FGHC by using frozen representations of all terms and explicit libraries of substitutions. The overhead is plainly enormous, but the suggestion is that by applying an FGHC partial evaluator to the combination of even an inefficient interpreter of frozen Prolog in FGHC and a frozen Prolog program much of that overhead can be reduced. The result is a general compilation strategy for Prolog programs to FGHC. However, the complex FGHC translation products of even very simple Prolog clauses clearly show that it does not yet provide an efficient method for supporting don't know non-determinism indirectly in a CLP language.

The price of interpreting exhaustive search in a CLP language is an order of magnitude loss of efficiency in performance and high and not very tractable consumption of memory used in continually building new complex terms to represent goals. Partial evaluation can improve the performance efficiency of meta-interpretation by specialising the clauses relative to the meta-interpreter [33]. However, specialisation does not solve the problem of the inefficient use of memory by exhaustive search meta-interpreters. These meta-interpreters in committed choice languages have to evaluate OR-parallel branches of the resolution tree by copying goals at OR-nodes. Each goal copy is a complex term claiming memory in persistent storage space which can only be recovered by garbage collection, because the absence of backtracking precludes the natural stack popping reclamation of memory achieved by Prolog engines on exploring alternative branches. Thus meta-interpreting Prolog in CLP languages is not an efficient method for sustaining the don't know non-determinism of multiple solutions search.

6.2 Compiling Away a Complete Search

Ueda has proposed compiling away a complete search over Horn clauses into committed choice resolution using continuations [35] chapter 7. Under this scheme the exhaustive search goal over the Prolog program

```
:- bagof( (X,Y), append(X, Y, Z), S).

append([], A, A).
append([A|X], Y, [A|Z])  :- append(X, Y, Z).
```

with only Z as input is transformed into the continuation processing form goal over a GHC program

```
:- app(Z, cl0, S, []).

app(A, Cont, S0, S2)  :- true |
    app1(A, Cont, S0, S1),  app2(A, Cont, S1, S2).

app1(A, Cont, S0, S1)  :- true |
    cont(Cont, [], Z, S0, S1).

app2([A|B], Cont, S0, S1)           :-          true
    | app(B, cl1(A, Cont), S0, S1).
app2(A, _, S0, S1)        :-          otherwise
    | S0 = S1.

cont(cl0, X, Y, S0, S1) :-          true
    | S0 = [ (X,Y) | S1 ].
cont(cl1(A, Cont), X, Y, S0, S1)              :-          true
    | cont(Cont, [A|X], Y, S0, S1).
```

The clauses of *append*/3 become the conjunctive goals *app1*/4 and *app2*/4. Their first argument accepts the input list, their second the continuation and their last two arguments collect solutions as a difference list. *cont*/5 does the

continuation processing. cl1 continuations have A prepended to the output
X and recursively continue. cl0 continuations insert the two outputs received
into the difference list.

However, compilation strategies like these cannot handle the full spectrum of
requirements of multiple solution search. Mode of use information must be
supplied with the Horn clauses being searched. The mode of use distinguishes
whether each argument supplies a value or has a value matched with it, and
Ueda's transformation requires that input arguments of goals be grounded on
invocation and output arguments be grounded upon satisfaction. Plainly this
precludes the use of partially instantiated data structures like difference lists
and the kind of multi-moded use of Horn clauses which is often necessary for
knowledge based systems applications. Furthermore where logical variables
exist which may be written upon by resolution with more than one literal,
the so-called multiple writers case, these transformation techniques cannot
be applied at all.

6.3   Delayed Goal Extensions to Prolog

Coroutining extensions to Prolog realised by when declarations in NU-Prolog
[25], control annotations in IC-Prolog, and by the *freeze*/2 primitive in
Prolog-II [5], offer a limited form of interacting concurrent execution of conjoined goals. In coroutining Prologs producer consumer relationships can be
established for concurrent evaluation by means of their goal delay mechanism. In NU-Prolog when declarations associated with a relation delay a
goal when called with that variable uninstantiated. Suppose the following
query is made over the NU-Prolog clauses below it.

```
:-  producer([A|B], 1),  consumer([A|B], 10).

?-  producer(X, N)  when  X.
producer([X|Y], M)  :-  solution(X, M, N),  producer(Y, N).
producer([], _).

?-  consumer([X|Y], M)  when  X.
consumer([X|Y], 1)        :-        test(X),  Y = [].
consumer([X|Y], M)        :-        test(X),  N is M - 1,
     Y = [U|V],  consumer(Y, N).
```

The top level *producer*/2 goal reduces to the goal *solution*(X, M, N), which
binds A to the Mth solution and updates the index M to N, and a *producer*/2
goal which suspends. The top level *consumer*/2 goal is then run, and reduces

on its second clause to its body. Given that *test*/1 succeeds for its argument, the third goal in that body wakes the suspended *producer*/2 goal, which begins the cycle again. The cycle continues until the second argument of *consumer*/2 has been reduced to 1.

This program demonstrates bi-directional communication using the [A—B] stream in the fashion of the systems programming interpretation of resolution. However, the program does not escape its potential for don't know non-deterministic search in finding a suitable satisfier of *solution*/3. If this search is not contained to resatisfying *solution*(*A*, *M*, *N*) for a given value of M, it could cause backtracking involving earlier and earlier parts of the computation in complex non-local search. This potential for unrestricted search muddies the tidy model of producer consumer relationships, making it hard to capture systems programming notions in a modular, scrutable fashion.

Parallel NU-Prolog is a preprocessor for a parallel extension of NU-Prolog. It was proposed to make it easy to write stream and-parallel code which avoids search which creates uncommitted bindings, and to provide an integrated way of reconciling stream and-parallelism and don't know non-determinism. Parallel NU-Prolog takes advantage of the binding deterministic subset of NU-Prolog to produce code which can be run in parallel. Binding determinism means that variables shared between goals can only be bound by one goal sharing the variable, and that binding cannot be undone without the whole computation, which created the shared variable, failing. Relations for parallel execution are declared to be eagerly or lazily deterministic and the intended mode of use of each argument of being either input or output is also specified in a Parlog-like way. This information is used to place in the clause body instantiation tests, like *nonvar*/1, which can suspend, as well as a cut in place of a commitment operator and unifications on which to match input or to output arguments to the goal. when declarations to delay execution of a goal invoking the relation until its input arguments are bound are also added to ensure the code is binding deterministic for goals. This enables the relation to be executed in parallel. The effect is to transform Parlog-like relations into Prolog which can be co-processed in a stream and-parallel-like fashion. Parlog code for *append*/3

```
mode append(?, ?, ^).
append([D|E], B, [D|F])  :-  append(E, B, F).
append([], B, B).
```

becomes in Parallel NU-Prolog

```
?- eagerDet append(i, i, o).
```

```
append(D.E, B, D.F)  :-  !,  append(E, B, F).
append([], B, B)  :-  !.
```

which is translated into NU-Prolog

```
?- append(A, B, C) when A.
append(A, B, C)  :-  nonvar(A),  A = D.E,  !,
    C = D.F,  append(E, B, F).
append(A, B, C)  :-  nonvar(A),  A = [],  !,  B = C.
```

Input matching is performed by the *when* declaration and the information in each clause's "guard" (the part before the cut) enables NU-Prolog's compiler to determine with which clause to reduce the goal.

In parallel NU-Prolog don't know non-deterministic code can call binding deterministic code synchronously, and the deterministic code can even spawn delayed goals which persist afterwards. Binding deterministic code can call non-deterministic code, so long as the call does not share unbound variables with other deterministic calls executing in and-parallel. Don't know deterministic code can also be called by binding deterministic code before cuts so long as inputs to it are ground and outputs to the call are performed after the cut. These combinations allow layered mutual invocations of both kinds of code subject to the stipulated execution restrictions. This enables some quite sophisticated admixtures of a complete search with stream and-parallelism to be achieved. However, the restricted form of stream and-parallelism supported by NU-Prolog is a much less expressive form of stream and-parallelism as compared with CLP languages. In Parallel NU-Prolog

- clause search is always sequential

- guard (pre-cut) goals are always executed and-sequentially

- input matches are

  - sequential and not concurrent
  - delayed between shared variables until goal variables are ground
  - delayed until the goal variables in user guard (pre-cut) goals are ground

Clause search is always sequentially in order from top to bottom unlike with the CLP languages Parlog, GHC and FCP, where the default assumption is parallel search. Guard goals are executed in order from left to right. This is necessary to perform various goal delay tests before input matching unifications. This is in contrast to CLP languages where no and-sequential restrictions on executing conjunctions of goals need exist. The sequencing of execution of guard goals also means that input matching on head arguments is sequential and not concurrent. This means that, where a goal's first argument is uninstantiated but subsequent arguments are instantiated, it is possible for a goal to suspend upon the first argument input match even though a subsequent argument input match cannot succeed. Input matching on shared head argument variables as on the arguments of the clause

```
member(A, [A|_]).
```

depends in Parallel NU-Prolog upon delaying execution of the goal until the first argument and the head of the list of the second argument of the goal are ground, and then testing whether they are the same. This precludes using the clause to reduce a goal like

```
| ?- member([2|A]-A,
        [ [2|B]-B, [2,3|C]-C, [2,3,5|D]-D ]).
```

using partially instantiated data structures like difference lists. Furthermore where Parallel NU-Prolog's analogue of deep guard evaluation for CLP languages is employed, which allows calls to non-deterministic code, the stricter delaying condition, that variables used in user defined guard goals are ground, is used. This again heavily limits use of partially instantiated data structures.

Parallel NU-Prolog is an interesting attempt to support a form of stream and-parallelism in a simple fashion on a multi-processor. It can support both complete search and a kind of concurrency suitable for programming systems. While it lacks direct tools for interactive task control like control meta-calls, it can use flavoured meta-interpreters to support interactive task management. However, its ability to express stream and-parallelism is significantly limited compared with the CLP languages. Or-parallelism is not supported at all, and scheduling over processors is highly constrained by the rules for combining the execution of don't know non-deterministic code with binding deterministic code. Furthermore the parallel extension to NU-Prolog relies upon an execution strategy for Prolog which does not accord execution quotas to goals and their offspring so that it lacks a means for striking a fair balance among the various demands for multi-tasking. Thus fair multi-tasking is not achieved, which undermines the prospects for sustaining a fair distribution of opportunities for execution to multiple users on a concurrent knowledge based system programmed in NU-Prolog.

7   Integrated Language Approach

At least two languages, Andorra, and Pandora, have been proposed which aim to support systems programming capabilities like stream and-parallelism along with don't know non-determinism in an integrated way.

7.1   Andorra

Andorra distinguishes between a deterministic goal, which can only match a single clause, and a non-deterministic goal which can match more than one clause [38]. Goals which can be reduced deterministically are always executed in parallel first. When no more deterministic reduction can be performed, the leftmost non-deterministic goal is selected and forked, making a branch point, each or-branch is executed one step and then deterministic reduction is begun again if possible. Or-branches are only created when there are no more deterministic goals to reduce. Thus the don't know non-determinism is lazy. The advantages of making don't know non-determinism lazy are that every binding made to and-parallel goals, sharing a common variable during the deterministic phase, is unique to its or-branch, and that search spaces are reduced by limiting the creation of choice points. Andorra's or-branches need not be Prolog-like choice points. They can be or-parallel forks in the computation. However, they are created and explored in a left to right fashion. For better control of the phases of execution Andorra allows relations to be declared as AND-relations or OR-relations. AND-relations are only executed during deterministic phases of execution, and OR-relations are only executed during non-deterministic phases.

Andorra's approach depends for its success upon how good it is at recognising whether a goal is deterministic or not. Compile time analysis along with simple run-time type tests on arguments, are intended to determine whether a goal is deterministic or not. The Andorra philosophy is to try to extract full and-parallelism transparently using compile time analysis without either using the CLP languages' control constructs of guards or using their (implicit) mode declarations or wait annotations to specify input matching requirements on head arguments. Andorra aims to avoid recourse to compiler annotations, and to use as far as possible compile time examination of head arguments and early use of built-in primitives in the clause body, in order to formulate conditions for deciding whether a goal is deterministic or not. In other words annotationless Andorra is intended to have an expressive power similar to flat committed choice languages in programming stream and-parallel applications. An Andorra example of stream and-parallelism would be the following query over the Andorra clauses beneath it.

```
:- producer([A|B], 1), consumer([A|B], 10).

:- and producer/2.
producer([X|Y], M)  :- solution(X, M, N), producer(Y, N).
producer([], _).

consumer([X|Y], 1)      :- test(X), Y = [].
consumer([X|Y], M)      :- not(test(X)), N is M - 1,
    Y = [U|V], consumer(Y, N).
```

This program works much like the NU-Prolog program before except that the and declaration ensures that *producer/2* goals are only executed during deterministic phases of execution, and the form of *consumer/2* goals ensures that they are only executed during non-deterministic phases of execution. The alternation of execution phases switches activity between *producer/2* and *consumer/2* goals. Without this phase restriction on executing producer/2 goals the risk would be that they would be executed during non-deterministic phases even though their first argument was unbound.

Andorra's deterministic and-parallelism enables it to handle multiple threads of execution. Furthermore Andorra clauses can be written to use the deterministic goal test to synchronise interacting tasks on dataflow among them. And declarations can be used to make sure that such goals are not executed over alternative clauses during non-deterministic execution. Andorra's ability to handle suspending primitives also enables it to handle asynchronous input/output. However, Andorra's approach to branch points means they are created lazily one at a time. This policy makes it impossible to guarantee to run concurrently in a fair fashion knowledge base queries for two different clients as might be required by a multi-user logic database system. Andorra only executes all deterministic goals in and-parallel. As soon as both searches run out of deterministic goals to execute, Andorra settles down to expanding the search tree and continuing execution for only one of the query searches. Only when it finishes will Andorra continue execution on the other. The required effect might be achieved if Andorra's execution model could be applied to independent sub-computations so that the subcomputations could be executed concurrently, but it is hard to see how such execution could be organised to guarantee fairness in execution opportunities to these concurrent tasks without introducing control annotations foreign to the Andorra approach.

Naive global synchronisation of Andorra's execution phases would be likely to result in rather inefficient use of multiple processors. Only when the last processor had finished executing the last deterministic goal could the non-deterministic phase begin. In the meantime the other processors would be waiting doing nothing. It remains to be seen how Andorra can be executed without naive global synchronisation and what effect local synchronisation has on concurrent execution of high level tasks.

7.2   Pandora

Pandora [1] extends Parlog towards Andorra's execution model. Pandora adds deadlock procedures and a non-deterministic fork primitive to Parlog. A deadlock procedure is a single extra clause for a Parlog relation preceded by a deadlock mode declaration. When a Parlog computation, i.e. a top level or a meta-called computation, deadlocks and at least one of the deadlocked goals is defined by a Parlog relation extended by a deadlock procedure, then an arbitrary one of these deadlocked goals is executed over its deadlock procedure. A non-deterministic fork primitive is a specially delimited n-wise concatenation of conjunctions of Pandora goals. When executed, it causes the computation to split into n or-branches, each branch defined by its respective conjunction in the concatenation. To avoid the inefficiency pitfalls of P-Prolog the ability to combine general or-parallelism with and-parallelism is restricted so that non-deterministic forks are only allowed to appear as the sole body goals of deadlock procedures.

Pandora is like Andorra in that it waits until a computation deadlocks before it engages in non-deterministic execution. It differs from Andorra in that it allows this lazy non-deterministic execution in each meta-called subcomputation. Pandora is limited by its Parlog origins, which requires all Pandora relations to be expressed by guarded definite clauses with their compulsory commit and to be given mode declarations. This limits multi-moded use of relations. Pandora also inherits the limitations of the Andorra approach in respect of scheduling biases. The lazy non-determinism of its deadlock relations would not guarantee fair opportunities for execution to concurrent queries being executed at the same time over a knowledge based system implemented in Pandora. Pandora's main advantage over Andorra for programming concurrent knowledge based systems is its systems programming capabilities derived from its Parlog origins. A significant disadvantage is the much greater overheads in supporting don't know non-determinism via deadlock relations and backtracking over Parlog-like execution rather than by stack based execution using choice points in an efficient Prolog-based manner.

8　Coupled Resolution Engines

An obvious compromise between the inability of particular kinds of resolution engines to combine the required capabilities together is to couple different kinds of resolution engines together in such a way that both kinds of capability can be realised together. The two main representatives of this approach are

- Parlog and Prolog United

- Coupled GHC and RBU Engines

Parlog and Prolog United was advocated by the developers of Parlog [10] and a coupled GHC and Retrieval-By-Unification strategy would seem to be the current approach of the FGCS project [18].

8.1　Parlog and Prolog United

Parlog and Prolog United advocates coupling resolution engines exhibiting systems programming behaviour and don't know non-determinism by interfacing Parlog with multiple Prologs [10]. Six interfaces are defined. Three interfaces enable a Parlog computation to call a Prolog computation

- eager all solutions predicate $set(List?,Term?,Conj?)$

- lazy multiple solutions predicate $subset(List?,Term?,Conj?)$

- single solutions predicate $prolog\_call(Conj?)$

$set/3$ and $subset/3$ are eager and lazy multiple solutions constructors like Prolog's $findall/3$. They deliver solutions instances of $Term$ to the goal $Conj$ incrementally as elements of $List$. $subset/3$ binds solution elements of $List$ as variable list elements are given to it whereas $set/3$ extends $List$ autonomously. The third interface $prolog\_call/1$ can have its variables bound at any time during its execution either by other Parlog goals executing concurrently with it or by the Prolog computation it represents. These new bindings may not be rescinded by the Prolog computation once made. Since the multiple solutions constructors can be defined using $prolog\_call/1$ (and destructive assignment), it embodies the functionality underlying all three interfaces. Three interfaces are also defined which enable Prolog to call Parlog

- deterministic conjunction prolog-conj :: parlog-conj

- eager non-deterministic conjunction prolog-conj <> parlog-conj

- lazy non-deterministic conjunction prolog-conj << parlog-conj

Each represents co-routining conjunctions. :: /2 spawns the Parlog conjunction immediately on execution and continues executing the Prolog conjunction. The Prolog conjunction may engage in backtracking so long as no bindings passed to the Parlog conjunction are undone. :: /2 succeeds when both conjuncts succeed. When the Prolog conjunct is *true*, Prolog is just synchronously invoking Parlog. The second and third interfaces allow failures in the Prolog conjunction to fail and undo bindings to variables shared with the Parlog conjunction. This rolls back the Parlog computation to the point at which the uncommitted binding, which was undone, was made. If the Parlog computation itself fails, the goal which caused the most recent uncommitted binding in the Prolog conjunction is supposed to be failed. <> /2 allows the Prolog conjunction to carry on making uncommitted bindings to variables shared with the Parlog computation eagerly. << /2 allows the Prolog conjunction to make deterministic bindings to shared variables eagerly yet delays making a binding it could undo on backtracking, and only proceeds if and when the Parlog conjunction deadlocks. The non-deterministic interfaces <> /2 and << /2 represent the really radical departure. They entail extending Parlog to allow bindings in a Parlog computation to be undone and the computation rolled back. However, the interest here is in programming concurrent knowledge based systems in logic. This kind of application only requires the *prolog_call*/1 and the :: /2 interfaces, which disallow the Prolog computation from revoking bindings made to shared variables. The possibility of backtracking in the Parlog computation would be a positive disadvantage in that it would undermine the systems programming interpretation of resolution based upon deterministic signalling via shared variable bindings.

Deterministic coupling of Parlog and Prolog can be realised under Unix by executing the multiple Prologs and the Parlog engine as separate Unix processes which share memory. This allows coupled pairs of Parlog and Prolog computations to bind shared variables in each others heaps. Parlog and Prolog United allows multiple concurrent calls to be made to Prolog from Parlog.

```
| ?-  prolog_call(task(one)), prolog_call(task(two)),
      prolog_call(task(three)).
```

This enables multi-threaded execution. Dataflow synchronisation can be achieved by giving Prolog a primitive *data*/1 which suspends that Prolog computation until the argument is bound. Thus Parlog can manipulate Prolog computations through *prolog_call*/1 interfaces using *data*/1. These goals can be suspended in Prolog using the *freeze*/2 mechanism. Interactive task control can be realised through the Unix operating system by sending Unix inter-process signals to Prolog computations. This could be manipulated by Parlog by adding extra arguments to *prolog_call* to achieve this.

```
prolog_call(Goals, Control, Status).
```

Fairness of scheduling is ensured by the Unix operating system. Shared memory multi-processing is achieved relatively straight-forwardly by a multi-processing version of Unix like Dynix.

8.2 Coupled GHC and RBU Engines

The Japanese Fifth Generation Computer Systems or FGCS project aims at producing a highly parallel knowledge processing machine. In its last phase of development, its research strands are being brought together into a prototype of a fifth generation machine. The parallel inference sub-system [27] and the parallel knowledge base sub-system [18] are to be merged to form an integrated parallel machine which executes a variant of flat GHC called KL1. The design of the parallel knowledge base sub-system will be mainly based upon enhancements of the Mu-X system and work on a parallel interface to knowledge bases from GHC [18]. Mu-X is a multi-processor backend for adapted PSIs, which execute an extended version of Prolog. Mu-X executes term-relational queries (extended relational queries which replace equality checking with term unification) over full unit clauses held on large scale multi-port page memory [39]. The parallel interface to GHC is a special predicate *rbu*/1 which handles a stream of term-relational algebra commands for retrieving and updating knowledge via a dedicated term-relational knowledge base.

The parallel knowledge base sub-system will execute FGHC on the same dedicated multi-processor machine as the parallel inference sub-system. However, an *rbu*/1 call will enable it to exercise a dedicated system for operating a knowledge base by means of *retrieval by unification* operations added to an *rbu*/1 stream. They will be compiled into lower level operations, and farmed out to other processing elements to execute in parallel over clause storage. Multiple solutions will be delivered incrementally as a list to *unification restriction stream* or *unification join stream* commands. Thus the one element stream *rbu*/1 goal

```
| ?- rbu([urs(teacher, [1], student(female,$(1)),
    [1], X)]).

X = [student(female,science($(2))),
     student(female,arts(history)), ...]
```

contains a unification restriction stream operation *urs*/5. It initiates a search of the first attribute of the term relation teacher for terms unifiable with the condition *student(female,* $(1)). The first attribute is derived as a result. Results are returned as a stream bound to the variable X. An occurrence of (N) where N is an integer signifies a variable. The one element stream *rbu*/1 goal

```
| ?- rbu([ujs(teacher, [2], employee, [1], [3], X)]).

X = [salary(5000,part_time),
     salary(12300,fulltime), ...]
```

contains a unification join stream operation *ujs*/5. It is used to derive the third attribute of a result operation generated by a search of the second attribute of the term relation *teacher* and the first attribute of the term relation *employee* for unifiable terms. Results are returned as a stream bound to the variable X. Retrieval by unification is not just applied directly to term relations but may use rules to perform shallow inference.

Thus the FGCS project is using a coupled resolution engine approach to combine extended relational algebra or RBU operations with committed choice resolution in order to reconcile deductive capabilities with systems programming capabilities in a parallel processing framework. Input resolution is possible in terms of RBU operations, and an algorithm is given in [39] for realising breadth first search by RBU operations. This approach executes RBU operations from within FGHC instead of using Prolog to realise resolution. This allows a bottom up query evaluation approach to be used, which ensures completeness and termination for recursive query processing. However, it is less efficient because it does not allow the query to restrict the search space in the way in which top down query evaluation procedures can. Query and program transformation methods will be used to mitigate this problem.

Calls to *rbu*/1 serve much the same role in an FGHC program on a PIM as calls to the transiently communicating interface *prolog_call*/1 would from a Parlog engine to Prolog in a coupled resolution architecture. They both enable a committed choice computation to get back multiple solutions to a query over a clause database as a stream. Furthermore their macroscopic processing structure would also seem to be similar. Each time an *rbu*/1 predicate is executed, a new RBU process is created which is able independently to retrieve and update relations [40] p.12. Equally each time a call is made to *prolog_call*/1 from within a Parlog computation on a coupled resolution architecture, a new (lightweight) process is created with its own retrieval and update functionality. So long as the scheduling mechanisms of the parallel knowledge base sub-system complement the rough fairness of multi-tasking on the KL1 implementation, overall processing of concurrent knowledge based systems should preserve multi-tasking fairness. Interactive task control will be ensured by the mechanisms of PIMOS [6].

By going for a dedicated knowledge base approach, the FGCS project is losing a lot of flexibility in programming querying over the knowledge base. The functionality of *rbu*/1 is hard-wired, whereas the functionality of a Prolog computation invoked from a Parlog computation is open to a rich and powerful panoply of Prolog computation techniques which can fully exploit its backtracking (or-parallel) mechanisms and full logical unification. Furthermore by eschewing an interface to a programmable SLD resolution engine like Prolog, the FGCS project's approach is losing the rich possibilities of plugging into or-parallel Prolog implementation technology [37]. A dedicated knowledge base exercised by an *rbu*/1 interface enables the dedicated knowledge base to be optimised for performance at both the software and the hardware level. A disadvantage is lack of flexibility in programming use of the dedicated knowledge base. This may not be wise in a next generation machine. Lack of flexibility in handling the knowledge base through a rbu/1 interface may soon be exposed by innovation in query evaluation procedures, parallel algorithms, knowledge representation techniques, and application needs.

8.3 Limitations of Coupled Resolution

Table 1 briefly contrasts approaches to reconciling don't know non-determinism and and-parallelism.

Coupled resolution has some general limitations as a way to reconcile parallel execution, stream and-parallelism and don't know non-determinism.

- the solution provided is a hybrid rather than an integrated one
- its multi-threaded query search concurrency is coarse grained

Coupled resolution is at heart a hybrid solution. It seeks to reconcile di-

Language	Guard Depth	And-parallel style	Style of don't know non-determinism	Synchronisation	And-parallel & Search Couplir
Andorra	shallow	goal reduction determinism	lazy or-parallelism & backtracking	phased execution	fine
Flat Concurrent Prolog	shallow	stream	compiled or interpreted away	dataflow	fine
Compiled GHC & RBU engines	shallow	stream	bottom up evaluation	dataflow	coarse
Committed Bindling Parlog-Prolog United	deep	stream	backtracking	dataflow	coarse
Parallel NU-Prolog	shallow	binding deterministic	backtracking	dataflow	coarse
Pandora	deep	stream	lazy backtracking	dataflow and phased execution	fine

Table 1: Languages for Programming Systems and Search Problems in Logic

verse types of resolution by interfacing inference engines which support each type of resolution. This eclecticism lacks the integrated harmony which one would expect of a true synthesis of parallel execution, systems programming capabilities and the kind of resolution proof procedure needed for knowledge based applications. Coupled resolution rather manifestly fails to transcend its heterogeneous origins by preserving unamended the programming styles appropriate to each component resolution engine. Andorra does rather better than coupled resolution approaches in this respect.

Developing an integrated language solution would seem to have been a major part of the motivation why Gregory has tried to go beyond coupled resolution in creating a language Pandora which aspires to integrate stream and-parallelism and don't know non-determinism more closely [1]. Lack of integration in coupled resolution undermines coupled resolution's claim to be an ultimately satisfactory solution intellectually. However, even a language like Pandora does not dissolve away all heterogeneity between the contending demands of stream and-parallelism and don't know non-determinism. Pandora preserves that heterogeneity by substituting distinct phases of Parlog-like execution with don't know non-determinism for coupled stream and-parallel and don't know non-deterministic computations. It remains to be seen whether Pandora can be implemented in a memory efficient fashion.

A second general limitation of coupled resolution is that the style of concurrency achieved among don't know non-deterministic searches is basically coarse grained. Coupled resolution shares this characteristic with Parallel NU-Prolog. Because Prolog computations have significant overheads in start up times and in their static memory requirements, it is not practical for coupled resolution systems to create or have in existence large numbers of Prolog computations at the same time. Nor is it efficient to incur the communications overheads with a Prolog computation only for trivial calls to Prolog. These limitations can be recognised by programmers, and programs written to minimise their effects. However, it is not apt that implementation and efficiency issues should influence the programming style that much.

9 Conclusion

Concurrent knowledge based systems must be able to make complete searches over their knowledge to sustain an adequate knowledge base querying capability. Under certain assumptions sequential and parallel Prologs can do this efficiently, because they are able to exhibit don't know non-determinism in resolution. Since the CLP languages cannot exhibit don't know non-determinism, they cannot support an adequate knowledge base querying capability directly. It was also seen that the CLP languages cannot efficiently support general don't know non-determinism indirectly, even by compilation using continuations, meta-interpretation by copying, or using libraries of substitutions.

Logic programming languages must also be able to support the systems programming requirements of concurrent knowledge based systems. Some form of this capability can be realised if resolution can be interpreted as the execution of concurrent communicating processes. This can be done so long as individual goals can be delayed on data-flow synchronisation constraints and some form of stream and-parallel execution is supported for communicating among these processes. CLP languages are the most expressive way of doing this, but analogous capabilities can be demonstrated by and-parallel and co-routining Prologs. However, a systems programming interpretation of logic program execution requires variable bindings to be deterministic vehicles for sending messages. This conflicts with using them with trial values in a don't know non-deterministic search. Furthermore, co-routining and and-parallel Prologs, like NU-Prolog, are incapable of sustaining other important kinds of systems handling capability required by interactive knowledge based systems like fair scheduling of users' tasks. The same applies to other attempts to reconcile stream and-parallelism with don't know non-determinism like Andorra's lazy non-determinism. Thus while Prolog-like languages can program the deductive aspects of concurrent knowledge based systems by exploiting don't know non-determinism, and while the CLP languages can sustain systems programming capabilities using stream and-parallelism, none of several canvassed possibilities looks plausible for sustaining the combination adequately.

The only kinds of candidates suitable for combining the knowledge querying with the systems programming capabilities needed by concurrent knowledge based systems were the approaches of Parlog and Prolog United and the FGCS project's combination of GHC and Retrieval by Unification. Each approach was limited by the artificiality of using a hybrid solution. The Coupled GHC and RBU Engines approach lacked the flexibility of a coupled programming language strategy using a means like Prolog for knowledge processing and lost efficiency in trading top down search for bottom up recursive query processing. On the other hand its approach handled the completeness of search problem more expressively and efficiently than Parlog and Prolog United. An adequate non-hybrid solution to programming concurrent knowledge based systems in a resolution based computing paradigm has yet to be devised.

Acknowledgements

I would like to thank colleagues at Heriot-Watt university and members of the Parlog group at Imperial college. This research was funded by Alvey project IKBS 90.

References

[1] R. Bahgat and S. Gregory. Pandora: Non-deterministic parallel logic programming. Technical report, Department of Computing, Imperial College, London, November 1988.

[2] F. Bancilhon and R. Ramakrishnan. An amateur's introduction to recursive query processing strategies. In *Proceedings of the 1986 ACM SIGMOD International Conference*, pages 16–52, 1986.

[3] W. Bibel and Ph. Jorrand, editors. *Foundation of AI*, volume 232 of *LNCS*. Springer-Verlag, 1986.

[4] J. Bocca. EDUCE a marriage of convenience: Prolog and a relational dbms. In *Proceedings of the 1986 Symposium on Logic Programming*, Salt Lake City, Utah, September 1986.

[5] M. Carlsson. Freeze, indexing and other implementation issues in the WAM. In Lassez [22], pages 40–58.

[6] T. Chikayama, H. Satoh, and T. Miyazaki. Overview of the parallel inference machine operating system (PIMOS). Technical Report TR-483, ICOT, Tokyo, June 1989.

[7] K. L. Clark. Negation as failure. In H.Gallaire and J.Minker, editors, *Logic and Databases*, pages 293–322. Plenum Press, New York, 1978.

[8] K. L. Clark and S. Gregory. Notes on the implementation of Parlog. *Journal of Logic Programming*, 2(1), July 1985.

[9] K. L. Clark and S. Gregory. PARLOG: Parallel programming in logic. *ACM Transactions on Programming Languages and Systems*, 8(1):1–49, January 1986.

[10] K. L. Clark and S. Gregory. Parlog and Prolog united. In Lassez [22], pages 927–961.

[11] J. S. Conery. *Parallel Execution of Logic Programs*. Kluwer Academic Publishers, 1986.

[12] J. A. Crammond. *Implementation of Committed Choice Logic Languages on Shared Memory Multiprocessors*. PhD thesis, Department of Computer Science, Heriot-Watt university, Edinburgh, Scotland, May 1988.

[13] I. T. Foster. *Parlog as a Systems Programming Language*. PhD thesis, Department of Computing, Imperial College, University of London, March 1988.

[14] H. Fujita. FGHC partial evaluator as a general purpose parallel compiler. Technical Report TR-386, ICOT, Institute for New Generation Computer Technology, Tokyo, Japan, May 1988.

[15] S. Gregory. *Parallel Logic Programming in Parlog — The language and its Implementation*. Addison-Wesley, London, February 1987.

[16] S. Gregory, I. T. Foster, A. Burt, and G. A. Ringwood. An abstract machine for the implementation of parlog on uniprocessors. *New Generation Computing*, 6(4):389–420, 1989.

[17] N. Ichiyoshi, T. Miyazaki, and K. Taki. A distributed implementation of flat GHC on the Multi-PSI. Technical Report TR-230, ICOT, Institute for New Generation Computer Technology, Tokyo, March 1987.

[18] H. Itoh, H. Monoi, and H. Seki. Knowledge base system towards logic programming and parallel processing paradigms. Technical Report TR-435, ICOT, Tokyo, November 1988.

[19] M. Kishimoto, A. Hosoi, K. Kumon, and A. Hattori. An evaluation of FGHC via practical application programs. Technical Report TR-232, ICOT, Institute for New Generation Computer Technology, 1987.

[20] R. A. Kowalski. *Logic for Problem Solving.* North-Holland, 1979.

[21] R. A. Kowalski and K. A. Bowen, editors. *Proceedings of the 5th International Conference and Symposium on Logic Programming,* Seattle, USA, August 1988.

[22] J-L. Lassez, editor. *Logic Programming, Proceedings of the Fourth International Conference,* Melbourne, May 1987.

[23] J. W. Lloyd. *Foundations of Logic Programming.* Symbolic Computation Series. Springer Verlag, 2nd, extended edition edition, 1984.

[24] N. Miyazaki, H. Yokota, and H. Itoh. Compiling Horn clause queries in deductive databases: A Horn clause transformation approach. Technical Report TR-183, ICOT, Tokyo, June 1986.

[25] L. Naish. Parallelizing Nu-Prolog. In Kowalski and Bowen [21], pages 1546-1564.

[26] M. Nilsson and H. Tanaka. A flat GHC implementation for supercomputers. In Kowalski and Bowen [21], pages 1337-1350.

[27] M. Sato, H. Shimizu, A. Matsumoto, K. Rokusawa, and A. Goto. KL1 execution model for PIM cluster with shared memory. In Lassez [22], pages 338-355.

[28] E. Y. Shapiro. Systems programming in concurrent Prolog. In *Proceedings of the 11th ACM Symposium on Principles of Programming Languages,* pages 93-105, 1984.

[29] E. Y. Shapiro. Concurrent Prolog: A progress report. Technical Report CS86-10, Department of Computer Science, The Weizmann Institute of Science, Rehovot, Israel, April 1986. Reprinted in [3].

[30] E. Y. Shapiro. An or-parallel execution algorithm for Prolog and its FCP implementation. In Lassez [22], pages 311–337.

[31] L. Sterling and R.D. Beer. Meta-interpreters for expert system construction. *Journal of Logic Programming*, 6:163–178, 1989.

[32] A. Takeuchi and H. Fujita. Competitive partial evaluation — some remaining problems of partial evaluation. Technical Report TR-361, ICOT, Tokyo, March 1988.

[33] A. Takeuchi and K. Furukawa. Partial evaluation of Prolog programs and its application to meta programming. Technical Report TR-126, ICOT, Tokyo, July 1985.

[34] H. Tamaki and T. Sato. Old resolution with tabulation. In E. Y. Shapiro, editor, *Proc. of 3rd International Logic Programming Conference*, pages 84–98, July 1986.

[35] K. Ueda. Guarded Horn clauses. Doctor of engineering thesis, University of Tokyo, Graduate School, Tokyo, March 1986.

[36] L. Vieille. A database-complete proof procedure based on SLD-resolution. In Lassez [22].

[37] D.H.D. Warren. The Aurora or-parallel Prolog system. In *Proceedings of FGCS 1988*, Tokyo, November 1988.

[38] R. Yang. Programming in Andorra-I. Technical report, Department of Computer Science, University of Bristol, Bristol, September 1988.

[39] H. Yokota and H. Itoh. A model and an architecture for a relational knowledge base. In *Proceedings of the 13th Annual Symposium on Computer Architecture*, Tokyo, June 1986.

[40] H. Yokota, H. Kitakami, and A. Hattori. Knowledge retrieval and updating for parallel problem solving. Technical Report TR-380, ICOT, Tokyo, June 1988.

The Wivenhoe Computational Model: In Search of More Parallelisms

Jiwei Wang   Simon Lavington

Abstract

This paper proposes a model which enjoys the possible bene-fit of parallel unification, yet also parallelises unification and the costly housekeeping operations (e.g. choice-point creation, environment management and backtracking etc.). The model, named the Wivenhoe model, is based on a widely suggested idea in Automatic Theorem Proving, i.e. separating unification from inference.

In the model, a logic program is viewed as consisting of two components, namely, logical relations and structure relations, which are actually separable. The logical relations (specified by logic connectives) which do not contain any variables are extracted out of the source program with a rewriting formalism, so that performing logic deductions turns into rewriting a certain symbol. Refutation plans are generated in the rewriting, ready for validation by unification. This allows all the unifications in one refutation to be done in one go; and thus, with respect to unification, the nature of terms to be unified is changed with maximum sharing of constants, variables and structures, which makes the terms more suitable for parallel unification. The structure relations (the construction of terms and variable sharing) can be represented as a labeled directed acyclic graph(dag) to speed up unification.

Taking the idea of separating unification from inference, the Wivenhoe model benefits not only from parallel unification (subsuming And-parallelism), Or-parallelism, and pipeline parallelism between housekeeping and unification, but also from an automatic control over inference in the intelligent backtracking style. It is shown that the Wivenhoe approach to compilation and execution admits a clearer declarative semantics than that of Prolog, whilst having interesting possibilities for run-time parallelism and implying a new hardware organisation. This paper is mainly concerned with the theoretical part of the Wivenhoe model.

1 Introduction

Unification is the essential operation in logic programming, taking the greater part of the computation in executing a logic program. It has been argued that the complexity measure of logic programs should be based on the number of unifications performed [18]. For most practical purposes, unification can also be the measure of the computation performed by a logic program. Thus it is sensible to classify various computational models for logic languages in terms of the scale of computation. According to the size of the terms to be unified (the granularity of unification) and the quantity of unifications, current logic programming computational models can thus be roughly classified as:

1. Small grain,[1] Small quantity (SGSQ).

2. Small grain, Large quantity (SGLQ).

SLD-resolution is a typical SGSQ model, as each step of its inference (computation) involves the unification of only two user-defined literals, and one deduction is performed at a time. It is generally admitted that the SGSQ models are difficult for efficient parallel implementation.

Most models exploring And-parallelism,[2] or Or-parallelism, or both (e.g. [12], Parlog [11], Concurrent Prolog [34]) and set-based resolution [21] increase the quantity of unifications performed, but each unification remains independent as to its user-defined size. (For And-parallelism, the unifiers of two related unifications should be joined. The join operation is not regarded as part of the unification.) The granularity of the unification is not changed. Thus they are SGLQ models. A persistent problem in these models is that, when the number of processes becomes much larger than the number of processors, most of the work performed by the system is wasted in administration (c.f. the experience of Concurrent Prolog [34]). Here, we shall propose a computational model, the Wivenhoe[3] model, with another dimension of computation scale:

3. Large grain, Large quantity (LGLQ).

This is achieved by increasing the granularity of unification. The basic idea of this model is to find a refutation plan first and postpone the unifications

---

[1] Each user-defined literal, if regarded as an individual, is relatively small in size. So the unification for two user-defined literals is said to manipulate small grain data.

[2] As defined in [12]

[3] It is named after the Wivenhoe Park where the University of Essex is located.

for each pair of potentially complementary literals until the last step. Thus, all the unifications in a refutation are done in one go. They can be regarded as one super-unification for two huge terms. The granularity of unification changes from small grain to large grain. Also, many independent refutation plans can be generated to provide a large number of these super-unifications.

Increasing the scale of computation allows parallel implementation of unification effectively. It is well known that in the worst cases, generally unification contains basically sequential operations [15, 44]. However, [39] shows that parallel treatment of unification has great advantage for terms having non-sparse dag representations. A non-sparse dag has many more edges than nodes, which is the result of much sharing of constants, variables and structures. [17] also reveals that parallel unification on terms of large arity is beneficial. Doing all the unification of a refutation in one go achieves maximum sharing of constants, variables and structures, and virtually increases the arity of the terms to be unified. Thus it is more suitable for parallel implementation.

To separate unification from inference is actually to part computation from management of computation states. This gives a good treatment of managing computation states which can eliminate the ordering amongst clauses and amongst literals within a clause that causes the problem of inconsistency between declarative and procedural semantics of a logic language. More importantly, it can also provide a powerful automatic control over inference. The failure of unification indicates wrongly combined clauses. In the common approaches, the failure of a unification denotes the wrong selection of only one clause. Furthermore, it may not denote the genuine one — resulting in much redundant computation. Doing all the unifications in a refutation in one go offers a global view on the interrelations of clauses caused by sharing of variables. With this global view, the Wivenhoe model can precisely identify wrongly selected clauses. This kind of automatic control has been addressed in the form of intelligent backtracking [7]. The Wivenhoe model provides another more powerful approach.

The idea of (totally or partially) separating unification and inference was widely proposed (e.g. [35, 2, 9, 13, 4, 8]) in theorem proving researches in the school of the Matrix method [31]. Unlike Resolution which provides a proof by repeatedly generating new clauses from previous ones until the empty clause is generated, Matrix methods identify a proof by analysing the structure of the given formulae with respect to pairs of complementary literals.

The Wivenhoe model adopts the rewriting technique proposed in [9]. Two notions, *viz. potentially complementary literals* and *refutation plan*, are important in this approach. Two literals are *potentially complementary* if one is positive, the other negative, and they have the same major predicate and arity; but the question of the unifiability of their arguments is ignored. A *refutation plan* for a set of formulae is a set of potentially complementary literals which makes the formulae unsatisfiable if there exists a set of substitutions which simultaneously makes each pair of potentially complementary literals complementary.

In order to understand the model, we take a special view of logic programs. Abstractly, a logic program can be viewed as comprising two components, viz. *logical relations* and *structure relations*.[4]The *logical relations* are the relations among literals indicated by logical connectives. The *structure relations* include the structures of functions, predicates, and sharing of variables between literals within a clause. Logical relations are used to construct refutation plans, while structure relations are used to verify the validity of the refutation plans.

In resolution-based models, the logical relations and structure relations are mixed up in use. The Wivenhoe model manipulates them separately. Under this model, logical relations are extracted from the program in the form of a set of rewriting rules, leaving the structure relations represented in the form of a labelled dag. In evaluating queries, the logical relations generate sequences of refutation plans by rewriting a special symbol, which performs the abstract inference; the structure relations are used in unification. The process of extracting the logic relations from a program is actually a compilation of the source program. The target codes are not a sort of machine code, but instructions and data structures for a high level inference engine.

We restrict our discussion to a pure Horn clause language, that is, a language without negation and extra logic features (e.g. addition and deletion of clauses), and especially no ordering among literals or clauses. For convenience, we shall follow Prolog's conventions.

The paper is organised as follows: Section 2 describes how to extract the rewriting rules from a logic program; Section 3 discusses directed acyclic graphs representation for a logic program and its usage for a unification algorithm; Section 4 shows how control of inference is performed with unification failure messages and its advantages; Section 5 briefly sketches a simulator of the Wivenhoe model and discusses some implementation issues. Due to the space limitation, the readers are referred to [40] for the proofs of the theorems.

---

[4]The two notions are not meant to be precise, but to catch the intuitive idea.

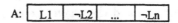

A:

Figure 1: A clause

2 Logical Relations in a Logic Program

The rewriting formalism extracting logic relations from a logic program is essentially [9]'s approach in a simplified form. Kowalski's procedural interpretation of Horn clauses is employed to assign meaning to the rewriting rules.

2.1 Extracting Logical Relations from a Program

The procedure of extracting logical relations from a program comprises of two steps: one is to build up a connection graph for the program and assign directions to the connections in the graph; another is to generate rewriting rules with the connection graph by following certain cases.

A logic program with variables disjoint for different clauses is represented in a connection graph where each clause has only one copy and each pair of potentially complementary literals is connected with a connection. For clear reference, we mark a clause with a label, and the literals within the clause are named with their order. Connections are arbitrarily labelled with a unique t_i. A clause, L1 :- L2, ..., Ln. ($n > 0$, Li are literals), is represented in Figure 1.

A is the label for the clause. The first literal is referred as $A1$, the i-th literal as Ai. The *direction* for each connection is from its positive literal to its negative literal. Here we call the positive literal a *premise literal*, and the negative literal a *goal literal*.

This step is exemplified with the program **append** and query :- append([1],[2,3],X):

```
:- append([1],[2,3],X).
append([],A,A).
append([B|C],D,[B|E]):- append(C,D,E).
```

After processing, it looks like that in Figure 2.

In Horn clauses, the directed connections coincide with the potential procedure calls in the procedural interpretation of Horn clauses [Kowalski 74].

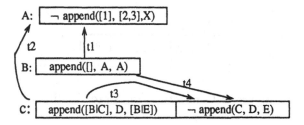

Figure 2: append after processing

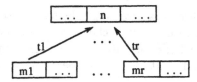

Figure 3: Connections for a goal literal

The meanings of the rewriting rules can be given with Kowalski's procedural interpretation, where the connections denote the mapping between procedure calls and procedure declarations.

The domain for the rewriting system consists of two categories of terms: literals as *non-terminals* (terminology imported from the formal language theory), e.g. literal $\neg append(C, D, E)$ in clause C is a non-terminal represented as $N(C2)$, and connections as *terminals*.

Rewriting rules can be obtained from the connection graph by following the four cases as follows:

1. For a goal literal n, if $m1, \ldots, mr$ are premise literals of n, and $t1, \ldots, tr$ are labels of connections between n and $m1, \ldots, mr$ respectively, as in the situation shown in Figure 3.

   A rewriting rule is obtained as: $N(n) \Rightarrow t1 * N(m1) + \cdots + tr * N(mr)$. This rule means: there are r possible approaches to complete the procedure call $N(n)$; for each approach i, the mapping ti should be made and the procedure $N(mi)$ be called. A $*$ denotes an And-relation, which can be omitted for convenience, while a $+$ indicates an Or-relation. They are both commutative, associative and distributive.

2. For a premise literal $m0$ in a clause shown in Figure 4, where $r > 0$:

   A rule is obtained as: $N(m0) \Rightarrow N(m1) * \cdots * N(mr)$. This rule means: procedure $N(m1)$ contains procedure calls $N(m1), N(m2), \ldots, N(mr)$.

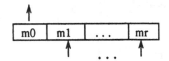

Figure 4: Connections for a premise literal

Note that for Horn clauses, a literal cannot be both a goal literal and a premise literal in one clause.

3. For each unit clause m, a rewriting rule is obtained: $N(m) \Rightarrow \varepsilon$, which means: the procedure of a unit clause does not contain any procedure calls. It is a special case of Case 2. The ε represents an empty string, so it is the left and right identity of operations $*$ and $+$.

4. For the query consisting of literals $m1, \ldots, mr$, its respective rewriting rule is: $S \Rightarrow N(m1) * \cdots * N(mr)$. This rule means: to answer the query, all the procedure calls in it should be done. S is called *start symbol*, and the rule *start rule*.

Using these rewriting rules to generate a refutation plan is simply to rewrite the start symbol and use the distributive properties for $*$ to simplify the rewritten terms. A string $(ti\,tj \ldots tk)$ of terminals is a refutation plan if it is of the form, $S \Rightarrow \Pi + ti\,tj...tk + \Gamma$, where Π and Γ are any strings of terminals and non-terminals.

Again, the append program with the query are used to show the procedure of obtaining rewriting rule:

rule 1: $N(A) \Rightarrow t2N(C1) + t1N(B)$

rule 2: $N(C2) \Rightarrow t3N(C1) + t4N(B)$

rule 3: $N(B) \Rightarrow \varepsilon$

rule 4: $N(C1) \Rightarrow N(C2)$

rule 5: $S \Rightarrow N(A)$

Rule 1, 2 are derived from goal literals with case 1, while rule 3, 4 are obtained from premise literals with case 2 and 3. Rule 5 is the start rule. The rules are rather long-winded with respect to the original program. In fact, they can be simplified as follows:

$$
\begin{aligned}
S &\Rightarrow N(A) \text{ from rule 5} \\
&\Rightarrow t2\,N(C1) + t1\,N(B) \text{ from rule 1} \\
&\Rightarrow t2\,N(C1) + t1 \text{ from rule 3} \\
N(C1) &\Rightarrow N(C2) \text{ from rule 4} \\
&\Rightarrow t3\,N(C1) + t4\,N(B) \text{ from rule 2} \\
&\Rightarrow t3\,N(C1) + t4 \text{ from rule 3}
\end{aligned}
$$

Thus, rules for evaluating the query with append program are:

$$
\begin{aligned}
S &\Rightarrow t2\,N(C1) + t1 \\
N(C1) &\Rightarrow t3\,N(C1) + t4
\end{aligned}
$$

These rewriting rule can generate a sequence of refutation plans, $\{t1\}$, $\{t2\,t4\}$, $\{t2\,t3\,t4\}$, ... , $\{t2\,t3\ldots t3\,t4\}$ ..., which can be verified to be correct refutation plans. The simplification can be done mechanically, which dramatically reduces the number of rules (refer to [40]).

2.2   Indexing Duplicated Clauses

A refutation plan is denoted by a string of terminals (i.e. connections). The duplicated terminals indicate the duplication of clauses. It is essential to identify to which instance of a clause a terminal belongs. Indices are attached to connections to indicate the duplications. An index is a pair (X,Y), where X is the instance number for the clause which the goal literal of the connection belong to (in short goal clause), Y is that for the clause of premise literal (premise clause, in short). The method of assigning indices to the connections in a refutation plan is based on the principle that every time a clause is invoked, a new instance of it should be provided. It has been observed that after simplification, each clause appears in the rewriting system with the non-terminal of its head, and it is invoked by a particular terminal. In the start rule, a non-terminal being rewritten means one more instance of that clause should be provided, and hence it is feasible to index the terminals in the clause when it is being rewritten. The algorithm is as follows:

1. Set up a counter for each clause and initialise it to 1;

2. Initialise the start rule, that is, assign 1 to Xi in $\{(Xi, Yi)\}$ where $\{(Xi, Yi)\}$ is the set of indices of all the terminals in the start rule.

3. In rewriting, for a non-terminal Nt to be rewritten, take the counter for its corresponding clause; let the value of the counter be C; assign C to Xi in $\{(Xi, Yi)\}$ where $\{(Xi, Yi)\}$ is the set of indices of all the terminals in the rule related to Nt; also assign C to Y in (X, Y) which is the index of the terminal invoking Nt.

An indexed connection is thus represented as a quintuple (T, G, P, X, Y), where T is the connection name, G is its goal literal, P is its premise literal, (X, Y) is its index. The indexing of a refutation plan is actually a renaming scheme for the variables in duplicated clauses involved in the refutation.

2.3   Properties of the Wivenhoe Model

Definition 1 *A refutation plan for a logic program is* acceptable *iff there is a set of substitutions which simultaneously makes every pair of literals (denoted by a connection) complementary, after variables being renamed by the indexing scheme.*

Theorem 1 (Completeness and Soundness) *A query Q and a Horn logic program P is unsatisfiable iff there is an acceptable refutation plan for $P \cup \{Q\}$.*

The rewriting system for $P \cup \{Q\}$ is actually a context-free grammar with extra features. Given a term rewriting system, two important properties should be investigated, namely, *Noetherian* (uniform termination) and *confluence* (unique termination). Considering these two properties, we have the following theorems.

Theorem 2 *For any Horn clause program P and a query Q, their corresponding rewriting system R is confluent.*

The confluence property corresponds to the theorem on the independence of computation rule in SLD-resolution based models [27]. Only some of the rewriting systems have the termination property. These rewriting systems are related with non-recursive sets of Horn clauses. A set of Horn clauses is *recursive* if there is a path of directed connections (shown in Section 2.1) starting from and ending up with the same clause.

Theorem 3 *A Horn clause program P is not recursive, iff its corresponding rewriting system R is Noetherian for any query Q, and thus Canonical.*

3 Structure Relations in a Logic Program

After logic relations have been extracted from a program, the remaining is the structure relations. Supporting unification is the only usage of structure relations. Thus, the representation of structure relations should be at the discretion of unification algorithms. The well-known linear unification algorithm [30] employs dag. The parallel unification algorithms in [39] also use dag. Dag, rather than string or tree, is chosen by these algorithms because it has the virtues of representing shared terms and revealing the relationships among terms. Sharing terms reduces much equality checking (in dag, two identical objects have only one occurrence).

Because of the indexing scheme, duplication of clauses is not done in the dag representation, but with the indices of connections. Thus, only one copy of the program is represented in dag form, saving considerable memory and computation.

3.1 Unification with Labelled Dag

[15] and [22] show that the major difficulty of unification lies upon the variable sharing and non-linearity of the two input terms. If a variable appears in both input terms, these terms are described as *sharing variables*. A term is *linear* if no variable appears in it twice. Two pair of terms with the same set of variables are said to be *equivalent in unification* iff the unifications for them yield the same MGU. Some input terms sharing variables can be converted to linear terms, some cannot. For example, unifying $f(X, Y)$ and $f(a, X)$, which are non-linear, is equivalent to unifying $f(X, X)$ and $f(a, Y)$ which are linear, while $f(X, X)$ and $f(a, X)$ are not convertible.

A refutation plan denotes two sets of literals to be unified. The two sets of literals can be viewed as two huge terms. These two huge terms do not increase the difficulty of unification, as it is possible to rearrange pairs of literals in a refutation plan to form two huge terms which are non-linear without variable sharing, or vice versa, and still equivalent in unification to other arrangements. This is done by putting literals of the same copy of a clause into one input term. Because with the indexing scheme, there is no cycle in a refutation plan, the rearrangement is always possible.

Here we are going to present a unification algorithm. The algorithm may not be the most efficient one, either in sequential or in parallel. The major purpose of the algorithm is to show how the Wivenhoe model may require unifications to be performed, and how unification failures are detected. We shall leave the choice of unification algorithm open for the reason that better algorithms may turn up and specialised hardware units may be used.

In the Wivenhoe model, two literals to be unified are connected with a connection containing a unique name and information which instance of the clauses the literals are. Due to the need of precisely locating where possible unification failures are, the Wivenhoe model requires that the tuple of each connection should be carried along when the literals are decomposed into sub-terms. And if a newly formed connection arises from several connections, all those connection names should be carried along in the new connection. If a unification fails, there must be two constants, or a constant and a function unmatchable. The connections between the unmatchable constants or constant-function form a *failure pattern*. If we consider the unification for finite terms only, the failures of occur-check also generate failure patterns. Therefore, the quintuple of a connection is thus changed from (T, G, P, X, Y) to $(\{(T, A, B)\}, G, P, X, Y)$ where (T, A, B) is the ancestor connection.

The algorithm consists of two procedures, viz. the rewriting procedure and the chaining procedure. A connection denotes two literals to be unified. Usually a connection denotes two compound terms. The first step of unification is to decompose those pairs of compound terms to atomic terms. With the dag representation of structure relations, decomposing a pair of compound terms is to rewrite the connection, according to the structure relations, to the connections for their sub-terms. The newly generated connections in the rewriting still hold the same meaning as the original. The second step of the unification is to check whether two different function nodes are connected together directly or indirectly; if so, the terms are not unifiable. The procedure is in fact to check the transitive consistency of the connections, that is to chain up all the connected connections to see if more than one different non-variable node is involved in the chain. The procedure is called the chaining connection procedure. It starts after the forwarding procedure finishes.

There are several data structures employed in the procedures. Connections to be rewritten are stored in a queue, called *r-queue*. Connections to be chained are collected in a pool, called *c-pool*. A queue, called *c-queue*, is also created for indicating the starting connections of chains. We also define a *hyper-connection* for a chain, which is a relation of two sets: $\langle c, v \rangle \in \{c : c \in F\} \times \{v | v \in V\}$, where V, F are the sets of variables and functions respectively, and the indices of c and v may also be attached.

The *rewriting connection procedure* is as follows:

1. Take a connection $(\{(T, X, Y)\}, G, P, X, Y)$ from the r-queue.

2. If $G \in F$, $P \in F$, and $G \neq P$, unification fails with $\{(T, X, Y)\}$ as the

failure pattern.

3. If $G \in V$ (or $P \in V$) and $P \in F$ (or $G \in F$), put connection $(\{(T, X, Y)\}, P, G, X, Y)$ (or $(\{(T, X, Y)\}, G, P, X, Y)$) into the c-pool; If both $G \in V$ and $P \in V$, put connection $(\{(T, X, Y)\}, P, G, X, Y)$ and $(\{(T, X, Y)\}, G, P, X, Y)$ into the c-pool.

4. If $G = P$ and $arity(G) = arity(P) = n$, which arity is a function returning the arity of function symbols, assume $G1, \ldots, Gn$ and $P1, \ldots, Pn$ are the respectively sub-nodes of G and P, put into the r-queue the following new connections, $(\{(T, X, Y)\}, G1, P1, X, Y), \ldots,$ $(\{(T, X, Y)\}, Gn, Pn, X, Y)$; otherwise report failure of that connection with the failure pattern $\{(T, X, Y)\}$.

5. Carry on step 1, 2, 3 and 4 until the r-queue is empty.

At Step 3, the connections are assigned a certain direction. A connection for two variables is bidirectional, while in other cases, a connection is directed from the function to the variable. With the directed connections, the chaining procedure can always start from constants and functions, and hence the efficiency can be enhanced.

The *chaining connection procedure* is to carry out steps as follows:

1. Take a connection $(\{(T, X, Y)\}, G, P, X, Y)$ from the c-queue; Do transitive closure on the connections in the c-pool by regarding a connection as a relation $\langle (Gi, X), (Pi, Y) \rangle$; The transitive closure is called a chain; Connections in a chain are removed from the c-pool and the c-queue; Form a hyper-connection $\langle \{(Gi, X)\}, \{(Pi, Y)\} \rangle$ from the chain where

$$(Gi, X), (Pi, Y) \in \{z : \text{there is a connection } (\{(T, X, Y)\}, z, P, X, Y)$$
$$\text{or } (\{(T, X, Y)\}, G, z, X, Y) \text{ in the chain}\}$$

   and $Gi \in F$, and $Pi \in V$. If $\{(Pi, X)\} \neq \emptyset$, also check the existing hyper-connections: if there is a hyper-connection $\langle R, S \rangle$ that $\{(Pi, X)\} \cup S \neq \emptyset$, merge them to form a new hyper-connection $\langle R \cup \{(Gi, X)\}, S \cup \{(Pi, Y)\} \rangle$.

2. In the case that $1 \geq |\{(Gi, X)\}|^5$, the hyper-connection succeeds.

3. In the case that $|\{(Gi, X)\}| = S > 1$, put the S nodes in a line in an arbitrary order, and check the adjacent $(S - 1)$ pair of nodes; For any pair of nodes, $(N1, X1)$ and $(N2, X2)$, let the set of connections in the

---

[5]$|(Gi, X)|$ is the cardinality of $\{(Gi, X)\}$.

shortest path between $(N1, X1)$ and $(N2, X2)$ in the chain be $\{TT\}$; Establish a new connection $(\{TT\}, N1, N2, X1, X2)$ and save it into the r-queue.[6]

4. (Occur-check) For a hyper-connection $\langle \{(Hf, X)\}, \{(Hv, Y)\} \rangle$, for each (f, n) which $(f, n) \in \{(Hf, X)\}$ and $arity(f) \neq 0$, do transitive closure on the dag for the arcs $\{\langle f, i, ai \rangle\}$ where i range from 1 to $arity(f)$; If there is a variable v that $\langle b, j, v \rangle \in \{\langle f, i, ai \rangle\}^*$ where $\{\langle f, i, ai \rangle\}^*$ is the transitive closure of $\{\langle f, i, ai \rangle\}$, and $\langle v, n \rangle \in \{(Hv, Y)\}$, the hyper-connection fails the occur-check with the failure pattern as the set of connections in the shortest path between (f, n) and (v, n).

5. Repeat Steps 1, 2, 3 and 4 till the r-queue and c-queue are both empty.

The MGU (or a subset of it, the answer substitution to the query) can be obtained from the hyper-connections. Some variable substitutions may not be found from the hyper-connections. Those variables are connected only to other variables, and remain in the c-pool. Those variables should be treated as the uninstantiated.

Remarks 1 At Step 3, it is not necessary to establish $S * (S - 1)/2$ new connections because connections for function nodes are bidirectional. But this requires us to purge the ancestor connections of a new connection. And even occurrences of an ancestor connection should be removed from the name set of the new connection. This is justified by that travelling forward and back via a connection means that the connection is redundant.

Remarks 2 The connections in our algorithm are quite similar to the equations in other algorithms, e.g. [28, 20]. However, the connections are based on a dag of the programs, thus having a flavour of graph operations. This also make the occur-check a bit easier. Another difference is that the algorithms in [28, 20] maintain a Frontier for the set of equations to be solved, and the rewriting and chaining are done in one procedure. In our algorithm, the functionality of the Frontier is replaced by r-queue and c-queue, and the rewriting procedure does the decomposition of pairs of terms thoroughly.

Remarks 3 In order to find all the unification failure pattern, both procedures should not terminate when one clash in input terms is found, but

---

[6]The consistency check of the nodes is left with the rewriting procedure.

rather carry on till the r-queue and c-queue are empty. This method is intractable in the worst case, that is, the number of failure patterns may be exponential in the number of unifications to be unified [42].

It is not difficult to see that the unification algorithm terminates for terms of finite size. Because the dag is acyclic, no rewritten connections will be led to the r-queue for rewriting again. Accordingly, no identical connections can be generated in rewriting more than once. The chaining procedure only starts from constant or function nodes. A finite term will only have a finite number of function nodes. This guarantees the termination of both procedures.

This approach to unification has its particularities, and may be advantageous in certain implementations. We note that:

1. Variables are not allocated any actual memory. The whole unification process only creates pointers for variables to indicate their instantiations.

2. The unification procedure is suitable for parallel implementation; there are three places that parallelism can easily be applied, namely, rewriting the connections in the r-queue, chaining the connections in the c-queue and doing occur-check for the hyper-connections. In fact, [39] have shown that a similar algorithm can be parallelised to have the time complexity $O(c(E/P + V))$ where E and V are the number edges and nodes in the dag respectively, P is the number of processors and c is a very slow growing function (can be regarded as a small constant).

3. The data processing is, comparatively, large scale. This makes parallelism more advantageous. Furthermore, the most general unifiers (MGU) for each individual unification within the refutation plan need not to be generated and maintained, saving considerable amounts of computation and memory.

3.2 A Working Example of the Unification Procedure

We shall demonstrate the whole unification by evaluating the query

```
:- append([1],[2,3],X)
```

with the rewriting rules developed in Section 2. The structure relations for the append program and the query is shown in Figure 5. (# indicates the name of the node; in the case of implementation, it can be the actual address of the node.)

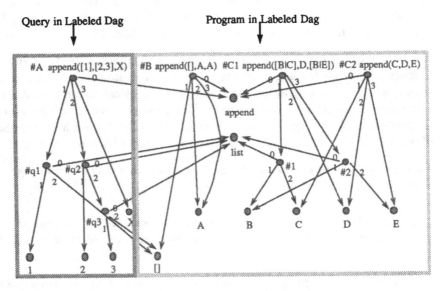

Figure 5: The append program again

At the second level, the refutation plan is $\{t2\,t4\}$, where $t2 = (t2, \#A, \#C1,$ $1, 1)$ and $t4 = (t4, \#C2, \#B, 1, 1)$. So initially, there are only two connections in the r-queue, none in the c-queue and the pool. After one round of rewriting, the connections in the r-queue are:

$(\{t2\}, \#q1, \#1, 1, 1)$.

$(\{t2\}, \#q2, D, 1, 1)$.

$(\{t2\}, X, \#2, 1, 1)$.

$(\{t4\}, C, [], 1, 1)$.

$(\{t4\}, D, A, 1, 1)$.

$(\{t4\}, E, A, 1, 1)$.

After another round of rewriting,

In the r-queue:	In the c-queue:	In the c-pool:
$(\{t2\}, 1, B, 1, 1)$.	$(\{t2\}, \#q2, D, 1, 1)$.	$(\{t2\}, \#q2, D, 1, 1)$.
$(\{t2\}, [], C, 1, 1)$.	$(\{t2\}, \#2, X, 1, 1)$.	$(\{t2\}, \#2, X, 1, 1)$.
	$(\{t4\}, [], C, 1, 1)$.	$(\{t4\}, [], C, 1, 1)$.
		$(\{t4\}, D, A, 1, 1)$.
		$(\{t4\}, E, A, 1, 1)$.

The third round of rewriting just moves the connections in the r-queue to the c-pool. Four hyper-connections are found.

$$\langle\{1\},\{B\}\rangle$$

$$\langle\{[]\},\{C\}\rangle$$

$$\langle\{\#q2\},\{D,A,E\}\rangle$$

$$\langle\{\#2\},\{X\}\rangle$$

They are all consistent and the occur-check succeeds. So the answer substitution is generated from the hyper-connections as follows:

$$X \;\leftarrow\; \#2 = [B|E]$$
$$B \;\leftarrow\; 1$$
$$E \;\leftarrow\; \#q2 = [2,3]$$

Thus $X \leftarrow [1,2,3]$.

4   Control over Inference

It has been gradually realised that performing inference is not difficult, while controlling inference is very hard. Many criticisms of Prolog are about its control facilities [23, 29]. It may be concluded that the failure of Prolog on being a declarative language is caused by its heavy reliance upon the user providing control information, i.e. ordering of clauses, ordering of literals (subgoals), and cut. This requirement forces programmers to think about their programs procedurally. On the other hand, this requirement does enable Prolog to run fast enough to be recognised.

The control of inference is also very critical to the Wivenhoe model, because the idea of separating refutation plan generation and unification introduces a problem, that is, the refutation plan generation algorithm never terminates in evaluating a query which involves recursive clauses. The problem results from ignoring the unification failure message. In fact, unification failure messages are the only control information that a logic programming system can possibly obtain from a pure declarative program.

In this paper, we confine the model to accepting pure declarative programs to see how far it can go. This may provide an acceptable base for users who do not wish to put any control information into their programs. But generally, it is admitted that user-provided control information can greatly enhance the execution efficiency. Such control facilities are perhaps desirable for advanced users, who, whilst programming in a declarative style, often have definite "computational intentions", e.g. recursive or iterative computation, if-then-else statements, etc. Supporting the "computational intention" annotations by altering rewriting strategy is out of the scope of this paper. More results can be found in [40].

4.1 A Level Rewriting Strategy

A *rewriting strategy* is a method that in rewriting a string decides which rule should be applied, or equivalently, which non-terminal in the string should be rewritten. Due to the confluence property of the rewriting system (Theorem 2), many rewriting strategies can be adopted. The confluence property actually corresponds to the well-known independence of the computation rule. Compared with the one-literal-at-a-time approach of SLD-resolution, the Wivenhoe model has more flexibility on choosing computation rules. For instance, the rewriting strategy in the Wivenhoe model can indicate two or more non-terminals being rewritten simultaneously.

The rewriting strategy should be decided by the desirable properties (e.g. efficiency, completeness, etc.) of the model. Here we emphasise completeness. It is noticed that if a program has several nested recursions, the rewriting process is quite easily trapped in a small loop and some unifiable refutation plans may never be achieved, i.e. the model is incomplete. This is the similar pitfall that Prolog's depth-first search strategy meets. Thus, we propose a level rewriting strategy to tackle this problem. Assume that a set of rewriting rules are simplified. Let the start rule be the first level start rule: $S1 \Rightarrow \Gamma$.

Definition 2 *Let the i-th level start rule be $Si \Rightarrow Gi$. Assume that $Nt1$, ..., Ntn are all the occurrence of non-terminals in Γi. A level of rewriting is to rewrite $Nt1, \ldots, Ntn$ one step simultaneously in Γi, and get the result $\Gamma i'$. The strings of terminals are removed from $\Gamma i'$ as refutation plans, and the remaining, $\Gamma i + 1$, form the next level start rule $Si + 1 \Rightarrow \Gamma i + 1$.*

With the unsimplified rule set, rewriting of one non-terminal in the start rule corresponds with going one-step down in a branch of the SLD-tree [3] of a program. With the simplified rule set, rewriting of one non-terminal becomes searching one or several steps down in one or several branches of the SLD-tree. This is because rewriting each LHS of a simplified rule represents creating one more instance of a clause. The level rewriting strategy rewrites all the non-terminals in the start rule, thus it acts as a kind of breadth-first search.

However, it is not exactly the same as breadth-first search in SLD-tree. The difference is that one step of level rewriting is to search all the possible refutation plans with one additional instance of all the non-unit formulae. Since it is a breadth-first search, the problem of ordering among clauses is solved. And since it is done level by level, it contributes to termination by preventing some branches being trapped into infinite loops.

4.2   Termination Condition of Evaluations

As remarked for the unification procedure, the label of a connection should be carried by connections in the rewriting connection procedure and the failure pattern are returned. The same unification failure will happen in any other refutation plan containing the failure pattern. Thus the doomed refutation plan can be safely removed from the start rule without affecting completeness. Based on this observation, a principle of deleting strings in the start rule is formed as follows:

Deletion of String: If a string (terminals and non-terminals related with
 *) in a start rule contains a failure pattern, the string should be deleted
 from the start rule.

More deletion can be applied if the behaviour of certain rules is taken into account. For a recursive rule of the form $N \Rightarrow \Phi N \Theta + \Pi$,[7] where Φ and Θ are strings of terminals and non-terminals, Π is a string of terminals, we define its *recursion pattern* as $\Phi^i \Pi \Theta^i$, where i is the number of levels. A rule of the form $N \Rightarrow \Phi N \Theta + \Pi 1 + \cdots + \Pi n$, where Φ and Θ are as above, Πi are strings of terminals, can be decomposed into n rules of the form $N \Rightarrow \Phi N \Theta + \Pi i$. So, n recursion patterns can be obtained. For rules of more complex forms, we still do not know what to do exactly. But it is predictable that the result may not be very promising, since the termination of recursive evaluation is generally undecidable.

Deletion of Rule 1: If the recursion pattern of a rule contains a failure
 pattern, the rule should be deleted and any strings in the rule set
 containing the LHS non-terminal of the rule should also be deleted.

Deletion of Rule 2: If the RHS of a rule is of the form, $\Phi 1 + \cdots + \Phi n$,
 where Φi contains at least one non-terminal, it will not contribute to
 any refutation plan and should be deleted.

---

[7]The rule corresponds to a clause having only one recursive call for itself and one termination case. It includes recursions such as tail-recursion, right recursion, which can be optimised in Prolog.

Termination Condition: If at a certain level n, all the strings in the start rule are deleted with the deletion of strings/rules principles (i.e. the start rule is of the form $Sn \Rightarrow \varepsilon$), the evaluation terminates.

Definition 3 *For a evaluation strategy E, let T_E be the set of $P \cup \{Q\}$ which has a finite proof tree with E. T_E is called a* termination set *for E.*

Let the termination set for the Wivenhoe model with the deletion of string and the deletion of rule be $T_{Wivenhoe-DS}$ and $T_{Wivenhoe-DR}$ respectively; let the termination set for Prolog with fixed computation rule be T_{SLD}; let the termination set for MU-Prolog with dynamic computation rule [29] be $T_{MU-Prolog}$; let the termination set for GLD-resolution with computation rule selecting a set of literals [43] be T_{GLD}. We have:

Theorem 4   *1. $T_{SLD} \subset T_{MU-Prolog} \subseteq T_{Wivenhoe-DS}$; and*

2. $T_{GLD} \subseteq T_{Wivenhoe-DS}$; and

3. $T_{Wivenhoe-DS} \subset T_{Wivenhoe-DS} \cup T_{Wivenhoe-DR}$.

Remarks   The Wivenhoe approach of control is actually a kind of intelligent backtracking with the detection of minimal non-unifiable subsets of unifications. The deletion of string is a top-down view (viewing connections from query) of evaluation; while the deletion of rule is a bottom-up view (viewing connection from the unit clause of a recursive procedure). The deletion of rule 2 is a simple loop detecting facility. The two principles make the Wivenhoe approach more powerful than the intelligent backtracking which is solely top-down [7], e.g. it can terminate for evaluating :- p(b) with

```
p(a).
p(A):- p(f(A)).
```

[3] employs the notion of *finite failure set (FF)* to characterise Negation-as-failure. As defined by them, a ground literal L belongs to the FF of program P iff any proof tree constructed for L is finite and has no empty clause. By [24], the level rewriting strategy has the property which makers it suitable for Negation-as-failure [10].

Theorem 5 *The level-rewriting strategy and the deletion of string principle is sound and complete with respect to finite failure.*

Let's use append with the query again to illustrate the whole termination situation of the query :-append([1],[2,3],A). Using level rewriting strategy, three levels of start rules are obtained:

$$S1 \Rightarrow t2N(C1) + t1$$
$$S2 \Rightarrow t2t3N(C1) + t2t4$$
$$S3 \Rightarrow \implies t2t3t3N(C1) + t2t3t4.$$

At the first level, the refutation plan is $\{t1\}$. Unification fails and no string can be deleted. At the second level, the refutation plan is $\{t2t4\}$. Unification succeeds with the result $X = [1, 2, 3]$. At the third level, the refutation plan is $\{t2t3t4\}$. After unification, a chain, $[] - (t2) - C - (t3) - [B|C] - (t4) - X$, fails as $[]$ cannot be unified with $[B|C]$. The connections involved are $t2$ and $t3$. (Note that $t4$ is not involved although $t4$ is connected with this chain.) So the failure pattern is $\{t2, t3\}$. Thus, $(t2t3t3N(C1))$ is deleted and the level 4 start rule is $S4 \Rightarrow \varepsilon$, indicating the termination of the evaluation.

5   Implementation Techniques

5.1   A Wivenhoe Inference Engine

A Wivenhoe simulator, including a compiler and a Wivenhoe inference engine, has been implemented in C-Prolog. The Wivenhoe inference engine is a virtual machine simulating the Wivenhoe computational model. It is a sequential implementation of the model, comprising three components, namely, the rewriting, the unification and the control components. Their functionalities and relations are: the rewriting part rewrites the start symbol with the rewriting rules and feeds refutation plans to the unification part; the unification part unifies the received refutation plans using the dag and reports unification failure messages to the control part; the control part makes use of the messages to trim down doomed strings in the start rule and returns the new start rule to the rewriting part. This forms a cycle of the execution of the Wivenhoe inference engine as shown in Figure 6.

5.2   Parallelism

There are three kinds of parallelism in the Wivenhoe model. The first is the *pipeline parallelism* between the three components. This is in the same spirit of parallelising bookkeeping and unification in WAM [36], but more flexible. The second is the *conservative parallelism* which includes the parallelism in

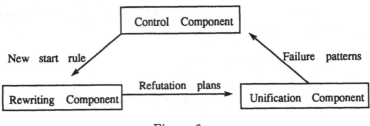

Figure 6:

rewriting and the unification parallelism. The confluence property (Theorem 2) of the rewriting system allows partitioning the rewriting rules and performing rewriting in parallel. The control component may also follow the same partition to work in parallel.

It has been shown in Section 3.1 that the unification algorithm has many opportunities for parallel processing. More sophisticated algorithms can be found in [39, 17]. Intuitively, the Wivenhoe approach to operating unification creates many opportunities for unification parallelism. To quantify the increase of parallelism, an empirical experiment has been done on measuring the potential parallel factor (PPF) for the common terms in practical logic programs. The *potential parallel factor (PPF)*, proposed in [17], defines the maximum possible speed increase of the parallel algorithm over the sequential one on a certain application domain. In other words, for an algorithm, the PPF = (speed of its parallel version)/(speed of its sequential version). The experiment is to compare the PPF of the whole refutation plan as one unification and individual unifications in the refutation plan. The data obtained from [44]'s algorithm[8] are shown in Table 1. The results indicate that for programs with recursive data types, e.g. naive reverse, the improvement is limited; whereas for programs with simple data structure, e.g. fib and ancestor, the PPF is linear to the number of unifications. For programs with complicated recursive structures, e.g. 8 Queen program, the result varies with different cases. However, generally, the improvement of PPF is quite significant.

The third parallelism is the *speculative parallelism* which exists in doing several refutation plans in parallel, a kind of Or-parallelism. Achieving speculative parallelism introduces redundant computation. For instance, overlapping of refutation plans makes duplicated unifications. If unification fails at the common part of overlapped refutation plans which are done in parallel, the waste is obvious as the refutation plans can be deleted with the

---

[8]We choose the data for Yasuura's algorithm here because they reflect the change of PPF directly. More test data for other algorithms can be found in [40].

Program	No. of unifications in a refutation plan	Average PPF for individual unifications	PPF of the whole refutation plan
Naive reverse (65)	2211	1.971	114.88
Quick sort (50)	637	2.037	79.04
Intersection (40-40)	275	1.609	76.19
Fibonacci 13	1161	1.599	1253.80
Ancestor	198	1.500	173.25
(of 100 generations)			
Ackerman(3,3)	6051	1.805	6051.20
8 Queens program 1	134	2.017	32.70
8 Queens program 2	39	1.863	26.00
8 Queens program 3	159	1.733	113.97
8 Queens program 4	146	2.138	145.12
8 Queens program 5	166	1.787	200.10
8 Queens program 6	151	1.795	284.33
Hamilton	170	1.765	23.97
Color map	91	1.565	37.37
Scene	8	2.187	11.40
Farmer	42	1.531	299.29

Table 1: PPFs of various programs

$$S \Longrightarrow \begin{pmatrix} B\ C\ D \\ E\ F\ B \\ G \end{pmatrix} \text{ and } B \Longrightarrow \begin{pmatrix} A\ C \\ D\ E \\ F\ G \end{pmatrix}$$

Figure 7: Matrix representation of rules

failure pattern of one unification. Thus achieving the speculative parallelism does not necessarily enhance run-time efficiency. This is a "parallelism vs. redundant computation" dilemma. Nevertheless, the experiment with the Delphi model [1], which pursues Or-parallelism and has redundant computation, showed it is still advantageous even when having some recomputation. Storing the result of successful parts of a refutation plan can ease this problem. In addition, grouping refutation plans according to their overlaps can also be applied. Only one refutation plan in each group is run in parallel. How to effectively balance this kind of Or-parallelism still needs further investigations.

5.3   A Matrix Representation of Rewriting Rules

The Wivenhoe simulator employs a string representation for the rewriting rules. After several levels of rewriting, the terms in the start rule become very large as there are too many duplications. The string representation is not practical even for a small program (e.g. the 8-queen program). An alternative is to represent the rules in a matrix form and abandon applying the distributive property of $*$ and $+$ in rewriting. Paths are used to indicate refutation plans. A rule can be converted into a matrix by representing $A*B$ as $[AB]$ and $A+B$ as $\begin{bmatrix} A \\ B \end{bmatrix}$, where A and B are strings of terminals and non-terminals. Rules such as, $S \Rightarrow BCD + EFB + G$ and $B \Rightarrow AC + DE + FG$, are represented as the matrixes in Figure 7.

Let the first rule be start rule, and apply the second to it. If the distributive properties of $*$ are not used, the rule remains as the matrix in Figure 8.

A refutation plan is a path through the matrix constituted only by terminals. Matrix representation is equivalent to string representation but solves the duplication problem, although not thoroughly for multi-recursive programs. Due to the confluence property of the rewriting system, each part of the matrix can be manipulated independently without violating soundness and completeness. The matrix can also be partitioned and handled in parallel.

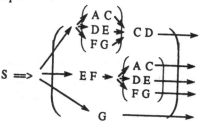

Figure 8: After the application of the second rule

5.4 Other Techniques to Improve Efficiency

A simple way to reduce the number of connections at compile-time is to require potentially complementary literals to be unifiable. For instance, in evaluating the query, :- append([1],[2,3],L), the connection between the query and the clause, append([],L,L), should not be established. This kind of compile-time unification can also be done on the dag, so that the unification results, the rewritten connections and the hyper-connections, can be stored for run-time use, which can save the first round rewriting procedure in unification. Static type checking for variables can reduce unification failures and thus enhance efficiency and give users extra confidence on the correctness of their programs. Furthermore, partial unification on the group of connections in rules is also worth considering. Program transformation techniques (e.g. [6]) can also greatly enhance the efficiency of the Wivenhoe model for data-intensive programs.

6 Concluding Remarks and Further Work

Tarnlund [37] has pointed out the possible advantages of separating unification from inference. Bibel et al [6] also showed the possible advantages for this kind of approach. However, to our knowledge, no complete system has been developed.

The Wivenhoe computational model may be distinguished from other models (from the low level models such as the WAM [41], to the high level ones e.g. Concurrent Prolog [34]) on its **explicit** representation of computation states (in the start rule). It combines several existing logic programming techniques, such as intelligent backtracking, control-flow analysis, loop detecting, building graph for procedure calls and compile-time unification, etc., nicely into a uniform framework. It has been shown that this can lead to the gain of large scale parallelism, and the tight control over inference. The parallelism includes the pipeline parallelism between unification and bookkeeping operations which takes 30% – 80% of the total execution time in a

WAM machine [36].

A problem with the model is the duplicated computation which needs deliberated balancing. Further practical experiments with the model are required. Nevertheless, the model shows good signs for practical implementations as follows:

1. The separation of unification and the computation state management avoids several conventional problems in other models, for instance, the heavy shallow backtracking as identified by Tick [38], and conflict unifier resolution in AND-parallel models [12] (even when the arity of predicates is no larger than 3, optimally scheduling AND-related goal is NP-complete in the worst case [14]).

2. The unification performed in the Wivenhoe model has a certain simplicity. The most general unifiers (MGU) for each individual unification within the refutation plan need not be generated and maintained, saving a considerable amount of computation and memory. Only one copy of the program is required in the form of a dag, and all the objects in the program have literally only one occurrence. The pointers (connections) are processed in a uniformed fashion, making garbage collection relatively easier.

3. Set and graph operations are frequently involved in the model, e.g. identifying strings containing failure patterns is the set inclusion operation, and the unification procedure basically comprises many graph operations. Direct support from fast hardware for such operations is possible (e.g. [25, 33]) .

Although the Wivenhoe model has imperfections, further development certainly seems profitable in respect of the following areas.

The Wivenhoe model has been extended to a two-level setting, viz. the meta-level and the object level [40]. It thus can accommodate built-in predicates, computational annotations and different kinds of rewriting (searching) strategies. Moreover, it can also support general Horn clauses programs (with negative clause in the program and definite clauses in the query, e.g. HORNLOG [16], general logic programs (Horn clause with negative literal inside the body), equational logic (using narrowing as inference rule [32]), and constraint logic programming systems [19]. It can incorporate with some program transformation techniques. Some study on employing the techniques of [6] shows that the enhancement is very effective. The model may also be extended to full FOL if so desired.

The investigation of feasible supporting architecture for the model is also on-going. The Wivenhoe model generates no intermediate MGU, and hence has no binding environment to maintain; goals are managed as a tree (graph) rather than a stack. These may suggest an alternative to the classical environment-stacking architectures. As unification is carried out in a large scale in the model, we consider that it is best suited to systems with hard-wired unification units, or with some special hardware support, e.g. for graph operations and relational operations. An existing machine, the IFS (Intelligent File Store) [25], provides fast associative memory searching and a special unit known as RAP (Relational Algebraic Processor) [26] which is fast at set operations and graph traversing. We intend to investigate how a future, re-designed, IFS-like machine can support our model and in the meantime keep an open mind on other novel architectures.

Acknowledgments

The authors are grateful to W. Clocksin (Cambridge), Y.J. Jiang (Imperial College), A. Ramsay (Dublin), J. Reynolds (Essex), J. Schumann (Munich) for their helpful comments. Thanks are also due to the IFS group at Essex for providing a stimulating working environment.

References

[1] H. Alshawi and D. B. Moran. The Delphi model and some preliminary experiments. In R. A. Kowalski and K. A. Bowen, editors, *Proceedings of the 5th International Conference and Symposium on Logic Programming*, pages 1578–1589, Seattle, USA, August 1988.

[2] P. B. Andrews. Refutation by mating. *IEEE Transactions on Computers C-25*, pages 801–806, 1976.

[3] K. R. Apt and M. H. van Emden. Contributions to the theory of logic programming. *JACM*, 29:841–863, 1982.

[4] W. Bibel. *Automated Theorem Proving.* Vieweg, Braunschweig, 1982.

[5] W. Bibel and Ph. Jorrand, editors. *Foundation of AI*, volume 232 of *LNCS*. Springer-Verlag, 1986.

[6] W. Bibel, R. Letz, and J. Schumann. Bottom-up enhancements of deductive systems. Technical Report ATP 67, Forschungsgruppe Kuenstliche Intelligenz, Techn. Universitaet, Munchen, 1986.

[7] M. Bruynooghe and L. M. Pereira. Deduction revision through intelligent backtracking. In J. A. Campbell, editor, *Implementations of Prolog*, pages 194–216. Ellis Horwood, 1984.

[8] R. Caferra. Proof by matrix reduction as plan + validation. In *Proc. of the 6th Intl. Conf. on Automated Deduction*, volume 138 of *LNCS*, pages 309–325. Springer-Verlag, 1982.

[9] C. L. Chang and J. R. Slagle. Using rewriting rules for connection graphs to prove theorems. *J. AI*, 12:159–180, 1979.

[10] K. L. Clark. Negation as failure. In H.Gallaire and J.Minker, editors, *Logic and Databases*, pages 293–322. Plenum Press, New York, 1978.

[11] K. L. Clark and S. Gregory. PARLOG: Parallel programming in logic. *ACM Transactions on Programming Languages and Systems*, 8(1):1–49, January 1986.

[12] J. S. Conery and D. F. Kibler. Parallel interpretation of logic programs. In *Proc. ACM/MIT Conference in Functional Programming Languages and Computer Architecture*, pages 163–170, 1981.

[13] P. T. Cox and T. Pietrzykowski. Deduction plans: a basis for intelligent backtracking. *IEEE Transactions on Pattern Analysis and Machine Intelligence, PAMI-3*, pages 52–65, 1981.

[14] A. Delcher and S. Kasif. Some results on the complexity of exploiting data dependency in parallel logic program. *Journal of Logic Programming*, 6:229–241, 1989.

[15] C. Dwork, P. C. Kanellakis, and J. Mitchell. On the sequential nature of unification. *Journal of Logic Programming*, pages 35–50, 1984.

[16] J. H. Gallier and S. Raatz. HORNLOG: a graph-based interpreter for general Horn clauses. *Journal of Logic Programming*, 4:119–155, 1987.

[17] J.H. Harland and J. Jaffar. On parallel unification for Prolog. *New Generation Computing*, 5:259–279, 1987.

[18] Itai and J. Makowsky. Unification as a complexity measure for logic programming. *Journal of Logic Programming*, pages 105–117, 1987.

[19] J. Jaffar. Efficient unification over infinite terms. *New Generation Computing*, 2:207–219, 1984.

[20] J. Jaffar, Michaylov, P. J. Stuckey, and R. H. C. Yap. The clp($\mathcal{R}$) language and system.

[21] Y.J. Jiang. An algebraic technique for deductive database systems. In *IEEE, COMPSAC-88*, pages 329–342, 1988.

[22] P.C. Kanellakis. Logic programming and parallel complexity. In G. Ausiello and P. Atzeni, editors, *Proc. ICDT'86*, volume 243 of *LNCS*, pages 1–30. Springer-Verlag, 1986.

[23] R. A. Kowalski. *Logic for Problem Solving*. North-Holland, 1979.

[24] J-L. Lassez and M.J. Maher. Closures and fairness in the semantics of programming logic. *Theoretical Computer Science*, 29:167–184, 1984.

[25] S.H. Lavington. Technical overview of the intelligent file store. *J. Knowledge-Based Systems*, 1(3):166–172, 1988.

[26] S.H. Lavington, J. Robinson, and F-Y. Mok. A high-speed relational algebraic processor for large knowledge bases. In Delgado-Frias and Moore, editors, *VLSI for Artificial Intelligence*, pages 133–143, Oxford, July 1988. Kluwer Academic Press.

[27] J. W. Lloyd. *Foundations of Logic Programming*. Symbolic Computation Series. Springer Verlag, 2nd, extended edition edition, 1984.

[28] A. Martelli and U. Montanari. An efficient unification algorithm. *ACM Transactions on Programming Languages and Systems*, 4(2):258–282, 1982.

[29] L. Naish. *Negation and Control in Prolog*, volume 238 of *LNCS*. Springer-Verlag, 1986.

[30] M.S. Paterson and M.N. Wegman. Linear resolution. In *Proc. 8th ACM Symp. on Theory of Comp.*, pages 181–186, 1976.

[31] D. Prawitz. Advances and problems in mechanical proof procedures. In D. Michie and B. Meltzer, editors, *Machine Intelligence 4*, pages 59–71. Edinburgh University Press, 1969.

[32] U.S. Reddy. *Logic Languages Based on Functions: Semantics and Implementation*. PhD thesis, Univ. of Utah, 1986.

[33] J. Robinson and S.H. Lavington. A transitive closure and magic functions machine. In *The Second International Symp. on Databases in Parallel and Distributed Systems*, Dublin, July 1990.

[34] E. Y. Shapiro. Concurrent Prolog: A progress report. Technical Report CS86-10, Department of Computer Science, The Weizmann Institute of Science, Rehovot, Israel, April 1986. Reprinted in [5].

[35] S. Sickel. A search technique for clause interconnectivity graphs. *IEEE Transactions on Computers*, C-25(8):823–835, 1976.

[36] A. Singhal and Y.N. Patt. Unification parallelism: How much can we exploit? In *The North American Conference on Logic Programming*, 1989.

[37] S-A. Tarnlund. Logic programming — from a logic point of view. In *Proc. IEEE Symposium on logic programming*, pages 96–113, 1986.

[38] E. Tick. *Studies in Prolog Architectures*. PhD thesis, Stanford University, 1987.

[39] J.S. Vitter and R.A. Simons. New classes for parallel complexity: a study of unification and other complete problems for P. *IEEE Transactions on Computers*, C-35(5):403–418, 1986.

[40] J. Wang. *A New Computational Model for Logic Languages and its Supporting Architecture*. PhD thesis, Dept. of Computer Science, Univ. of Essex, 1990.

[41] D. H. D. Warren. An abstract PROLOG instruction set. Technical Note 308, SRI, 1983.

[42] D. A. Wolfram. Intractable unifiability problems and backtracking. In E. Y. Shapiro, editor, *Proc. of 3rd International Logic Programming Conference*, pages 107–121, July 1986.

[43] D. A. Wolfram, M. J. Maher, and J-L. Lassez. A unified treatment of resolution strategies for logic programs. In *Proc. 2nd International Logic Programming Conference*, pages 263–276, Sweden, 1984.

[44] H. Yasuura. On parallel computational complexity of unification. In *Proc. of the fifth generation computer systems*, pages 235–243, 1984.

Printed in the United States
by Baker & Taylor Publisher Services